SELECTED COMEDIES

Elizabeth Inchbald

Introduction and Notes by
Roger Manvell

UNIVERSITY
PRESS OF
AMERICA

LANHAM • NEW YORK • LONDON

Copyright © 1987 by

University Press of America,® Inc.

4720 Boston Way
Lanham, MD 20706

3 Henrietta Street
London WC2E 8LU England

British Cataloging in Publication Information Available

Library of Congress Cataloging-in-Publication Data

Inchbald, Mrs., 1753-1821.
Selected comedies.

I. Manvell, Roger, 1909-   . II. Title.
PR3518.A6   1987   822'.4   87-21248
ISBN 0-8191-6635-9 (alk. paper)

C

All University Press of America books are produced on acid-free
paper which exceeds the minimum standards set by the National
Historical Publication and Records Commission.

To

Françoise

CONTENTS

Introduction

Note on the Texts of the Plays

I'll Tell You What (1785)

Such Things Are (1787)

Everyone has His Fault (1793)

The Wedding Day (1794)

Wives As They Were and Maids as They Are (1797)

Notes

MRS. INCHBALD

ENGRAVED BY HEATH FROM AN ORIGINAL PICTURE.
PUBLISHED BY LONGMAN AND CO

Portrait of Elizabeth Inchbald

vi

Introduction

Elizabeth Simpson had been stage-struck since early adolescence. Reared during the 1750s and 1760s in a country district near Bury St Edmunds in Suffolk, some forty miles north of London, member of a Catholic farming family with two sons and six daughters, she had finally run away from home in 1772 at the age of eighteen in order to be in London, where her four married sisters now lived. London was the centre for outstanding achievement in the English theatre, at that time still dominated by David Garrick who was soon to retire. After marrying that same year Joseph Inchbald, a man twice her age but an established professional actor, she had managed to become an actress solely because he enjoyed modest success and relatively continuous employment in the provincial theatres of England and Scotland. Her beauty rather than the possession at this stage of any outstanding talent soon made her well-known and well-liked in the various companies she joined, but her husband's untimely death in 1779 had left her a youthful widow of 25 who had somehow to make a living for herself in the theatre.

Elizabeth Inchbald was a young woman of considerable determination and good sense. Her brief marriage had scarcely been altogether happy, and she was instinctively opposed to marrying again, even though several suitors, mostly unconnnected with the stage, eagerly sought her hand. She wanted above all to retain her independence, and her other ambition, to become a professional dramatist, gained ground with her since she realized she would never become a star talent in the London theatre, as her friend Sarah Siddons was to be, and that her miniscule earnings as an actress in the provincial theatres would condemn her to a life of near poverty and homeless residence in the lodging houses of Bristol, York, Hull or Edinburgh, towns and cities where there were theatres ready to employ her as much for her good looks and good manners as for her acting skill. So she began to write plays, having tried her hand without immediate success in composing a novel while still appearing in the provinces. When in 1780 she finally secured an engagement at London's Covent

Garden Theatre, she began to write the long series of comedies which were to bring her so much acclaim in the 1780s and 1790s.

It was not easy for a woman to gain acceptance in the male-dominated profession of playwrighting. The success of women in the theatre since the time of the Restoration, over a century earlier, had been virtually confined to acting. There had, however, been two or three instances of women succeeding as writers for the English stage--the maverick adventuress Aphra Behn,[*] for example, in the 1670s, who had written indistinguishably from her male contemporaries, could certainly be called a professional, and there had been Mrs Susanna Centlivre, who had completed nineteen plays, including such successes as *A Bold Stroke for a Wife* (1718), much earlier in the 18th century. The century was, in fact, to produce a cultural climate more accommodating for women writers, though they mostly preferred to write the more accessible and less demanding form of fiction designed to entertain the expanding middle classes, with their many ladies of leisure who had received some modicum of education and were alert to establish their own, more cultivated place alongside their menfolk in Georgian England. Elizabeth Inchbald had been preceded in this endeavour, for example, by Mrs Elizabeth Griffith, whose best comedy had been *The School for Rakes* (1769), adapted from Beaumarchais' bourgeois drama, *Eugénie* (1767), and by Fanny Burney, with her novel *Evelina* (1778). Mrs Hannah Cowley's best play, *The Belle's Stratagem*, had appeared in 1780. Another authoress, Mrs Ann Ward Radcliffe, was to publish her celebrated 'gothic' horror story, *The Mysteries of Udolpho* (1794) three

---

[*]Aphra Behn (the widow of a Dutch husband) is commonly held to be the first professional woman writer in Britain. Her plays, full of baudy humor, such as *The Rover* (1677) had their success, but her literary reputation rests more on her novels, notably *Oroonoko* (1688). She was a notable feminist, championing women's right to live as freely as men.

years after Elizabeth Inchbald's principal novel, *A Simple Story* (1791) came out.

Mrs Inchbald gradually abandoned her stage career and during the 1780s and 1790s became a prolific writer, producing no less than fifteen plays in the ten years 1785-1794, only one of which, *The Massacre*, a short tragic subject set in France at the time of the massacre of St Bartholomew's Day, was neither staged nor published in her lifetime, while of the remaining fourteen, eleven received publication at the time of their presentation on the London stage or shortly after. *I'll Tell You What*--the title imposed by George Colman the Elder, himself a dramatist of merit mid-century with the comedies of manners, *The Jealous Wife* (1761) and *The Clandestine Marriage* (1766), and now manager of the Little Theatre in the Haymarket--was presented with great success in July 1785. The play brought its author three hundred pounds (equal to two years salary for a supporting actress in the provincial theatre) and enabled her to begin her lifelong practice of purchasing stock and building up capital on the interest from which she would later be able to live in modest comfort at the time of her retirement. She was never to marry, in spite of the many offers other women might well have considered attractive.

Part of her conception of independence included a carefully developed plan for reading contemporary and classical literature. Like many middle-class women of the time, she had received no formal education outside the home, and was entirely self-taught, though she was soon, as an established actress and well-known writer in London, to form friendships with men of letters as well as with the more distinguished members of London society, whose sophisticated conversation was rapidly to widen the experience of so intelligent and observant a woman as she.

As dramatists, her more immediate contemporaries were Richard Cumberland (*The Brothers*, 1769; *The West Indian*, 1771), Hugh Kelly (*The School for Wives*, 1773), Oliver Goldsmith (*She Stoops to Conquer*, 1773), Richard Brinsley Sheridan (*The Rivals*, 1775; *The School for Scandal*, 1777), Thomas Holcroft (*The Follies of the Day* or

The Marriage of Figaro, 1784, adapted from Beaumarchais; and the celebrated serious drama, *The Road to Ruin*, 1792), George Colman the Younger (*The Iron Chest* , a melodrama, 1796; *The Heir at Law* , 1797) and, as we have seen, Hannah Cowley (*The Belle's Stratagem*, 1780; *Which is the Man?*, 1782). Among all these Goldsmith and Sheridan championed a return to the traditional comedy of manners (Jacobean and Restoration) against the overwhelming school of sentimental comedy which had prevailed in the earlier 18th century theatre.

Elizabeth Inchbald's work straddled the prevailing schools, but at her best her plays are comedies of manners, humours and intrigue that reflect the influence of Congreve and Farquhar rather than the strictly sentimental comedy of her 18th century predecessors. Her judgment was too influenced by common sense entirely to relapse into merely fashionable sentiment or 'sensibility.' She shared this characteristic with her lesser contemporary, Mrs Cowley, and her range extends to farce in *The Midnight Hour* (1787) and, above this, *The Wedding Day* (1794), which Professor Allardyce Nicoll likens to *The School for Scandal* in its attack on the excesses of 'sensibility' (*History of the English Drama 1660 to 1900*), Vol. III p. 190).

When Sheridan withdrew from playwrighting after his brief, brilliant output in the 1770s, he left a way clear for her, and she took full advantage of it in the succeeding decades. The five Inchbald plays I have selected span the years 1785 to 1797, and all of them are in one way or another concerned with intrigues surrounding marriage and relationships between the sexes; we find here wives compliant and wives rebellious; marriages done and marriages undone; unsuitable marriages to older men planned by parents and guardians only to be frustrated by evasive wards or eloping daughters with younger, more attractive men in view, all occurring in those ranks of society that are infested by libertine lords with boundless fortunes doomed to be lost at the gaming tables while they seek to conquer in the bedrooms, seducing beauties whose marriages have staled. These are the situations of Restoration comedy, but with actions and conversations toned down for the gentler or more genteel tastes of 18th century bourgeois society, the fashionable upper classes who fancied being seen at the theatre alongside the well-known, the notorious, and the genuine nobility. Aphra Behn's comments would have been interesting.

Considering the difficulties of divorce in 18th century England, the interest in broken marriages and their consequences can scarcely be wondered at. Upper class marriages involved property--on the one hand the inherited property of the estate-owning aristocracy and the landed gentry, and on the other the growing wealth of the money-owning urban classes involved in trade at home and abroad. The formal separation of married couples and their ultimate divorce led to formidable complications. It was possible to secure an initial phase of divorce called *divortium a mensa et thoro* (divorce from bed and board) from the ecclesiastical courts under Canon Law. This was in effect a judicial separation, though it might be termed divorce, but the partners involved, innocent or guilty, were not free to marry again. If they were adamant that they wanted freedom to remarry, then they needed to secure a decree of 'nullity,' establishing that the marriage had been null and void in the first place, as a result, for example, of affinity of blood (consanguinity) or impotence, or because some previous contract could be claimed to have existed.

However, by the 18th century it was possible through a private act of Parliament presented in the House of Lords to petition for a *divortium a vinculo matrimonii,* a full divorce from the marriage bond, normally following on a separation under Canon Law. Needless to add, such a proceeding was extremely expensive and tedious to negotiate. It was not until 1857 that the Matrimonial Causes Act made it possible to obtain a full-scale divorce without such an act of Parliament. Wilkie Collins, in his novel, *Man and Wife* (1870), exposes very fully the 'corruptions which exist in the Marriage Laws of Great Britain and Ireland' and also peculiarities of the Scottish custom of 'marriage by consent,' without any formal license or contract. Readers of Elizabeth Inchbald's *Every One Has*

His Fault need to keep these conditions in mind as they would affect the society people she portrays in 1793.

Another aspect of 18th century life in England involved British interests abroad, which were increasing, and this is reflected in many of her plays--for example, Irwin and his wife Lady Eleanor in *Every One Has His Fault* return to England after a prolonged period abroad, and so do Euston and his brother Antony in *I'll Tell You What* and Tom Contest in *The Wedding Day*, while *Such Things Are* is actually set on the island of Sumatra in the East Indies. British involvement in North America and the West Indies went back some century and a half; it was the Dutch, however, attracted by the Asian spice trade of the East Indies who had developed a monopoly in that area early in the 17th century; in competition, the British had set up their East India Company in India itself, and by the 18th century the British presence in India was considerable, extending to Bengal. Moreover at the time of Elizabeth Inchbald's play, *Such Things Are* (1787), the British government was increasingly taking over administrative control in these areas not only in terms of trade but also politically. Sumatra, the second largest island of Indonesia, though Dutch controlled since the 17th century, saw increasing British infiltration in the later 18th century in order to establish bases from which to develop British trade with China. In 1786 the British government had established a naval station in Penang on the Malayan archipelago, but in Act I, Scene i (p. 18), Mrs Inchbald still appears to identify Sumatra (where she has set her play) with India.

Turning to the plays themselves, although Elizabeth shared with her greater contemporaries, Sheridan and Goldsmith, the (to us) irritating habit of using type-names for what in the end prove to be interesting and entertaining

supporting characters,[*] and although most of her original
plays are dominated by people drawn from the English
aristocratic (or pseudo-aristocratic) class and the wealthy
gentry-about-town, there is a very solid and observant
human base to virtually all her dramatic characterization.
Her aim, based on years of acting experience on the stage, is
to produce readily playable characters (type-named or not)
given the considerable skill to be expected among the
regular actors and actresses available for work in the
leading London and provincial theatres. Her plays, well-
constructed and smooth-running as they are, depend on the
development of amusing confrontations between the dozen
or so people she assembles in each piece to entangle and
disentangle themselves in the pursuit of their interests,
which are usually marital or financial or both.

Some of the type-names convey only a hint for
characterizations--Lady Raffle, Mr Haswell, Tom Contest,
Lord Rakeland, Lady Autumn, Sir Luke Tremor, Mr
Twineall--whereas Miss Spinster, Mr Solus, Mr Harmony,
Colonel Downright, Sir Harry Harmless and Lord Flint
have the main spine to their characters fully revealed on
entry, though Mr and Mrs Placid in *Every One Has His
Fault* act contrariwise, since they are always at loggerheads
and remain faithful to each other only because they are
inured to confrontations. But Elizabeth Inchbald's
characters offer considerable scope for talented actors and
actresses. Sir Robert Ramble, for example, in *Every One
Has His Fault*, is in a hopeless state of confusion; having got
rid of the wife he always neglected, he now discovers he is
really in love with her, and his secret remorse for the

---

[*]Tony Lumpkin in *She Stoops to Conquer*, Sir Benjamin
Backbite, Lady Sneerwell, Careless and Snake in *The
School for Scandal*. The habit was carried forward into the
next centruy and after; for instance, Canon Chasuble and
Miss Prism in Wilde's *The Importance of Being Earnest* or
characters in plays by Bernard Shaw: Alfred Doolittle in
Pygmalion, Mrs Lutestring in *Back to Methuselah*, Hector
Hushabye in *Heartbreak House*, or General Bardo
Bombadone in *Geneva*.

manner in which he has treated her is in conflict with his *amour propre*. Having made such a fuss in society about separating from his wife, his pride makes him feel he ought to maintain his independence in the eyes of the world. However, he cannot bear the thought of her marrying anyone else. Elizabeth Inchbald handles this character with considerable subtlety and understanding, so that the audience can be made by a skillful actor to feel for him in his psychological dilemma. In the short piece *The Wedding Day*, the elderly Sir Adam Contest is full of doubts on the very day he has married his frivolous young bride--he cannot help perpetually reminding himself, and her, of the fond memories he still holds of his first wife's excellence, while the new Lady Contest would much rather respond to the advances of the attractive Lord Rakeland, who cannot resist trying to seduce her, especially on her wedding day. The situation is full of rich opportunities for comedy.

In *Wives as They Were and Maids as They Are*, Maria represents one of Mrs Inchbald's most spirited heroines whom, in her brief Remarks preceding the published version of the play, she compares to Miss Milner, heroine of her novel, *A Simple Story*, who in turn is commonly regarded, in her show of independence, as having some at least of the characteristics of Elizabeth herself. Under the irresponsible influence of her older companion and chaperone, Lady Mary Raffle, Maria runs up bills and gaming debts to the consternation of her correct and kindly guardian, Mr Norberry. The two women end up in a debtors' prison. In the same play, Mrs Inchbald introduces yet another comic study of an ill-matched married couple--Lord and Lady Priory, the husband desperate in his endeavours to keep his carefully nurtured and compliant wife free from the contaminations of London society, while she delights in a vagrant kiss bestowed on her in a darkened corridor in Mr Norberry's house and a secret rendezvous with a would-be seducer, whom she foils by producing her knitting and maintaining her virtue strictly on her own terms. Even in what was only her second play, written and produced in 1785, *I'll Tell You What*, Mrs Inchbald devises a brilliant comic situation: Lady Harriet, who has been divorced from her former husband, Sir George

Euston, and has married her lover, the libertine Major Cyprus, finds that he is intent now on seducing the new Lady Euston, while Sir George is chronically jealous of his former wife's involvement with any man other than himself. Lady Harriet, enjoying the situation in which she has the whiphand, lures Sir George into precisely the same compromising situation in her bedroom in which he had originally discovered Major Cyprus. The two men, Sir George and Major Cyprus, are fully stretched characters, fraught by their obsessions, while Lady Harriet takes delight in exploiting their weakness. Character and situation combine as in all Elizabeth Inchbald's best work, to create good comedy. *I'll Tell You What* is a Restoration comedy of manners cleaned up to please an 18th century bourgeois audience, exciting them without too much embarrassment. The dialogue, though frank, is never gross.

Nor was Mrs Inchbald's capacity to write sparkling, highly playable dialogue less than her ability to create amusing, highly playable characters. Her dialogue flows on rapidly, but with natural, 18th century elegance of speech rhythm, each line cuing naturally and racily into its response:

Col. Downright.   Pray, sir, do you live in the house?

Sir Harry Harmless. I have been on a visit here this six weeks.

Downright.   And during that time--

Harmless.   I have seen such things! Enough to terrify me from marrying; for wives are sometimes so provoking, I am sure I cou'd not keep my temper. Now, here is Lady Harriet Cyprus, you cannot think how provoking she is--she sometimes says such terrible things to her husband, that, I am sure, if she was my wife--

Downright.	Why, you'd not beat her, would you, or lock her up?
Harmless.	No--but perhaps I might kick her lapdog, or do some outrage to her dress.
Downright.	You would make an admirable soldier, Sir Harry.
Harmless.	I must own Colonel, I am positive you wou'd be obliged to *press* commissioned officers were it not for the becomingness of some of their dresses.
Downright.	Give me your hand, Sir Harry. I like you much; and could I see you master of a firelock, or a wife--
Harmless.	No. While my neighbors marry, I never shall.
Downright.	Why so, Sir Harry?
Harmless.	Their wives will do for me.

There is nothing of exceptional literary quality about this dialogue except for its immediacy and vitality. Such dialogue almost speaks itself, and in the hands of skillful players, such as the leading theatres commanded, it would spring to dramatic life from the stage.

So, too, the continuity of her plots and sub-plots, which are always carefully interwoven, each sustaining the other. In *Every One Has His Fault*, the pathetic vein (the impoverished Irwin and his wife Lady Eleanor returned to London after a prolonged absence abroad to seek the forgiveness and help of her father, Lord Norland, from whom she has been estranged following her runaway match) is contrasted by the purely comic (Sir Robert Ramble's ill-suppressed jealousy because Lord Norland, guardian of his divorced wife, is only too anxious to marry her off again, and therefore needs to claim her dowry back from Sir Robert, which in turn would lead to his impoverishment), all of these complications accompanied by the comic involvements of Solus, the confused and frustrated bachelor, Miss Spinster, the frustrated bride-for-someone-or-other, and Harmony, trying to do his best for everyone, but at the expense of getting entangled himself. And behind these there are the Placids, quietly getting on with their marital differences. To keep this, and more, in smoothly laced continuity requires a considerable measure of dramatic skill, the same skill that weaves plot and sub-plot together in *Wives as They Were and Maids as They Are*: Maria's extravagances, which are the despair of her kindly guardian, Norberry, and the bane of Maria's unrecognized father, visiting Norberry with his identity kept a strict secret; and the sub-plot involving Bronzely's ludicrous attempt to seduce Lady Priory, the seemingly compliant wife of Norberry's other friend, the absurd Lord Priory. What a houseful they all make up! Elizabeth Inchbald, like a juggler, keeps in fluid and harmonious motion the variously coloured balls of her comic contrivance.

Her best plays, I think, would stand on the modern stage, played as elegant comedies of manners after the style of Sheridan, whose outstanding work was so unfortunately curtailed when he deserted the theatre for politics. Although Elizabeth Inchbald's work is sometimes marred by the sentimentality or 'sensibility' of her times, the Kotzebue touch, at their best her comedies are virtually free of these taints, and conceived more nearly in the spirit of Jonson, Congreve and Sheridan. It is a century since they were made readily available in a popular edition for readers and actors, and they should, at least in this writer's view, be given a chance to renew their former popularity with our contemporary audiences.

I would like to express my gratitude for the encouragement and help I have received from Vice-President Gerald Gross of Boston University, from Mr John P. Laucus, Boston University's Librarian, and from Boston Public Library. I am especially grateful to my wife Françoise for her constant help, and to Dr Ann Marie Barry for help in the preparation of the camera-ready script; also to Ms Helen Hudson who advised on and supervised book production.

ROGER MANVELL

NOTE ON THE TEXT OF THE PLAYS

The texts as reproduced here in slightly magnified facsimile are taken from Elizabeth Inchbald's plays as they appeared in collections she edited: *The British Theatre*, London 1806-09; and *The Modern Theatre*, London 1811. (See below.) These texts are in the writer's possession. Following is the bibliographical history of the five plays involved.

	Staged	Published	Irish Editions Dublin	US Editions
I'll Tell You What	1785	1786	1787	–
Such Things Are	1787	1788 (13 editions by 1805)	1788	–
Every One Has His Fault	1793	1793 (7 editions by 1805)	1793, 1795	Philadelphia 1794, 1822, 1827 Boston 1809
The Wedding Day	1794	1794	1795	New York 1819
Wives as They Were and Maids as They Are	1797	1797 (reprinted five times)	1797	New York 1813, 1825

Manuscripts of all five plays are held in the Larpent Collection at the Henry E. Huntington Library, San Marino, Pasadena, California, USA.

Subsequent Publication of the Plays:

The British Theatre, edited by Elizabeth Inchbald, London
1806-09, Vol. XXIII:
>   *Such Things Are*
>   *Every One Has His Fault*
>   *Wives as They Were and Maids as They Are*
>>   Note: A facsimile reprint of The British
>>   Theatre in 25 volumes was published by
>>   Georg Olm Verlag of Hildesheim in 1970
>>   ($983.00)

Collection of Farces and Afterpieces, collected by Elizabeth
Inchbald, London 1809, Vol. I:
>   *The Wedding Day*

The Modern Theatre, collected by Elizabeth Inchbald,
London 1811, Vol. VII:
>   *I'll Tell You What*
>>   Note: A facsimile reprint of The Modern
>>   Theatre in 10 volumes was published by
>>   Georg Olm Verlag of Hildesheim in 1973
>>   ($373.00)

The London Stage, London 1834-37:
>   *Such Things Are*
>   *The Wedding Day*
>   *Wives as They Were and Maids as They Are*

Cumberland's British Theatre, London 1825-55:
>   *Every One Has His Fault*
>   *The Wedding Day*
>   *Wives as They Were and Maids as They Are*

Dick's Standard Plays, London 1883-:
>   *Such Things Are*
>   *Every One Has His Fault*
>   *The Wedding Day*
>   *Wives as They Were and Maids as They Are*

Note: In the twentieth century, *Every One Has His Fault* appeared in *English Comedies of the 18th Century*, London, Oxford University Press, 1926, and in *Lesser English Comedies of the 18th Century*, London, Oxford University Press, 1927.

NOTES

I'LL TELL YOU WHAT (1785)

Pages 7, 44. Chocolate, tea, coffee, coffee-houses. Chocolate as a beverage was originally developed by the Aztecs and came to Europe via Spain. It had already become a fashionable drink in London around the 1650s. Tea as a social and ceremonial drink originated in China and came to Europe early in the 17th century. The British East India Company held a monopoly on imports to Britain until 1834. (The Boston Tea Party depopularized tea consumption in North America, its place being taken by coffee.) Coffee as a drink goes back to the 15th century in Arabia, Egypt and Turkey, and was originally associated in Christian eyes with the Muslim infidel. It was formally 'Christianized' by Pope Clement VIII, and introduced to Europe mid 17th century. In 18th century society the coffeehouses became like clubs for male gossiping and gambling, especially popular with literary coteries.

Page 11, 14. For conditions governing marriage, separation and divorce in the 18th century, see Introduction.

Page 13. *Mariage en militaire* . Perhaps the best rendering of this in English is 'shot-gun wedding.'

Page 15. Zounds! 'By God's wounds.' This oath dates from the 16th century, and was still in use in the 19th century.

Page 21. Regimentals: military dress or uniform. Press: enforced recruitment. Firelock: a gun-lock producing sparks that fired the priming.

Page 28. Egad! A mild oath, 'gad' being a softening of 'God.' In use 17th to 19th century.

Page 35. Post Office. The term first came into use in the 17th century in reference to an office for the mailing of letters.

Page 48. Wave was used as an alternative spelling for 'waive,' and accepted as such by Dr Johnson.

Page 57. Crim. con. An abbreviation used in the 18th and 19th century for 'criminal conversation,' meaning adultery.

SUCH THINGS ARE (1787)

For the setting of this play on the island of Sumatra in the East Indies, see Introduction.

Page 9. The reference is to the total eclipse of the sun in 1772. Politesse: courtesy. It is part of Lady Tremor's affectation to employ such elegant French terms.

Page 14. Fashionable undress: informal but still stylish clothing, though in Twineall's case necessarily over-eccentric.

Page 15. Hand: escort.

Page 50. Frisseur: hairdresser, hair curler.

Page 52. The scenes: this will refer to the side wings which projected a few feet onto the stage, and could be used for exits.

EVERY ONE HAS HIS FAULT (1793)

Page 13. Lord Mayor's Day. The Lord Mayor's Day celebrates the installation of a new Lord Mayor of London. He still rides in the state coach built in 1756 to Westminster to present himself to the Sovereign. A popular pageant forms part of the festivities of the day.

Page 21. Scotch lawyers. Marriage by consent, without license, made the Scottish marriage laws only more complex than the English. See Introduction.

Pages 43, 45. By the law of the time any money belonging to or earned by a wife became her husband's property after marriage. He could administer, invest, expend it as he chose, with or without her consent. However, on separation the sums involved could be assigned back to the lady. See Introduction.

Page 46. Lord Norland implies that it is the custom for men to offer their hand in marriage, and for women to accept or refuse, subject normally to parental or guardian consent on both sides.

Page 54. Mr Placid makes clear the necessary distinction between formal separation and an actual divorce. See Introduction.

THE WEDDING DAY (1794)

Page 43. The term 'mother-in-law' was frequently used for 'step-mother.'

Page 51. Cribbage: a card game, with scoring kept on a cribbage board. The game was said to have been invented by Sir John Suckling (1609-42), poet and gamester attached to the court of Charles I. Beggar-my-neighbor was another popular card game.

Page 55. Hottentot. The Hottentots were a pastoral people originally inhabiting areas on the coast of the Cape of Good Hope, but dispossessed by Dutch settlers during the 17th century. They were related to Bushmen and used the notorious Click language.

Page 64. *Robinson Crusoe.* Defoe's celebrated novel had appeared in 1719.

WIVES AS THEY WERE AND MAIDS AS THEY ARE (1797)

Page 10. Hotel. In French the word implies a large private mansion, or an official residence. This appears to be an early use of the word in the modern sense of a hostelry, a place for travelers or transitory guests to stay.

Page 11. Routs: originally a rowdy assembly of persons, but in the 18th and 19th centuries applied to more fashionable gatherings, such as an evening party--and so used by Fielding, Johnson and Smollett, among others.

Page 12. Piquet: a card game for two played with a 32-card deck or pack.

Page 26. A reference to Ovid's *Ars Amatoria* (*The Art of Love*) and to Sir William Blackstone (1723-80), the British jurist who compiled his great pioneer study of English law, *Commentaries on the Laws of England*, 1765-69.

Page 43. Tarquin; Lucretia. This of course is a reference to the legendary rape of the virtuous Lucretia, wife of Lucius Tarquinius, by Sextus Tarquinius Superbus, which drove her to commit suicide after pledging her husband to avenge her.

Page 49. Scenes: stage wings.

Page 51. Coxcomb: originally the cap worn by a professional clown or Fool, then used from the 16th to 19th centuries as a term for a vain or foppish person.

Page 65. Bond Street. Then, as now, a fashionable street for daytime strolling and shopping. Side boxes: the boxes at the side of the stage or auditorium for private parties attending the play.

Page 72. Public prints: newspapers.

EDINBURGH:
Printed by James Clarke.

DRAMATIS PERSONÆ.

Major Cyprus,	*Mr Palmer.*
Mr Anthony Euston,	*Mr Bensley.*
Colonel Downright,	*Mr Aickin.*
Charles Euston,	*Mr Bannister, jun.*
Sir George Euston,	*Mr Williamson.*
Sir Harry Harmless,	*Mr R. Palmer.*
Servants, *Messrs Ledger, Gaudry, and Lyons.*	
Mr Euston,	*Mr Parsons.*
Lady Euston,	*Mrs Bulkley.*
Lady Harriet Cyprus,	*Mrs Bates.*
Bloom,	*Mrs Riley.*
A Young Lady,	*Miss Farren.*

I'LL TELL YOU WHAT;

A

COMEDY,

IN FIVE ACTS.

AS PERFORMED AT THE

THEATRE-ROYAL, HAYMARKET.

BY

Mrs. INCHBALD.

I'LL TELL YOU WHAT.

ACT THE FIRST.

SCENE I.

A Room at SIR GEORGE EUSTON'S.

Enter MR. EUSTON, *followed by* SIR GEORGE.

Sir Geo. But, my dear uncle, why in such a passion?

Mr Eus. I can't help it—I am out of all patience! Did not I leave you one of the happiest men in the world?

Sir Geo. Well, and so you find me, Sir.

Mr Eus. 'Tis false—you are not happy—you can't be happy; 'tis false—and you shan't be happy.

Sir Geo. If you are resolved to make me otherwise, Sir—

Mr Eus. No, I am not resolved—'tis yourself
that is resolved. Did not I leave you one of the
happiest of men?—married to one of the most beautiful women in the world? Did not I give you my
blessing and a large fortune, and did I not stay and
see you father of a fine boy?—Then only just stept
over to visit my estate in St. Kitt's, and now, I'm
come back, here I find you married to another woman, and your first wife still *living*—and, egad, she
is married to another man!

Sir Geo. Dear uncle, I should certainly have
asked your opinion and my uncle Anthony's on the
subject, but your absence put it out of my power;
and it was universally believed the ship in which you
sailed was lost.

Mr Eus. Well, you will hear what my brother
will say to it.

Sir Geo. I trust, Sir, when I have explained
every thing, you will not only think me worthy of
your pardon, but even of being pleaded for to my
uncle.

Mr Eus. Not I, indeed—Nay, were it in my
power to do you any good, I would not; I shan't forgive you myself; much less ask him. But you are right
in fixing on me for a mediator; my brother pays
much regard to me, truly. I have been of infinite
service, to be sure, in reconciling him to his own poor
boy. Nay, did he not even (for my brother Anthony
would always be master, although he was the youngest) when I went to him to persuade him to forgive
poor Charles, his son, did he not even (instead of
my gaining him over, and getting something for the
poor boy,) did he not even draw me into a promise
never to do any thing for him myself? My brother
does what he pleases with me—but nobody else shall
—No, what I want in resolution to him, I'll make
up in obstinacy, to other people.

Sir Geo. Sir, if you will but hear the just pleas
I have to offer—

Mr Eus. I will hear no pleas—What do you think
my brother will say? Why, you inconsiderate boy!
He had designed you for his heir!

Sir Geo. I should be as sorry, Sir, to excite his
displeasure as I am at incurring yours; yet, give me
leave to add, I should derive very little enjoyment
from the possession of a fortune which his son, my
poor cousin, (but for a single act of imprudence)
had a right to expect. And be assured, Sir, that
if this seeming indiscretion of mine, when compared with that of his son's, shou'd be regarded so un-
favourably as to make *his* offence appear lighter to
my uncle, and move him to forgiveness, I will
contentedly support the burthen of his resentment.

Mr Eus. Why now, that's well spoken. You silly
young rogue, I am not angry with you for getting
rid of your wife (for that, I dare say, is what every
sensible man in the world wou'd do if he cou'd,) I
am only angry with you for getting another. Could
not you know when you were well off, you blockhead?

Sir Geo. Dear uncle, as you are a bachelor, and
can only speak of wives from theory, suppose we
drop the subject? Is my uncle Anthony come to
his house? He knows nothing of the alteration that
has taken place in my family, you tell me: Shou'd
I wait on him, or do you think he will favour me
with a visit first?

Mr Eus. Now, what a deal of ceremony! 'Tis a
fine thing to *look* like a man of consequence. My
brother Anthony has had more privileges from his
looks than I ever had from being eldest son—even
you, whom I love so well, and have given half my
fortune to, (and 'tis not long you know that you
have expected a sixpence from Anthony,) yet you

never meet *him* without a low bow. " How do you
do, Sir? I hope you are well, uncle! I am glad
to see you!" And you stumble over *me*, with " So
uncle, how is it? how is it, uncle?"—And when you
invite us both, " Uncle Anthony, I hope I shall
have the *honour* of your company:" While you give
me a nod, " Uncle, I shall see you."

Sir Geo. Dear Sir—

Mr Eus. Nay, with every other person 'tis the
same thing—If we are stuffed into a coach, with a
little chattering pert Miss, " Oh dear, Mr Anthony
Euston, you must not ride backwards, here is
room for *you* on this seat—and *Mr Euston*, I know,
will like one seat as well as another;"—and then am
I put with my back to the horses, though my head
is whirling all the time like one of the coach wheels.
Then if any thing be lost, or wanted, when no servant is by, " Mr *Anthony* Euston must not stir for
the world—but *Mr Euston*, they know, will be so
kind as to go for it." And this is all because I am
good natured. Egad! if this is my reward, no
wonder there are so few in the world of my temper.

Sir Geo. But, dear Sir, no jesting. Does my
uncle intend to call on me or not?

Mr Eus. Yes, I dare say he did intend it; and,
if he does not hear of what you have been doing,
before he gets to your house, he will.

Sir Geo. Why then, my dear uncle, will you
step home, and give orders that none of the servants
mention any thing to him this morning?

Mr Eus. There now!—" *I* step home and give
orders!" There 'tis, again!—Wou'd you ask my
brother to " step home, and give orders?" No, I
fancy not!—But I—poor I—will be so good as to do
it, you think—But, for once I won't. Besides, Anthony never asks questions of servants. We enquired of our house-keeper, indeed, how you did, last

night; she told, us both you and your lady were well, and so we thought all safe.   Anthony will ask no more questions; therefore, you may have the pleasure of explaining matters to him yourself, as you have to me.

Sir Geo. I shou'd be sorry if any imperfect account shou'd reach him; for, so sincere is my respect for him, I wou'd not even suffer for a moment in his esteem.   I will be with him in half an hour, but I am afraid——

Mr Eus. No, no, he'll not be out, nor have had any company in that time; for my brother is no sailor, and he'll be too fond of the exchange of a bed for a hammock to be stirring so soon.   However, I think I *will* step home, and give a caution to the servants that they don't mention your divorce to him.   As for myself, I'll keep out of his way—— I'll not go near him; for I will say this for my brother, although it was never in my power to persuade him to forgive an injury or an indiscretion in my life, yet I never said to him, " Brother Anthony, *don't* forgive a thing," that he did not take my advice.

Sir Geo. Come, uncle, walk into the parlour before you go; let me introduce you to Lady Euston— Do step in, and take your chocolate with her.

Mr Eus. And, by the time I have taken a turn in the Park, and eaten a mouthful of dinner, you'll, perhaps, have a new Lady Euston to introduce me to, and I may drink tea with *her.*

Sir Geo. Well, uncle, whether you stay or go, I must bid you a good morning; for I am obliged to attend a friend, who has a law-suit depending, and I fear I shall be waited for—my presence won't be required long, and I'll be with my uncle Anthony within half an hour.

Mr Eus. Very well, [*Going*] but you had better take an hour—Let me advise you to take an hour. Anthony is devilish sharp—he is not to be imposed upon. Take an hour, or an hour and half, before you see him—Anthony is a deep man, he is not to be deceived; for, I dare say, in his time, he has been as idle as yourself—and I *will* go on your errand.

[*Exeunt Mr Euston and Sir George, separately.*

SCENE II.

A Room at MAJOR CYPRUS'.

LADY HARRIET CYPRUS, *and* BLOOM, *waiting.*

Lady Har. Married!

Bloom. Yes, my Lady, as sure as death.

Lady Har. Amazing! It cannot be.

Bloom. O yes, my Lady, I have known of it these three months; but, as they kept out of town till within this fortnight, and your ladyship has been abroad most of that time, I thought I would not tell your ladyship till we returned to London, when your ladyship was sure to hear of it. Why they live but just by, madam; and my master, I know, has been several times in company where they have been visiting.

Lady Har. Ay, she was your master's intended.

Bloom. O yes, my lady, I know that.

Lady Har. Insignificant girl! I triumphed, when I snatched him from her, and now I suppose she thinks to triumph equally.

Bloom. No doubt, madam; but, if I was you, I wou'd let her see I cared nothing about him.

Lady Har. And do you imagine I do care? No, indeed, Bloom; my exchange is for the better, I am certain; and (*sighing*) entirely to my satisfaction.

Bloom. Indeed I think so, Madam: you certainly have changed for the better—and, bless me, I think, of all the husbands I ever saw, my present master is sure the fondest.

Lady Har. As for that—no one cou'd be fonder than Sir George, at first.

Bloom. Ay, my lady, but Major Cyprus is not so flighty as Sir George.

Lady Har. Not so flighty—(*sighs.*) I have been envy'd Sir George's gaiety a thousand times.

Bloom. Yes, my lady, when your ladyship married first, I suppose; but, you know, in a few months, Sir George altered so much, and seemed so miserable, I protest, every single rap that came at the door made my blood run cold, for I took it for the report of a pistol.

Lady Har. You need not have feared him, Bloom —he is too fond of the pleasures of this life—Dear pleasures, which he wanted to retrench me in.

Bloom. More shame for him, madam. Now my present master is a soldier ; and, what is more, I dare say will soon be call'd on to go abroad.

Lady Har. Ha!

Bloom. Nay, I beg your ladyship's pardon—I thought perhaps your ladyship wished to see the Major show himself a courageous gentleman in the field ; and that that was the reason of your preferring him to Sir George.

Lady Har. I prefer! Did not my brother, from Sir George's humiliating suspicions and cruel treatment of me, compel us to a divorce; and then, as a defence for my weakness, forced me into the arms of the Major; being, I suppose, convinced that no-

thing less than a soldier, should undertake the guard
of a lady's honour!

Bloom. Very true, madam—and I heard the
Major say, this morning, as your ladyship left the
room, that " your ladyship's honour would require
the guard of a file of musketeers."

Lady Har. Ungenerous man—even worse to
me than Sir George; for poor Sir George, from
my indiscreet partiality to this ingrate, had some
pretence for his unkind apprehensions; but Mr Cyprus, who knows what proofs of affection I have
given him, even in preference to the man I had
sworn to love—

Bloom. Nay, I fancy, that is what frightens my
master; for I believe he is a little fearful lest your
ladyship shou'd chance to be forsworn again.

Lady Har. Insolent supposition! He knows the
delicacy of my sentiments—my honour to Sir George
—knows that, although his unwearied artifices con-
quered my too susceptible heart, and hurried me to
indiscretions, I merited not that severe contumely
I have endured.

Bloom. Bless my soul! Well now, I assure you,
you surprise me! And so, my lady, there was nothing at all in it, when Sir George found my master in the closet?

Lady Har. What did you suppose?

Bloom. Oh, my lady, nothing—I hope I did not
distress your ladyship by the mention of Sir George's
second marriage.

Lady Har. Ridiculous!

Bloom. Nay, indeed, I always thought, as your
ladyship wou'd not live with him yourself, your
ladyship did not wish to prevent them that wou'd.

Lady Har. Don't mention that insignificant woman!

Bloom. If I was your ladyship, I am sure, I

wou'd not care—especially as I got married before
him.

Lady Har. Leave me.

Bloom. (*Aside.*) She'll have another husband
within half a year—and so have three all alive at
once.—Well, I will say, 'tis very hard that, because
I am poor, I never can have above one at a time.

[*Exit* BLOOM.

Lady Har. And so, Sir George has been married
these three months to another, and entirely forgot
me.   To be so soon forgotten!—I shall never
now forget him, I am certain.   He has behaved
like a man of resolution and spirit, in casting me
from his heart, and I feel the irreparable loss. Why
were we divorced?   I shou'd have disliked him still
had he been my husband; and yet how tender, how
patient to my failings to what Mr Cyprus is.   His
cruel and unjust suspicions of me are not to be borne.
How provokingly did he treat me last night—I was
too tame; but the next time he insults me, with his
jealousy, I will endeavour to augment rather than
pacify it—I'll try a reverse of conduct—Though,
indeed, I *am* tolerably provoking in all our wrangles:
—Yes, thank heaven, I can say as cool, spiteful
things, as any woman in the world.   [*Exit.*

SCENE III.

Another apartment in Maior Cyprus' house.

Enter COLONEL DOWNRIGHT, *followed by the* MAJOR.

Col. Down.   I assure you, Major, this is the first
visit I have made since I set my foot in London.—
Nay, and faith, no great compliment to you, neither;

for, as I parted with my fellow passengers at Portsmouth, I don't know that I have a friend or acquaintance in the whole town but yourself.

Major Cyp. I am happy in your want of friends, Colonel, if it gives you occasion to consider me as one.

Col. Down. As for that, I don't want friends, neither, I believe; only they are not here, at present. I have plenty of friends on the other side the Atlantic.—Zounds! I think it wou'd be hard for a man, who has been so long in the army, and borne a post like mine in it, not to have a *regiment* of friends, at least.

Major Cyp. Which is a great consolation to you, no doubt, Colonel.

Col. Down. The greatest in the world, Major. But what! you have changed your house since I was last in England : this is not the same, I think, tho' near the same spot.

Major Cyp. Yes, I have changed my house; and, what is more, changed my state too, Colonel.

Col. Down. Why, you are not married?

Major Cyp. What surprises you ?

Col. Down. Nay, I am not surprised at your marrying; only at your appearing so easy about it !

Major Cyp. And why not, Colonel? A valuable woman—

Col. Down. Very true, very true—and so I wish you joy, with all my heart. *(Shaking hands.)* But, who is the Lady, pray? Do I know her, or any of her family ?

Major Cyp. Did you know Sir George Euston ?

Col. Down. I have heard of him.

Major Cyp. She was his lady.

Col. Down. A widow !

Major Cyp. No—she was no widow.

Col. Down. Did not you say she was Sir George Euston's wife?

Major Cyp. Very true; but Sir George is still living.

Col. Down. What, the devil! is the man living, and you married to his wife?

Major Cyp. It was a divorce, Colonel.

Col. Down. A divorce!—Whu! Now I understand you. Why, that's *mariage en militaire.* You might well appear so easy.

Major Cyp. Fye, Colonel;—I assure you, Lady Harriet Cyprus and I are a most happy couple—and my having snatched her from " a dull, doating husband," gives superior pleasure and triumph to our bliss.

Col. Down. The husband is much obliged to you both.

Major Cyp. Why, poor fellow, that is the worst. In spite of the congratulations I receive from my friends, and my natural desire of fame, and propensity to conquest, I do feel, and cannot help it, a most deep sorrow and compassion for the thorns I have planted in his bosom.

Col. Down. But, I suppose, he used his lady very ill, before he provoked her to the divorce, and certainly preferred some other?

Major Cyp. Oh no, by no means! He doated on her, even to the day of their separation, notwithstanding it was he who sued for the divorce.

Col. Down. He who sued for the divorce—Oh! that was it! I understood you, that you had planted *thorns*—but you said *horns,* I suppose.

Major Cyp. (*Smiles.*) Ha! Ha!

Col. Down. Oh! I wish you much joy—

Major Cyp. Why ironically, Colonel? Depend upon it, I am the envy of all the men in town.: Lady Harriet Cyprus is a perfect beauty.

Col. Down. a Im glad she is perfect in some respect.

Major Cyp. Oh! (*With some inquietude.*) ridiculous, Colonel—Divorces happen now every day; and
the favoured lover is the most admired and envied
of mortals, while the poor husband becomes an object
of general pity.

Col. Down. Ay, the husband?

Major Cyp. Yes, the husband.

Col. Down. Ay, and *you* are the husband now.

Major Cyp. Pshaw! the forsaken husband.

Col. Down. You pity him?

Major Cyp. Certainly.

Col. Down. And, if he is a tender hearted man, I
suppose, he pities you.

Major Cyp. Ha, ha, ha!—Let me describe a scene
to you, where poor Sir George's situation must affect
the most obdurate heart. Lady Harriet Euston,
(now Lady Harriet Cyprus,) was, when I first became acquainted with her, a very loving wife: (We
are friends, Colonel, and I will venture to recount a
few anecdotes to you) a very loving wife, indeed;
and but for my insinuations—artful insinuations I
may call them—had continued her conjugal regard—
she had been to this hour an example to wives, if I
had not tempted her to stray.

Col. Down. Ay, you! or somebody else.

Major Cyp. (*Disturbed.*) Hear me out, Colonel.
She was long an example to wives—she was, I assure you. But to describe to you Sir George's piti-
able situation, and what was chiefly the cause of the
divorce.—One evening, we had prolonged the *tête-à-
tête* rather beyond the usual time; when, unexpectedly, Sir George and a party of beaux and belles
were rushing up stairs,—" Dear Major," cried my
wife——

Col. Down. Your wife? Sir George's, you mean.

Major Cyp. Yes, Sir George's *then,* but my wife *now.*

Col. Down. Ay, ay, and I most sincerely give you joy! (*Ironically.*)

Major Cyp. Pshaw! you put me out.—" Dear Major," cried my wife; or Sir George's, if you will have it so—" What will become of us," (for Sir George had given us some little proofs of his jealousy,) " what will become of us!" exclaimed the then Lady Harriet Euston. " Put me into your thimble; into the eye of your needle, madam," said I—Instead of which, cramm'd I was into that closet.

Col. Down. That closet!

Major Cyp. That very identical closet, which you see there; for Sir George never loved the house after, and so settled it on her Ladyship.—Screwed up in that closet, I believe I remained ten minutes; when old Lady Downfall, who was of the party, called for drops; the door was opened,—and out dropt your humble servant.

Col. Down. Zounds! it was enough to make you wish yourself—

Major Cyp. Nay, it was Sir George's place to wish. Every beau in the room was round me in a moment; and, in a whisper, " Give you joy, Major,"—" The happiest man in the world,"—" An Alexander,"—" A conqueror every where." Even old Sir Samson Shrivel, shook his head, and wished to be in my place.

Col. Down. Zounds! I would have thrust him into the closet, and kept him there for a month. But what did the husband say all this time?

Major Cyp. That is what I was going to tell you. What did he say? Why, he said nothing. You may depend upon it, he heard and saw all the half-stifled laughs, and was wise enough to know to whom they were directed: So, poor fellow, he turned pale,

c 2

bit his lips—looked at her ladyship—looked at me—
looked at his sword—and then cried "Heigh ho!"

Col. Down. Heigh ho! And what the deuce did
you say?

Major. What do you think I said? Egad, I *was*
a little confused.

Col. Down. Confused!

Major Cyp. And do you know I said—Faith, it
was an odd speech, and has been laughed at since in
a thousand fashionable circles—the conclusion of it
has been particularly marked.—" Dear Sir George,"
said I.—He was standing where you may be (here,
a little more this way,) and I just where I am
at present—" Dear Sir George," said I, (half stifling a laugh, for by my soul I could not help it,
though I pitied the poor devil, too,)—" Dear Sir
George," said I, " I'll tell you what,"—you will
find *nobody* to blame in this affair—I protest my being in that closet was entirely owing to—" I'll tell
you what,"—in short, to an—an *undescribable something*——There I made a full stop.

Col. Down. " An undescribable something."

Major Cyp. 'Tis true, upon my soul! those were
the very words.

Col. Down. Owing to an " Undescribable something," and " I'll tell you what," that I got into
this closet:—And so, I suppose, the next day Sir
George left both his wife and the closet, and you have
ever since held possession?

Major Cyp. After some other explanations, and
regular proceedings, I became the happy husband he
was never formed to be.

Col. Down. But I hope you keep the key of the
closet?

Major Cyp. You will have your joke, Colonel.—
Sir George, out of despair, is just married again; and
Lady Harriet's affection for me is such—yet faith, I
must confess to you too, Colonel, that notwithstand-

ing I am so very happy in my marriage—my wife so
very beautiful and so affectionate, yet I am a sad
wicked fellow; I have not forgot my old ways—no,
I am going to-morrow evening to meet a lady of un-
tarnished reputation—a married lady. Faith, 'tis
wrong—I know it is; but I cannot withstand the
temptation—no, I cannot forgot my old ways.

(Yawning.)

Col. Down. And do you suppose her Ladyship can
forget *her* old ways either? (*Yawning.*)

Major Cyp. For shame, Colonel! but you are so
fond of a joke.   Egad, I have a great mind to make
you laugh most heartily at the business I have now
on my hands—you wou'd say it was the most impudent thing of me.   I'll tell you another time, on purpose to make you laugh; no other design whatever.
(*A bell rings.*) That is her ladyship's bell—Come,
I will introduce you to her directly; and, I flatter
myself, you will admire my choice.

Col. Down. It does indeed excite my admiration,
most prodigiously!

[Exeunt.

ACT THE SECOND.

SCENE I.

Enter Mr Anthony Euston, *and a* Servant.

Ser. I'll let my master know immediately, Sir.
[Exit.

Mr Ant. Sir George has changed all his servants,
I think, as well as his house, for I have not seen one

that I know; and not one of them seems to know their old friend Anthony Euston.

Enter SERVANT.

Ser. I beg your pardon, Sir; I thought my master had been at home; but he is not.

Mr Ant. Is not he?

Ser. No, Sir; he has been gone out this half-hour.

Mr. Ant. He is gone to my house then, I dare say. Is your lady at home?

Ser. Yes, Sir.

Mr Ant. Be so kind as to let her know I should be glad to see her.

Ser. What name, pray Sir?

Mr Ant. Only say a relation she will be glad to see. [*Exit Servant.*] Sir George may not be gone to my house, neither; for, perhaps, my brother has not yet called on him, and he may be ignorant of our arrival.—This house is a handsome one; yet, I wonder Sir George should leave his other; for I remember my niece was remarkably fond of its situation.— Poor girl—if she knew it was Anthony, Anthony Euston, I believe she wou'd not be so long in coming. (*Goes to the side of the scene, and calls.*) Come, come, my dear! 'tis an old friend that wants to see you. (*He walks to the opposite side, and, when he hears Lady Euston entering, he returns and calls.*) Come, come—sure you have kept me long enough!

Enter LADY EUSTON.

(As Mr Anthony is going with great eagerness to salute her, he stops short, and she curtsies.)

Mr Ant. I beg your pardon, madam! I thought I had been speaking to my niece.

Lady Eus. Your niece, Sir?

Mr Ant. The lady of the house, madam.

Lady Eus. I have the honour to be mistress of this house, Sir.

Mr Ant. Madam?

Lady Eus. My name is Euston, Sir.

Mr Ant. Good Heaven! Is then my niece, that beautiful young woman, dead?

Lady Eus. The lady that was Lady Harriet Ogle, Sir?

Mr Ant. Yes.

Lady Eus. No, Sir, she is still living, and very well: I saw her the other morning.

Mr Ant. Madam, you rejoice me.

Lady Eus. You are only mistaken in the house, Sir; that's all.

Mr Ant. Madam, you make me happier than I can express. But how cou'd the mistake happen? They told me my nephew lived here. Indeed, I named no names at the door, but only ask'd the man if his master was within; and your name being Euston, madam, I suppose, first caused the mistake.

Lady Eus. Very likely, Sir.

Mr Ant. I beg pardon for the trouble I have given you.

Lady Eus. No apologies, Sir. Permit me to let one of my servants shew you to Lady Harriet's.

Mr Ant. No, I am much obliged to you. If it is the same house that Sir George Euston lived in, about two years ago, I know it very well.

Lady Eus. It is, Sir.

Mr Ant. Madam, I thank you—and once more beg pardon for the trouble I have given you, through a mistake.

Lady Eus. Dear Sir, no apology. Permit the servant to shew you to Lady Harriet's.

Mr Ant. No, madam, I thank you; I have been often there, and know the house very well.—Madam, good morning to you—I beg your pardon—good morning, madam.   [*Exit* MR ANTHONY.

Lady Eus. Good morning to you, Sir.—This is
certainly an uncle of Lady Harriet's, who is unacquainted with her divorce—and I cou'd not inform
him of it; 'twould have led to such disagreeable explanations, and such a long round-about story it must
have caused—" Sir, I am *second wife* to your *present
niece's first husband."* Lud! Lud! how ashamed I
shou'd have been. Lady Harriet had better explain
it by far.   [*Exit* LADY EUSTON.

SCENE II.

A Room at MAJOR CYPRUS'.

Enter COLONEL DOWNRIGHT *and* SIR HARRY
HARMLESS.

Sir Har. Now the Major is gone, Colonel—notwithstanding all he has been talking, of love, and
his vast happiness, you will hardly believe it, perhaps—but he is not so very happy.

Col. Down. No!

Sir Har. No, poor man : you will hardly think it,
but he is jealous.

Col. Down. What, already? And, for Heaven's
sake, of whom?

Sir Har. Nay, I assure you he has no cause—
Nor is he jealous of one alone alone—he is so of every body—and will be so of yóu; therefore, I tell
you, that you may be on your guard. I am constantly with his lady and him, and, because the poor
woman once shut him up in her closet, he now suspects a lover concealed in every part of the house ;
and I have known him, when the mad fit has been
upon him, search for a supposed rival even in her
drawers and band-boxes.

Col. Down. Pray, Sir, do you live in the house.?

Sir Har. I have been on a visit here these six weeks.

Col. Down. And during that time—

Sir Har. I have seen such things! Enough to terrify me from marrying; for wives are sometimes so provoking, I am sure I cou'd not keep my temper. Now, here is Lady Harriet Cyprus, you cannot think how provoking she is—she sometimes says such terrible things to her husband, that, I am sure, if she was my wife—

Col. Down. Why you wou'd not beat her, would you, or lock her up?

Sir. Har. No—but perhaps I might kick her lapdog, or do some outrage to her dress.

Col. Down. You wou'd make an admirable soldier, Sir Harry.

Sir Har. I must own, Colonel, I shou'd have no objection to a commission, where the regimentals were becoming.

Col. Down. Really!

Sir Har. And indeed, Colonel, I am positive you wou'd be obliged to *press* commissioned officers, if it were not for the becomingness of some of their dresses.

Col. Down. Give me your hand, Sir Harry. I like you much; and could I see you master of a firelock, or a wife—

Sir Har. No. While my neighbours marry, I never shall.

Col. Down. Why so, Sir Harry?

Sir Har. Their wives will do for me.

Col. Down. I am amazed, Sir Harry, that the Major, jealous as you describe him, should suffer you to remain in his house!

Sir. Har. I have often been surprised at it myself.

Col. Down. You have!

Sir Har. But he never was jealous of *me.* Zounds! it piques me sometimes. The ladies are fond of me, and yet the gentlemen are not jealous of me. But, indeed, my amours have all been managed so secretly, that none of them have ever yet come to light.

Col. Down. But who has been to blame there, Sir Harry?

Sir Har. I have paid regard to the reputation of the ladies, and none to my own. I expect an assignation to-morrow evening; and I question whether I shall mention it to above three or four of my acquaintance, notwithstanding the lady is reputed a woman of honour, and is, besides, a married lady.

Col. Down. And would you divulge the appointment sooner on that account?

Sir Har. Certainly! Had I a wish to build a reputation.

Col. Down. Who have we here? (*Looking out.*)

Sir Har. The Major and her ladyship! He has been following her into the Park, and is now conducting her home. I assure you their company at present will not be very desirable; so step this way, dear Colonel, and I will indulge you with a few more particulars. Egad, I can surprise you!

[*Exeunt* COLONEL DOWNRIGHT *and* SIR HARRY.

Enter LADY HARRIET CYPRUS, *followed by* MAJOR CYPRUS.

Major Cyp. So, Madam, I have followed you home, and now shou'd be glad to know, what unusual whim brought you into the Park so early?

Lady Har. How can you be so teazing as to ask questions? Especially when you see I am too fatigued to answer.

Major Cyp. Fatigued, madam? How is it possible—

Lady Har. Don't speak so loud.—I'm thinking of something else.

Major Cyp. Zounds, madam, I say—

Lady Har. How can you, Major? Sir George Euston, with all his faults, never asked me such impertinent questions!

Major Cyp. Sir George, madam! How dare you mention his name to me, madam? How dare you mention to me that contemptible —— ?

Lady Har. Dear Major, do not be severe—consider you are—a married man yourself now.

Major Cyp. Heavens! Madam, do not imagine—

Lady Har. And you know every gentleman is liable to—

Major Cyp. What, madam?

Lady Har. *Be* married. There is nothing certain in this world.

Major Cyp. Very well, madam! Very well—I believe I understand your insinuation; and I deserve it. I justly deserve it for venturing my happiness with a woman whose principles I *knew.*

Lady Har. How dare you, Major Cyprus, upbraid me, or think, because my unhappy partiality for you *once* betrayed me into indiscretions, I am not now an altered woman? I am sure I have most heartily repented of all my faults,. and wished a thousand times I had never seen you.

Major Cyp. Exceedingly well, indeed, madam! Exceedingly well. Repent you ever saw me! What am I to expect after such a declaration? And why repent you ever saw me? What, you won't speak! I believe you are the only woman who cou'd call me her husband, and be insensible of her happiness. When you consider, too, your release from Sir George.—What makes you smile, madam? Surely, after all your seeming contempt for Sir George, you

wou'd not, even in *idea*, put him in competition
with *me*?   Though, by heaven, your continual
mention of him is enough—did I not know how
much you despise him.   I am amazed how you
cou'd ever consent to marry such a being, and so I
have told you a hundred times—Not one accomplishment.

Lady Har. Now you provoke me—he had a thousand!

Major Cyp. That I am destitute of?

Lady Har. (*Sighs.*) Oh!

Major Cyp. Zounds, madam, what do you mean
by that sigh?   And in what quality, pray, did your
first husband, your *first* husband, madam—in what
quality did he eclipse your humble servant?

Lady Har. (*After a pause.*) He danced better
than any man I ever saw.

Major Cyp. Dance better!

Lady Har. And his bow was exquisite.

Major Cyp. (*Bowing.*) O—your most obedient!

Lady Har. Then, sometimes, he was the most
entertaining—

Major Cyp. You would have a husband entertain
his wife then?

Lady Har. Certainly—and entertain himself, at
the same time.

Major Cyp. I wish to heaven you had kept him,
with all his accomplishments!

Lady Har. (*Sighs, and shakes her head.*) Oh!

Major Cyp. Damnation!—(*After a pause, comes
up to her with a softened tone of voice.*) Come hither.—Come, tell me,—wou'd you?—and so you
wou'd really prefer your old husband to me?

Lady Har. Old! He was the youngest.

Major Cyp. Madam, madam, I'll hear no more—
I'll suffer no more.   Since you can compare that

contemptible animal to me, I have done with you—you are below even my resentment.

Lady Har. Dear Major, say what you will, Sir George had his virtues—He seldom asked me where I was going; or who visited me in his absence? Where I had been walking? What made me so remarkably cheerful, or why I looked so very ill-natured? In short, he was truly and literally, in every respect, a fashionable husband.

Major. Cyp. You are—

Enter SERVANT.

Ser. Sir, a gentleman below desires to see you; I did not know whether you chose to be at home or not, so I told him I believed you were gone out, but that I wou'd come and see.

Major Cyp. I *am* gone out—go and tell him so. [*Exit Servant.*] I am in too ill a humour to see any body—my temper is spoiled. I am neither fit for company, pleasure, business, nor any thing.

Lady Har. Nor I—I am spoil'd too.

Enter SERVANT.

Ser. The gentleman, madam, begs to see you. Do you chuse I should show him up?

Lady Har. Yes, show him up—he may be of service to my spirits. Who is he? What is his name?

Serv. I ask'd him, madam, but he would not say. He first asked me if my master was within; and when I return'd, and told him no, he said, tell your lady, Lady Harriet, I desire to see *her.*—He spoke as if he was acquainted with your ladyship.

La. Har. Show him up.

Major Cyp. You will please to take him into another room.

La. Har. It is not my intention to leave this room
till dinner.

Major Cyp. Nor mine.

La. Har. Then you'll have an opportunity of assuring the gentleman, *yourself*, you are not at home.

Serv. Shou'd I shew the gentleman into another
room, madam?

Major Cyp. No!   [*Exit angrily.*

La. Har. Shew the gentleman up. (*Exit Servant.*)
Who in the name of wonder can it be, that wants
both the Major and me? I thought our acquaintance had been all separate visitors.

Enter the SERVANT, *with* MR ANTHONY EUSTON
following.

La. Har. Mr Anthony Euston!—(*Mr Anthony
salutes her.*)—Is it possible I shou'd have the honour
of a visit from *you*?

Mr Ant. My dear lady, and why *not*? What,
you heard, I suppose, I was lost;—but have not
you heard again that I was found?

La. Har. No, upon my word, Sir; and the sight
of you amazes me.

Mr Ant. Was not my brother here this morning?

La. Har. No, Sir.

Mr Ant. Nor did not your husband expect me?

La. Har. No, indeed, Sir!

Mr Ant. My brother not here to tell your husband of our safety, after all the perils of shipwreck,
imprisonment, and a story fit for a romance!

Lady Har. Is Mr Euston too return'd safe?

Mr Ant. Certainly.—'Tis strange he has not been
here before me! Where is your husband?

Lady Har. Did you ask for him when you came
in?

Mr Ant. Yes, I asked the servant if his master
was at home, but he returned and said, no;—so I

then asked him for his mistress—and here I find you, my dear lady, as beautiful as ever! But where is my nephew? I am all impatience till I see him.

Lady Har. (*Aside.*) He does not know what has happened, I find.

Mr Ant. What is the matter, my dear?

Lady Har. You are just arrived from abroad, Sir?

Mr Ant. Only left the ship yesterday morning, came to London late in the evening, and, not having had a night's rest on shore for many months, went to bed as soon as I arrived; and, as soon as I rose this morning, came with my respects to you.

Lady Har. Then you have seen no acquaintance since you came to town?

Mr Ant. You are the first. Can you suppose I shou'd visit any one before I had seen you; or do you think any of my friends wou'd find me out the very night of my arrival.

Lady Har. And have you met with none of your English acquaintance while you have been abroad—nor read any of our English newspapers?

Mr Ant. I have seen neither since I left England. —Indeed, when I am at a distance from my friends, as I hate to be imposed on, I seldom ask a question concerning them, and never read a paragraph where their names are mention'd.

Enter COLONEL DOWNRIGHT.

Col. Down. I beg your Ladyship's pardon—I thought the Major had been here;—he promised he wou'd go with me into the city on some business—He is not gone out, I hope?

Lady Har. Mr Euston, you will excuse me a moment—I will send (*To the Colonel*) the Major to you immediately, Sir. (*Aside.*) Let him explain to Mr Euston—the task wou'd be too much for me.

D 2   [*Exit* LADY HARRIET.

Mr. Ant. My fellow traveller! Have you forgot me?   (*Going up to the* COLONEL.)

Col. Down. My good friend! Is it you?—I am heartily glad to see you—I thought it *was* you? and then again—Where is my friend your brother? Why you got to town before me—I am glad to meet you, faith!—So unexpectedly too!

Enter MAJOR CYPRUS, *and bows to* MR ANTHONY.

Major Cyp. Colonel, I beg your pardon; I am afraid I have tired your patience?

Col. Down Not at all—Sir Harry Harmless has been an excellent companion, but he has just left me. (*To Mr Anthony*) I shou'd have call'd on you in the afternoon—Who wou'd have thought of meeting you here?

Mr Ant. Why faith, Colonel, I do not know a more likely place to find a man at, than a relation's house.

Col. Down. What, are the Major and you related?

Mr Ant. Sir!

Major Cyp. Have I the honour of being related to you, Sir?   (*Bowing.*)

Mr Ant. Not that I know of, Sir.—   (*Bowing.*)

Major Cyp. If Lady Harriet has that honour, Sir, I presume to claim the same.

Mr Ant. You are related to Lady Harriet then, Sir?

Major Cyp. By very close ties.—

Mr Anthony. Sir I shall be happy to be better acquainted.

Col. Down. (*Aside to the* MAJOR.) Tell him the story of the closet—Egad 'twill make him laugh.

Major Cyp. (*Aside to the* COLONEL.) Fy, fy! He is a relation of my wife's.

Col. Down. (*Aside.*) He wou'd not like a good story the worse for that.—Would you, Mr Anthony, have any dislike to a good story?

Mr Ant. A story, Sir ?—

Col. Down. Ay, a good story of a—a—zounds
" I'll tell you what!" and " an undescribable something !"—

Major Cyp. For shame, for shame, Colonel !

Mr Ant. Why, my fellow traveller, you are at
your jokes ; the same as ever, I find. What is all
this ?

Major Cyp. Nothing, Sir ; nothing, I assure you.

Col. Down. As good a story as ever was told.
Tell it, Major ; I wou'd, but I cannot *look* it us you
do. Egad, you *look* it to the life.

Mr Ant. Well, gentlemen, I should be very happy
to hear this story, but I am obliged to defer it till
some other time. I have waited for Sir George as
long as possible, and, as I find he does not come,
I'm resolved to go in search of him—So, gentlemen,
your humble servant. If I meet with Sir George, I
shall return, I dare say, immediately ; and, if not, I
shall certainly call in the afternoon. My compliments to her ladyship—Your servant, gentlemen.

Maj. Cyp. Pray, Sir, who did you expect to meet
here ?

Mr Ant. Only Sir George, Sir.

Major Cyp. What Sir George, pray, Sir ?

Mr Ant. Sir George Euston, Sir.

Major Cyp. Sir George Euston, Sir! Did you expect to meet Sir George Euston *here ?*

Mr Ant. Certainly I did, Sir.

Col. Down. That's all for want of hearing the story.—Do, my good friend, come back and hear the
story of the " undescribable something,"—and of the
closet—that little closet—and, " I'll tell you what!"

Major Cyp. Colonel, permit me to speak seriously
to the gentleman.—Sir, (*to Mr Anthony*) you will
never see Sir George Euston in this house, I am certain.

Mr Ant. How so, pray Sir?

Major Cyp. I am now master of this house, and—

Mr Ant. You are master of this house!

Major Cyp. Yes, Sir.

Col. Down. He took possession of the closet, some time ago.

Mr Ant. But pray, Sir, does not Lady Harriet Euston then live here?

Major Cyp. That lady is no longer Lady Harriet Euston, Sir, but Cyprus: she is my wife.

Col. Down. You have spoiled the whole story, by beginning at the wrong end.

Mr. Ant. You astonish me!—I beg your pardon: I came but last night from the West Indies, where I have been for some time, and where not the smallest intelligence from England has ever reached me; therefore you will excuse my ignorance. But I think her ladyship, knowing how great a stranger I was, ought to have dealt a little more openly with me.

Major Cyp. I dare say, Sir, her ladyship——

Mr Ant. Yes, I suppose her ladyship was unwilling to be the first to acquaint me with the death of Sir George.

Major Cyp. The death of Sir George, Sir.

Mr Ant. Yes, Sir; for, while I give you joy on your marriage, give me leave to say, that mine is all damped by the loss of him: And my grief is doubly poignant; because, till this moment, I was not only unacquainted with Lady Harriet's second marriage, but, till this moment, I did not even know Sir George was dead!

Major Cyp. Sir George is not dead, Sir.

Mr Ant. What do you mean? Did you not tell me you were married to his wife?

Major Cyp. Very true, Sir; but you know that is no reason, now-a-days, why the lady's first husband should be dead.

Col. Down. Why, my brother messmate, you are just like me—I had forgot that a man in England might marry his neighbour's wife, and his neighbour living in the next street. And 'tis not the wives of their neighbours, only, these generous gentlemen assail, but more especially the wives of their *friends*.

Mr Ant. Shame on such friendship! Shame on such neighbourhood! Let every tender husband and virtuous wife desert it! (*To the Major.*) Sir, I wish you joy; and, though I know not who are the parties to be censured in this business, I wish her ladyship joy—But more, in particular, I wish *myself* joy, with the sincerest congratulation, that, amidst the depravity of the times, I have followed a beloved wife to her peaceful grave, (mournful as the day was) without seeing her wrested from my arms by the insinuations of a villain: or being myself that villain to force her to seek a refuge from my perjuries, in the protection of another!

Major Cyp. Dear Sir, let me assure you that, however Lady Harriet's conduct may meet censure from the unfeeling prude, the woman of sensibility and taste must applaud her spirit, which could no longer submit to the tyranny of Sir George.

Mr Ant. Did her Ladyship then sue for the divorce?

Major Cyp. No—Sir George, on some frivolous suspicion, was pleased to sue for it.

Mr Ant. Is Sir George married again?

Major Cyp. Yes, Sir, he is married. He has won the lady, and he has won her fortune; but for her affection—there, I believe, we must excuse Sir George—that is a stake now playing for by many noblemen of fashion.

Mr Ant. I suspect Sir George is the dupe of a fashionable gallantry. I know his virtues, and am sorry to find a man of merit so betrayed.

Major Cyp. Dear Sir, think on Lady Harriet, your relation.

Mr Ant. Thank heaven, all ties between Lady Harriet and me were dissolved when she was divorced from Sir George: and so they should, Sir, had she been my own daughter, and Sir George, with the principles I know he possesses, an utter stranger to me.

Col. Down. Why then, I believe, my friend, you are *not* at a relation's house.

Mr Ant. Colonel, you will call on me shortly.— Sir, (Mr Cyprus, I think you call yourself,) I assure you, Sir, as a particular friend of my nephew's, and of the family in general, I am, Sir, your most obedient servant—your humble servant, Sir. (*With contempt.*)   [*Exit* Mr ANTHONY.

Major Cyp. For heaven's sake! who is this man? I took him to be Lady Harriet's uncle! Explain to me who the brute is.

Col. Down. He came passenger from the West Indies in the same ship with me, and that was the first of our acquaintance. As he was no more reserved than I, we soon became intimate; and I learnt from him that his fortune, (a pretty good one) was designed for a nephew, whom I now recollect, (tho' the deuce take me if I thought of it before) to be this very Sir George Euston; and a son, an only child, by that wife he speaks so tenderly of, he disinherits.

Major Cyp. This is the very savage I heard Lady Harriet say the other day was drown'd. What, has his son been guilty of the criminality of a divorce?

Col. Down. No; his guilt is in being married— married to some poor girl, without friends or fortune. Thank heaven, I have neither child nor wife to offend me; but, if I had, I don't know which I would make the most obedient.

Major Cyp. And were you never a lover, Colonel? Never in the service of the ladies?

Col. Down. O yes—I have been in a closet before now—and under a bed, too ; but then I was never pull'd out by a *husband ;* and, on a discovery, I could always describe the something that brought me there.

Major Cyp. By heaven! you are so taken with that joke, I cannot reserve that which I before hinted at from you any longer : Rat me if I have not an appointment for to-morrow evening with Euston's *other* wife! Is it not the most impudent thing of me—

Col. Down. I'll be shot if I dont think so !

Major Cyp. The poor fellow thinks her as chaste as Diana ; and so she is at present, as far as I know. I was happy in her favour a few years ago ; but marriage not being then convenient, my passion was postponed. On her becoming Euston's wife, I renewed my addresses, and she has kindly allotted to-morrow evening for our first *tête-à-tête.*

Col. Down. Zounds, have a care, or you will be obliged to marry *her* too.

Major Cyp. No, no ; we shall be very circumspect in our conduct. But laugh! Why the devil don't you laugh !

Col. Down. No, I was thinking—

Major Cyp. On what?

Col. Down. Come, I must be gone, or I shall be too late for my business.

Major Cyp. I'll attend you immediately.   ut what were you thinking on ?

Col. Down. I was thinking on the happiness—of a married man.

[*Exeunt* COLONEL DOWNRIGHT *and* MAJOR CYPRUS.

ACT THE THIRD

SCENE I.

A Room at Sir George Euston's.

Enter Mr Euston *and* Sir George.

Mr Eus. Bless my soul! Bless my soul! Why, what did my brother Anthony say? Was not he in a dreadful passion? Only think of *his* being made such a fool of! It would not have signified had it been *me*. It had been a good joke if the mistake had happened to me; then you wou'd have had something to have laughed at.

Sir Geo. Dear Sir, let us think no more about it —my uncle has listened to reason, and approves my conduct in every circumstance.

Mr Eus. Ay, 'tis very well, George—'tis all very well—but I know, had you been his son, he wou'd not have forgiven you—he loved that boy so well, he wou'd never forgive him the smallest fault.

Sir Geo. A very cruel proof of his affection.

Mr Eus. 'Tis true, notwithstanding—you know it is. Poor Charles! George, you must do something for him—You know your uncle won't—and I am tied from it by a solemn promise. Many a letter and petition came from his wife to my brother and me, before we went abroad, but all in vain; for I had but just then given Anthony my word, and wou'd not equivocate, by causing the poor boy or his family to be relieved, in any shape, through my means; and therefore I forebore to mention their distress to you. However, now, though I have not forgot my promise, I will not be so *particular* about it; and, when the deviation from my word disturbs my conscience, I'll hush it to rest with having relieved a destitute family.

Sir Geo. Say no more, Sir; I understand you—and to find out my cousin and his family shall immediately be my care.

Mr Eus. (Shaking hands with Sir George.) That's right, George—Poor Charles is a lieutenant in the East Indies. His wife must be the first object of your bounty. Just before I left England, she wrote me a letter from a village near York—where he left her, with two children, and she styles them, in her letter, " the offspring of want and wretchedness." I was a hard-hearted fellow, not to listen to her complaint; but, I think, since I have been at sea, I have been more compassionate. I never knew, before, what it was to be cold or hungry.

Sir Geo. Can you tell me the name of the village, Sir, where I am to seek her?

Mr Eus. Write to her at the post office, Selby. If she should have left the place, they may still know where to send her letters. I wish some friend, that had not made a promise, would speak to my brother Anthony about them at present; perhaps, going to sea has changed his heart too.

Sir Geo. No, Sir; I touched on that subject when I was with him this morning.

Mr Eus. Did you? Did you? And what did he say?

Sir Geo. Asked if I meant to make him forbid me his sight—and, on my apologising, commanded me never to mention my poor cousin in his hearing again.

Mr Eus. Ay, that is what I must never do—

Well, so much the better ; for now, George, nei-
you nor I can tell tales one of another.

Sir Geo. You are right, Sir. Had my uncle Anthony an estate to bestow on each of his family, he
could not exact more obedience to his will than he
does at present.

Mr Eus. 'Tis very true, George. But what keeps
him so long away ?   I expected he wou'd have been
with your lady before this time, acknowledging her
for his niece : though, they have had one meeting,
it seems.

Sir Geo. My uncle cannot be introduced to Lady
Euston till to-morrow, Sir. Lord Layton, for whom
he settled some business when he was abroad, called
on him just as I came away, and, as his lordship
is going to Italy in a day or two, he entreated my
uncle to accompany him immediately to his country
house, (about ten miles from town) in order to look
over some papers he has there.

Mr Eus. Here comes your lady, so I'll leave
you.

Enter Lady Euston.

La. Eus. Dear Mr Euston, I hope I do not fright-
en you away—Sir George will be offended with me
if I do.

Mr Eus. No, madam—I am sure no man cou'd
be offended at being left in such charming company.
                                          [*Exit Mr Euston.*

Sir Geo. My uncle is grown a man of gallantry !

La. Eus. Yes, I inspire all the men.

Sir Geo. I believe you do.

La. Eus. Cou'd I only inspire you with reason to
listen to my arguments—

Sir Geo. 'Tis in vain—The Major shall now feel
my resentment. Did he imagine, because I was indifferent to the conduct of an *undeserving* woman,

that I am not to be roused at such an injury as this? An attempt on the principles of a woman of virtue! 'Tis done on purpose to try me, and by Heaven he shall find—That wretch too, Sir Harry!

L. Eus. Oh, pray have pity on poor Sir Harry.

Sir Geo. No, madam. I only defer my resentment till 'I have had some conversation with my uncle Anthony.

L. Eus. Do, my dear Sir George, suffer me to revenge my own cause this once—and ever after—

Sir Geo. I positively must!

L. Eus. Nay, Sir George, in a year or two, may, perhaps, have no objection to your fighting a duel; but only three months married—I do wish to keep you a little longer.

Sir Geo. Depend upon it, Lady Euston, death had never half the terrors I have beheld it with since I called you mine; but that life you have endeared to me——

L. Eus. You wou'd throw away immediately in my service. No, no, Sir George, a fond wife will never suffer her husband to revenge her wrongs at so great a risk: Besides, the exertion of a little *thought* and *fancy*, will more powerfully vindicate innocence, than that brilliant piece of steel, I assure you.

Sir Geo. Perhaps you are right.

L. Eus. Certainly I am! Now, suppose a gentleman makes love to me—I divulge the affront to you; you call my insulter to an account—*Your* ball misses; he fires into the air; and, to the fame of having dared to wound your honour, he gains that of presenting you with your life.

Sir Geo. But, why must these circumstances take place?

L. Eus. Well, then, we will suppose he kills you ; how do you like that ?

Sir Geo. (*Smiling.*) Hem !

L. Eus. Or, we will suppose, you kill him—even how do you like *that* ?

Sir Geo. Well, I confess that, if a severe punishment could be thought of, for such insolence—

L. Eus. There is as severe a punishment to men of gallantry, (as they call themselves,) as sword or pistol : laugh at them ; that is a ball which cannot miss ; and yet kills only their vanity.

Sir Geo. You are right.

L. Eus. Let me see ; we have been now only three months married ; and, in that short time, I have had no less than five or six men of fashion to turn into ridicule.   The first who ventured to declare his passion, was Lord William Bloomly ; his rank, joined to his uncommon beauty, had insured him success ; and wherever I went, I was certain to hear his distress whispered in my ear ; at every opportunity he fell even upon his kness ; and, as a tender earnest of my pity for him, begged, with all the eloquence of love, for "a single lock of my hair, which he wou'd value more than any other woman's person ; the wealth of worlds ; or (he is a great patriot you know,) even the welfare of his country."

Sir Geo. I am out of patience !

L. Eus. You will be more so—For I promised him this single lock.

Sir Geo. You did not !

L. Eus. But I did ; and added, with a blush, that I must insist on a few hairs from one of his eyebrows in return ; which he absolutely refused ;—and, on my urging it, was obliged to confess, " he valued that little brown arch more than the loc he had been begging for ; consequently, more han any woman's person ; the wealth of worlds ; or even the

welfare of his country." I immediately circulated
this anecdote, and exhibited the gentleman, both as
a gallant and a patriot ; and now his lordship's eye-
brow, which was once the admiration, is become
the ridicule of every drawing room.

Sir Geo. Your ladyship then wou'd not menace
your lover ?

L. Eus. Certainly not ; " You are the most beautiful woman I ever saw," said Lord *Bandy ;* " and
your lordship is positively the most lovely of mankind."—" What eyes," cried he ; " what hair," cried
I ; " what lips," continued he ;" " what teeth," added I ; " what a hand and arm," said he ; " and what
a *leg* and foot," said I ;—" Your ladyship is jesting,"
was his lordship's last reply ; and he has never since
even paid me one compliment. Prudes censure my
conduct ; I am too free—while their favourite, Lady
Strenuous, in another corner of the ball-room, cries
to *her* admirer—" Desist, my lord, or my dear Sir
Charles shall know that you dare thus to wound my
ears with your licentious passion ; if you ever presume to breathe it again, I will acquaint him with it—
depend upon it I will. *(Sighs and languishes.)*
Oh ! you have destroyed my peace of mind for
ever."

Sir Geo. There are too many such ladies, but
no such wou'd I hazard my life for—that I have
proved.

L. Eus. And, upon my word, Sir George, even
the virtuous wife, who wou'd not have some regard
to her husband's *life,* as well as his *honour,* if I
were a gentleman, I should not feel myself under
many obligations to.

Sir Geo. You wou'd protect both ?

L. Eus. And the guilty not escape. Now, with
your consent,) what must be the confusion, shame,
and disappointment, of my two masked lovers to-

morrow evening; the brutal audacity of one, and
insignificance of the other; both beneath *your*
resentment, yet deserving objects of mine. And,
indeed, Si George, it is my fixed opinion, that,
the man who wou'd endeavour to wrong a virtuous
wife, shou'd be held too despicable for the resentment
of the husband, and only worthy the debasement inflicted by our sex. I have already sent a letter to
Sir Harry, with the appointment at the masquerade;
and the Major has my promise of a meeting at the
same time. Come, come, Sir George, it is the first
petition I ever presented; do not refuse me!

Sir Geo. Give me till the morning to consider of
it?

L. Eus. With all my heart; and in the mean time
reflect on this—that, in regard to your terrible sex,
whether as licentious lovers or valiant champions—
women, of *real honour*, are not in danger from the
one; and, therefore, like me, ought to forego the
assistance of the other.

[*Exeunt Lady Euston and Sir George.*

SCENE II.

A Room at COLONEL DOWNRIGHT'S.

Enter COLONEL DOWNRIGHT and MR ANTHONY EUSTON.

Col. Down. My good friend, I was just going to
bed; but I am glad of your company, though I did
not expect it.

Mr Ant. Colonel, my errand at this time was
merely to ask a favour of you.

Col. Down. Command it, and you will make me proud.

Mr Ant. Why then, Colonel, with Lord Layton to-day, (at whose house I dined,) a circumstance happened, on which account I expect his lordship will call on me to-morrow for a fashionable satisfaction ; and though, depend upon it, I wish for no such rash means of ending a dispute ; yet, if his lordship *shou'd* call upon me, 'tis fit I be prepared with a second ; and I thank you for the friendly assurance you have now given me of your service.

Col. Down. You are as welcome to it—I was going to say, as my king ; but, zounds, if I shou'd be killed in a pitiful quarrel at home, I shou'd blush even in my grave ; for, when I die, I hope to have my knell rung by the groans of a score or two of our country's treacherous foes.

Mr Ant. The service I shall put you to, Colonel, will not prevent that hope.

Col. Down. But what, for Heaven's sake, has brought you into a quarrel ?

Mr Ant. The cause of our quarrel was—you will call it a very trivial one, I dare say—a woman !

Col. Down. Why, my old friend, you have not been quarrelling about a woman—Oh, if I shou'd be killed for a woman, I shou'd cut a noble figure, indeed ?

Mr Ant. Hear me, Colonel, hear me—and, as you may question my prudence, let me tell you the whole adventure.

Col. Down. Nay, nay, I did not mean to question your prudence, nor to speak against the women either. I like them as well as you do.

Mr Ant. I own I have a respect for their sex, which nites me to them as their father, their friend, and admirer. And I beg you will give me your sentiments upon the character of one whose behaviour, this day, has surprised me beyond measure; I will describe it to you, and you will then tell me whether you believe me imposed upon, or whether you think she really claims that extraordinary attention I have, some how, been compelled to give her.

Col. Down. Well, let me hear.

Mr Ant. Lord Layton and I had no sooner plac'd ourselves in his lordship's coach, than he exclaim'd, he had just seen the most beautiful girl his eyes ever beheld, to whom he had given a look of solicitation, and that she was returning her answer by making up to the coach. He begged a thousand pardons, .but, with my permission, (as he expected no other company at his country house,) he wou'd take her down to dine with us. I, knowing his lordship well, (and the girl being now arrived at the coach door) reluctantly assented, and she was immediately handed in.

Col. Down. Zounds, he shou'd have taken a companion for you too!

Mr Ant. Don't interrupt me. When she had been seated about a minute, I cast my eyes upon her—

Col. Down. 'Sdeath, I shou'd not have staid half so long.

Mr Ant. I was struck with her beauty—

Col. Down. And wish'd his lordship out of the way, I suppose.

Mr Ant. No, no; there was a sensibility in her countenance that amazed me; blushes on her cheeks; tears in her eyes. When his lordship spoke to her, she answered him with a forced smile, and a tremor on her voice. She avoided all conversation; and, when we alighted, I handed her out of the coach.

Col. Down. Ay, ay, I thought how it was.

Mr Ant. You misunderstand me. I perceived her hand tremble—

Col. Down. And so, I suppose, did yours.

Mr Ant. If you interrupt me, sir, you shall hear no more.

Col. Down. And, I believe, it will be for your credit if I don't.

Mr Ant. Let me tell you all that passed.

Col. Down. With all my heart—if you don't blush at it, I shan't.

Mr Ant. I believe her to be a woman of virtue.

Col. Down. Then what the devil were my lord and you—

Mr Ant. I have rescued her from him.

Col. Down. Why then, the deuce take me if you are not more in love than I thought you were.

Mr Ant. Oh, had you seen her countenance, so expressive of anguish! The hope with which she lifted up her eyes to me, for deliverance! The horror painted in her face, when I left the room! Heard her piercing cries, that called me back to her protection? The despair and earnest supplication that hung upon her tongue, while she entreated him to view her, not as an object of *love*, but *charity!* The grief! the pathetic tenderness with which she declared herself, " a virtuous, though forsaken wife! A poor, indigent, forlorn mother; perishing, with her children,—for whose sake she had been tempted by the first lure that offered (prompted by more than common grief,) to add the sense of guilt to all her other miseries!"

Col. Down. 'Sdeath—

Mr Ant. Cou'd I? Ought I to have gone and left her?

Col. Down. Left her! No. But what did you do?

Mr Ant. Returned to the chamber, and insisted on his lordship resigning her to me.

Col. Down. And did he?

Mr Ant. She hung upon me; and, in spite of his menaces, I led her to my coach, (which was then come for me,) and brought her safe away.

Col. Down. I hope she got safe home too.

Mr Ant. Perfectly so. As her tears interrupted her, whenever she attempted to tell me where she lived, or explain any circumstance of her life to me, I asked no questions, but took her to my own house— desired my house-keeper to show her an apartment, and treat her with attention—and, promising to see and speak with her in the morning, left her to the repose which she must greatly want.

Col. Down. And now you think his lordship will send *you* to repose for all this.

Mr Ant. He may attempt it, for which I wish to be prepared.

Col. Down. Well then, here is my hand; and, though I must acknowledge that you have had too little of the man of the world about you in the business, yet, as I said before, command me.

Mr Ant. Come then, Colonel, my coach is waiting for me at the door; will you go with me to the next coffee-house? I have to meet a gentleman there on a little business; and afterwards we will enjoy half an hour's conversation together.

Col. Down. With all my heart.

[*Exeunt* MR ANTHONY *and* COLONEL.

ACT THE FOURTH.

SCENE I.

A Room at MR ANTHONY EUSTON'S.

Enter MR EUSTON.

Mr Eus. Wonders will never cease!   Who wou'd have thought it!   Why surely it cannot be!   My brother Anthony to bring home a girl!— What wou'd he have said to *me* if I had done such a thing? For my part, I never durst think of such a thing. Perhaps it is some neighbour's child!   But if she is —the servant tells me she is very handsome, and Anthony wou'd not bring her home without some meaning. What wou'd my nephew George say to this? Why he would not believe it!   He wou'd a great deal sooner believe it of me.   And yet, I—I!—Lord bless me—how people may be mistaken!   Here he comes.

Enter MR ANTHONY.

Mr Ant. Brother, good morning to you.   Have you seen George this morning?

Mr Eus. No, brother.

Mr Ant. Are you going there?

Mr Eus. I believe I shall be presently, brother.

Mr Ant. (Sitting down.) Perhaps he may call here first.

Mr Eus. (Sitting down.) Perhaps he may, brother.

(Mr Anthony appears thoughtful, and leans on the table.)

Mr Eus. (After a long pause, and with significant looks.) It was a fine moon-shining night, last night.

Mr Ant. Yes, a fine night.

Mr Eus. (After another pause.) And 'tis a very fine day, to-day.

Mr Ant. Yes—it is.

Mr Eus. We have very fine weather, indeed.

Mr Ant. We have.—You have breakfasted, I suppose?

Mr Eus. Yes—and so, I suppose, have you?

Mr Ant. Yes, some time.—*(He begins writing.)*

Mr Eus. I interrupt you, brother—but I am going.—*(Rises.)*

Mr Ant. No, you do not. But tell Sir George, if you should see him, that I cannot call on him this morning, because I shall be busy.

Mr Eus. You shall be busy!

Mr Ant. Yes, I have got a little business to settle.

Mr Eus. To be sure, *business* must be minded.

Mr Ant. But be particular in delivering my apology, for I wou'd not have his lady affronted.

Mr Eus. One wou'd not affront a *lady* to be sure. No—no—no!

Mr Ant. I wou'd not have her think I slight her.

Mr Eus. No! I am sure you wou'd not slight a lady! *(He coughs.)* Good morning, brother!

Mr Ant. Good morning.

Mr Eus. We shall see you, perhaps, when your *business* is done! Good morning, brother.

[*Exit* Mr Euston, *coughing,*

Mr Anthony pulls a letter out of his pocke

Mr Ant. Yes, here is the challenge; and, truly, something noble in it. He applauds my taking away the lady, but says my manner was too rough. I must retract some words. My lord, that cannot be: (*Puts up the letter.*) And now for a few bequests to my relations, in case his lordship should prove victorious. It is well my will is already made--for he has scarcely given me time to—(*He writes, then throws down the pen.*) What paternal weakness! (*Rises.*) How strange it is, altho' I *have* resisted, and *can*, with manly firmness, resist every innate pleading for that ungrateful boy I once called my son; that careless prodigal of a father's peace, and his own welfare—yet—when I consider myself as shortly to be an inhabitant of another world, and without the power to assist him—I wish—I wish— What?—Why, that heaven may then raise him up a friend to deal more gently with him than I have done. A friend, whose temper, whose *place* it better may become to forgive his faults than an offended father. (*He takes the paper.*) In vain are the strugglings of nature. Justice—example—and my word irrevocably past, silence its pretences. (*He seals the paper, directs it, and looks at his watch.*) The time is almost expired, and I must pay a short visit to my new lodger, and be gone.—John!

Enter SERVANT.

Mr Ant. Is not this the time that the lady gave me permission to wait on her?

Serv. The lady sent word she wou'd wait on you, sir. This is the time; and, sir, she is coming.

Mr Ant. Shew her in.　　　　　[*Exit Servant.*

(*Mr Anthony walks two or three turns, and then the lady is shewn in.*)

Mr Ant. I hope, madam, my message did not disturb you?

Lady. Not at all, sir. I had asked permission to see you before I received it. *(He draws chairs, and they sit.)*

Mr Ant. Well, madam—Unless you have enquired of the servants, you are yet a stranger to my name and connections.

Lady. I am a stranger to them, sir. But your humanity must ever be engraved on my heart.

Mr Ant. Then, madam, for the service you are pleased to acknowledge I have rendered you, all I request, in return, is your confidence. Explain clearly to me the circumstances, the temptations that brought you into the situation from whence I released you! Declare them with frankness, and tax my humanity yet further; it shall not forsake you. To encourage you to this confession, my name is——

Lady. Hold, Sir! That is an information I cannot return—therefore let us wave it; and as I can remain grateful for your goodness, without knowing to *whom* I am indebted, so pity still my weakness, and my miseries, without a further knowledge of the wretched sufferer.

Mr Ant. Madam, you have imposed on me a task too hard. 'Tis true you have won my pity; but 'tis fit you shou'd *secure* it too. And while explanations are reserved, *Doubt,* that hardener of the human heart, must be your enemy.

Lady. Alas! *(Rises.)*

Mr Ant. Come—I wish not to exact too much; but I am a *man,* madam, and with every frailty incident to the species: *suspicion* has its place.

Lady. I know I am an object of suspicion; but you are deceived in me—indeed you are. Guilt never *harboured* in my heart. Maternal tenderness, for two helpless infants, hurried me in a moment to

do I know not what, rather than lose them : A
deed ! the horror of which (altho' by the mercy of
eternal Providence, I have escaped its direst consequences,) must ever cover me with blushes ; and,
shou'd indulgent heaven reserve me for a meeting
with my husband, must, with remorse, damp every
joy the fond, fond interview would give !

Mr. Ant. Be comforted. (*Leading her to her
seat.*) I mean not to increase, but soothe your grief.
Tell me but *who* you are, and *why* thus abandoned
by all your relations, friends, and husband ?   I can
excuse the feelings of a mother—the sudden starts,
or rather madness of resolution, formed by the excessive anguish of the soul.   Trust me, I can deal
tenderly with human failings. No frivolous curiosity,
but a desire to serve you, thus urges me to entreat
you will *unfold* yourself.

Lady. Oh, Sir, I have a husband, *I think*, who
loves me.   Once I am sure he did.   *My* heart has
never stray'd from *him*, since our fatal union. What
must that poor heart suffer, torn with remorse for
the rash step my mad despair suggested to preserve
my children?   Oh! in my bosom let his name lie
hid, that none may know his wretched fortune in a
hapless wife.

Mr Ant. Your reasons have satisfied me.   I do
not ask your name.   Tell me but the *circumstances*
that drove you to the state from whence I released
you :   Be so far explicit, and I will ask no more.

Lady. Most willingly ! · When first my husband
saw me, I was friendless.   Compassion caused his
love for me—Gratitude mine for him.   Forlorn and
destitute, no kind relation, no tender benefactor taught
my heart affection.   Unused to all the little offices of
kindness, could they but endear the object who bestowed them?   Sense of obligation, never before
excited, pressed on my thoughts, and soon was

changed to love. He scorned to violate the heart
that was his own, and we were married.

Mr Ant. I find no room for accusation here. Go
on—go on, madam. What has alienated your husband from you, and left you thus destitute at present? If you can resolve me that; if you still have
acted with equal propriety, I am your friend—I have
no censure for you.

Lady. But you will condemn my husband; even
I must own he was to blame. Born of wealthy parents,
the heir to large possessions, and I to none, when
he married, all were given up, and he changed his
state for mine. We had no friend, but in each other;
yet happy was that state to *me*, till poverty surprised
us; and the fond hope (which once he cherished) of
paternal forgiveness, vanished from my husband.
Then all our days were bitter as they had before
been happy; tears were my only food, and sighs
were his; even *reproach* I have endured from him,
for making him the friendless wretch he call'd himself. Yet—yet, at our parting, oh! then he can-
cell'd all; for when the regiment, in which he served, was ordered from the kingdom, he hung upon
me, clasped his poor children, begg'd our forgiveness for the thousand outrages distress at our misfortunes had caused him to commit; swore that affection for us, was the source of his impatience—prayed
heaven to bless *us*, whatever might be his fate—nay,
prayed that death might speedily be his doom, so
that it turned his father's heart to us.

Mr Ant. And have you never applied to his
father?

Lady. Yes, but all in vain; and two months since,
hearing my husband was made prisoner, (and destitute of every relief and every hope while he remained so,) I left my children and came to London, resolved, in *person*, to supplicate his father's bounty;

when I learnt (dire news,) his father, visiting an estate abroad, was lost, and we left to despair.

Mr Ant. What do you say?

Lady. Nay, do not blame him; I pardon him from
my soul. And as my husband, spite of his disobedience, loved him tenderly, I will ever give a tear in
tribute to his memory.

Mr Ant. Without hesitation!—without the smallest reserve, tell me your husband's name! Is it
Euston?

Lady. It is!

Mr Ant. His father is not dead! He lives, and
pardons him this moment! (*Embracing her.*)

Mrs Eus. You are his father! I know it! I
see it in your looks! (*Kneeling.*)

Mr Ant. And you shall henceforth see it in my
actions! Rise, rise, and behold (*Taking the paper
from his pocket,*) where I this moment again disown'd
him for my son, while the poor of every kind (except
himself) I ever styled my children—Oh! charity,
partially dealt, never more receive that heavenly virtue's title. Here (*Pointing to the paper.*) I provide
for you as a poor stranger, who never asked, and
might not have deserved my bounty; while, as a
daughter, begging for an alms, I shut my heart, and
sent your supplications back. Where was the merit
of my thousands given, while one poor wretch, from
proud resentment, petitioned me in vain?

Mrs Eus. I dare not call myself your daughter!

Mr Ant. You *are* my daughter; and, when I have
supplicated heaven to pardon my neglect of you, I'll
ask your pardon, too. You *are* my daughter—and
let the infamy you have escaped serve only to make
you more amiable; make you compassionate—compassionate to your own weak sex, in *whatsoever* suffering state you see them—They all were virtuous
once, as well as you—and, had they met a father,

F 2

might have been saved like you. For me—(*Pulls
out his watch.*) Bless me, how has the time flown!—
My dear, I have an engagement I cannot postpone
above half an hour; and that time I must dedicate
to——Now, methinks, I wou'd wish to live. (*Aside.*)
Retire to your chamber. I will, if possible, be with
you speedily.—Where your husband is, and in what
poor place your children, I am impatient till I know;
but now I cannot wait. Retire, my child. May we
meet again in safety. (*He leads her to the door, and
she withdraws.*)

Mr Ant. Now where's the Colonel? I have just
time to draw up a writing for him to sign when he
arrives; and I'll about it instantly. Oh! with
what transport does the human heart dislodge the
unnatural guests, malice, and resentment, to take to
its warm recesses the mild inhabitant, peaceful Charity. Yet even more welcome is the returning virtue, when thus 'tis strengthened by parental fondness.
                                    [*Exit.*

ACT THE FIFTH.

SCENE I.

An Apartment at MAJOR CYPRUS'.

Enter LADY HARRIET, *and* BLOOM, *meeting.*

La. Har. What success ? Will Sir George come ?
What a tedious time have you been gone !

Bloom. Dear madam, if you cou'd suppose how
obstinate Sir George was ; and how I had to beg,
and to pray——

La. Har. But will he come ?

Bloom. Yes, madam—at last he said he wou'd.

La. Har. Thank Heaven—Then I shall have the
unspeakable joy of giving him this ! (*Pulling out a
letter.*)

Bloom. What, Sir George, madam ?   Well, I declare, I was at my wit's ends to know what you cou'd
want with Sir George.

La. Har. To give him this letter, Bloom, from
Lady Euston to the Major, which you so luckily
found, and to have the extreme pleasure of informing
him that I am not the only object deserving his resentment ; but that even his wife of a few months——

r 3

she whom the world says he doats upon, and who has driven me from his remembrance, is indiscreet as I have been; to see with my own eyes his confusion—hear him reproach her conduct, and make him own—He promised he'd come?

Bloom. Yes, ma'am—but not till I knelt down and swore your ladyship was *dying*; suddenly taken ill; and cou'd not leave the world in peace till you had communicated something from your own lips to him.

La. Har. You did right; just as I ordered you— And what did he say to that?

Bloom. (*After a long pause.*) Why, he said,—" I will come to the poor unhappy wretch !"

La. Har. Wretch! Are you sure he said so?

Bloom. I am sure he said " Poor," and " unhappy," and then, you know, " wretch" follows of course.

La. Har. Who will be *most* wretched, in a few moments, he or I?

Bloom. Very true, madam; I believe he'll find he has not changed for the better.

La. Har. (*Looking at the letter.*) Confusion! What have you made me do? You told me this letter was for the Major; it is directed to Sir Harry Harmless.

Bloom. Oh that I shou'd not look at the direcon!

La. Har. No matter; this is even a greater dishonour to Sir George than were it to the Major, and will wound him deeper—But where is the Major then? He will not be engaged as I supposed—and may return.

Bloom. Oh, no, my lady, that I dare say he won't —you need not fear; go into your chamber, madam, and make yourself easy till Sir George comes, and make yourself easy when he does come too; for, though the Major may not be with Lady Euston, I dare say he has his appointments in some corner or another, as well as your ladyship.   [*Exeunt.*

SCENE II.

Mr Anthony Euston's.

Enter Mr Anthony Euston *and* Colonel Down-right.

Mr Ant. I have been waiting for you all day—What meant the few words in your letter?   Why is my meeting with his lordship deferred?

Col. Down. I am just come from Lord Layton—a friend of his lordship's, knowing I was acquainted with you, called and took me there ; and, to tell you the truth, I think this business between you and his lordship might be amicably and honourably settled—However, if you don't fight with *him*, you must fight with a mad-headed fellow I have left below—So which do you choose?

Mr Ant. What do you mean?

Col Down. Nay, you will have a worse chance than you wou'd have had with his lordship ; for this man is a soldier, one who has been fighting for these four or five years past ; besides, he's desperate—half mad; and has sworn, he'll either kill or be killed by you, *instantly.*

Mr Ant. Let him come—Who, and what is he? What has he to demand of me?   (*Angrily.*)

Col. Down. Nay, don't be too violent neither—He's
a poor unfortunate lad, I fancy ; and, notwithstanding all his blustering—he now and then looks so
heart-wounded, I cannot help pitying him.

Mr Ant. But what's his business?   What is his
quarrel with me?

Col. Down. Lord Layton is the innocent cause of
it; he told the young man, who came to his lordship's (somewhat sooner than I did) in search of the
lady whom you took away, that the lady had con-
fessed herself poor ; and even perishing for subsistence ; and that, consequently, she was willing to re-
sign herself to the most liberal; which, you proving,
in spite of his lordship's generosity, you carried off
the prize ; and, egad, I owned it was what I had
suspected, notwithstanding your grave countenance
last night.

Mr Ant. You told him you thought so?

Col. Down. Yes ; for I wished to turn the whole
matter into a joke with his lordship ; I did not think,
at the time, that the young fellow wou'd have been so
violent; for till this was explained he was as patient
as a lamb ; and only inquired, with *trembling* and
sighs, for the lady; but, when he heard what I said,
egad, he laid hold of me, and swore, till I brought
him to my friend, the " unpitying, vile purchaser of
innocence," (meaning you) he wou'd not quit me—
So here he has followed me through the streets ; and,
on condition that he wou'd be patient while I came
and announced him to you, I have promised him you
shall give him satisfaction.

Mr Ant. What is this gentleman's name? (*Anxiously.*)

Col. Down. He did not tell us.

Mr Ant. Does he know mine?

Col. Down. No; I thought it most prudent not to

tell him ; for, he is such a madman, he might have
bawled it as we came in the streets.

Mr Ant. (*Much embarrassed.*) What is he to the
lady ? Her brother ?—her cousin ?

Col. Down. Why, faith, I've a notion, (though he
did not say so,) I have a notion he is her husband.

Mr Ant: Indeed !—(*Starting.*)

Col. Down. Why you don't like the business the
worse for that ? 'Tis *crim. con.* now, and you'll be
quite in the fashion.

Mr Ant. Let the young man come up; I'll withdraw for a moment ; but do not give him to suppose
I have *not* injured him.

Col. Down. That you may depend upon; I never
tell a falsehood for myself, much less for another.

Mr Ant. Neither let him know my *name.* I'll
first send the lady to him, and then return myself.

Col. Down. He's coming.   [*Exit Mr Anthony.*

Charles. (*Without.*) Where is this gentleman ?

Col. Down. Walk in here, sir.

Enter CHARLES EUSTON.

Col. Down. The man you wish to see—and whom
you say has injured you—will be here and give you
satisfaction immediately.

Cha. I thank him—Then I shall die and never
see her more. (*Aside.*) Oh, sir! cooled with the
restraint you have thus long imposed on me! I wish
to ask a favour ; I thought I was resolved never
again to behold the wretch I have been deprived of;
but, my rage for a moment gone, I cannot think of
dying, and she so near me, without once looking on her;
I have come far to see her—suffered much—crossed
half the Eastern clime in poverty ; have endured
more pain, more toil, to gain my freedom, but to
starve with her—and, dying, comfort her, than, had
a throne been my waiting reward, my spirits could

have struggled with. And, after all, I feel, I feel
I could be repaid with a mere look. Then, why
refuse me? If I scape my antagonist, I have resolved on death! Let me then see her! I will not
exchange a word with her—will they refuse her
coming?

Col. Down. No—for here she is—

Enter Mrs Euston, *and stops* (*with emotion*) *as soon
as she enters.*

Mrs Eus. Oh! But I am commanded not to fly
to your arms—I must not run to you, and tell you
all I feel!

Cha. (*After a pause.*)   I said—I thought—I
wou'd not speak to you—but pity for your crimes and
miseries compel me ; and, I tell you, to alleviate
your remorse, I *pardon you*—nay, perhaps, love you
better, even in this agony of affliction, than if we had
been blest with prosperous, virtuous days! I know
what you have suffered! Your guilt convinces me !
I want no other plea from a heart like yours. But
where's your vile purchaser? My rage returns !
I must die soon—but first in his breast! (*Draws
his sword.*)

Col. Down. He's here!

Enter MR ANTHONY.

Cha. Then to his heart—(*Going to stab him, sees
it is his father, and after a pause, falls on his knees.*)
My father !

Mr Ant. Yes—I am the man, whose life you seek.
And, as your father, you might pursue your purpose
—But, as your wife's friend and preserver, still kneel
to me ; and receive her, virtuous, from my hands.

Cha. (*Embracing her.*) Virtuous ! Virtuous !—
O my father—Even groaning under your displeasure,

ever dear, and revered! What are you now, while
heavenly consolation pours from your lips?

Col. Down. Father and son! Why, then there's
to be no battle at last?

Mr. Ant. No—Hostilities are past—and may
their future days know only peace! My son—
(*Embracing him.*)

Cha. That tender name distracts me! Let me
be more composed—prepared—before I experience
such unexpected happiness. Maria, lead me from
my father—Hereafter I will thank him ; but now, I
cannot.

Mrs Eus. Oh! Yes, my husband, kneel to him
again!—Kneel for me! For your poor children!
Saved from want and wretchedness! From being
orphans! Kneel to him for us all!—preserved from
infamy!

Cha. O spare the recollection—I feel too much!
A poor, forsaken, desperate, dying man, restored to
love, to life, to *him*, too—whose anger, (even while
blest with thee,) plung'd me in constant sorrow. It
is too much!

Mr Ant. I thought my heart had been—but—
(*He faulters and wipes his eyes.*)

Col. Down. What? Do *you* weep?—Now, that
affects me more than any thing that has been said or
done yet. I don't like to see a woman cry, but I
can't bear to see a man : a man's tears flow from so
deep a source—they always appear to have come a
long journey, and therefore I notice them as strangers,
that have gone through fatigue, and trouble, on their
way. While a woman's tears I consider as mere
neighbours, that can call upon you when they like,
and generally drop in on all occasions.   [*Exeunt.*

SCENE III.

Major Cyprus'.

Enter LADY HARRIET *and* BLOOM.

La. Har. (*A loud rap.*)   That is Sir George—
Heavens !—

Bloom. Yes, my Lady, that it is—

La. Har. Heavens ! What a sensation—How am
I agitated at his approach !   Cou'd I have thought,
a few hours ago, I shou'd ever see him again?—
Speak to him again !   Oh this shame—

Bloom. Shame !   Bless me !   One does feel a
little ashamed sometimes on seeing a stranger ; but,
my lady, Sir George is (as one may say) an *old
acquaintance.*

La. Har. I must retire for a moment—Do you
receive him—and, before I return, give him to understand that I am *not* dying ; but will come to him
immediately.   [*Exit.*

Bloom. Well, now I declare I begin to be ashamed
myself—Own all I swore to him on my knees was a
falsehood ?   Why, what will he say ?   Dear me,
I'm quite alarmed !   I must retire for a moment
too ! (*Goes to the back of the stage.   A servant
shows Sir George in, and retires.*)

Sir Geo. How strange does it seem to me to find
myself once more in this house, especially when I
consider who resides here—Who ?   Perhaps, by this
time, poor Lady Harriet is no more—How amiably

did my dear Lady Euston enforce her dying request
—I doubted the *rectitude* of complying with it—but
she surmounted all my scruples, and her tenderness
and generosity have endeared her to me more than
ever.

BLOOM *comes down.*

Sir Geo. How does Lady Harriet?

Bloom. As well as can be expected, sir.

Sir Geo. How!

Bloom. I hope you won't be angry, sir—but she's
a *little* better.

Sir Geo. Angry! No; I am very glad to hear it!

Bloom. Are you indeed, sir? Why, then I believe she is a *great deal* better.

Sir Geo. Indeed! I am very glad; but then, if
my attendance can be dispensed with—I may as
well—

Major Cyp. (*Without.*) Let the chariot wait—
perhaps, I may go out again.

Bloom. Oh! Oh! Oh! Oh! Oh!—that's the
major—that's my master! my *other* master! Oh,
what will become of us all?

Sir Geo. How unlucky!

Bloom. Sir! Dear sir, hide yourself!

Sir Geo. Hide!

Bloom. On my knees I beg—Consider my poor
dying lady!

Major Cyp. (*On the stairs.*) Go with that note
immediately.

Bloom. Here! in here, sir, for Heaven's sake.
                    (*Opening the closet door.*)

Sir Geo. 'Sdeath! What shall I do? See *him?*
Damnation! And see him *here* too? No, I can't
bear it—I must avoid him.
                    (*Going towards the closet.*)

Bloom. Here, Sir—here quick! (*She puts Sir George into the closet, and shuts the door.*)

Bloom. There, there he is! thank Heaven! For, if my poor lady had lost the major, she might never have got a third husband. Lord bless me, I'm just as terrified as if I had never been used to these sort of things!   [*Exit to Lady Harriet.*

Enter MAJOR CYPRUS.

Major Cyp. Ridiculed, baffled—laughed at—disappointed! How Sir George will enjoy this! A fine figure I cut on my knees to Sir Harry, when the colonel and his friends were shown in! And then my ridiculous vanity in wishing him to be unmasked, confidently expecting it was Euston's wife! Oh, damn it! I'll think no more of it; but as I am deprived the satisfaction of revenge on the lady abroad, I'll e'en torment my lady at home! (*Calls*) Lady Harriet——Lady Harriet.

Enter LADY HARRIET *and* BLOOM.

Major Cyp. What's the matter? You tremble—you look pale!

La. Har. (*Trembling.*) Tremble! Bless me—I've been fast asleep—and such a dream! I thought I was falling—

Bloom. Ay, my lady, I always dream of falling too!

La. Har. (*Yawns and rubs her eyes.*) How long have you been come home? What's o'clock? How long do you think I have slept, Bloom?

Bloom. I dare say, pretty near an hour and half, my lady.

La. Har. A miserable dull book—fell out of my hand! and I dropp'd insensibly—

Bloom. And with the candles so near your ladyship! I'm sure your ladyship was very lucky, you
did not set yourself on fire!

, *Major Cyp.* Aye; does your ladyship consider
the danger with the lights so near you? You might
have caught fire, and I shou'd have had all my valuable pictures, and library, consumed in an instant!

La. Har. And I consumed too.

Major Cyp. Aye—and your ladyship.

La. Har. Very true—but I am fond of reading
melancholy books ; that set me to sleep.

Major Cyp. Then I desire, for the future, you
wou'd *not* read.

La. Har. And don't you desire I wou'd not
sleep too! I'm very sorry you disturbed me.—
Bloom, come and dispose the sofa, and the lights—
I'm resolved I'll finish my nap.

Major Cyp. But, Mrs Bloom, first order the
French horns up—I'm out of spirits. [*Exit Bloom.*

La. Har. And do you imagine your horns will
disturb my repose? I shall like them of all things
—they'll lull me to sleep.

Major Cyp. Like them or not—I will have them.

La. Har. You shall—you shall have them.
(*Significantly.*)   [*Exit.*

Enter SERVANT.

Ser. Colonel Downright, Sir, with two gentlemen,
strangers, desire to be admitted.

Major Cyp. (*Aside.*) What can bring them
here? They dare not come to laugh at me! No
matter—I'll see them. (*Aloud.*) Shew them up.

Enter COLONEL DOWNRIGHT, MR EUSTON, *and* MR ANTHONY EUSTON.

Col. Down. Major, these gentlemen, the Mr
Euston's, have begged me to introduce them to you,

late as it is, on business in which they are ma-
terially—

Mr Ant. Sir—Major Cyprus, I beg your pardon
—but I have received intelligence that my nephew,
Sir George Euston, is in this house, and I am come
to conduct him safe out of it.

Major Cyp. Sir!

Mr. Ant. In short, Sir—Sir George Euston has
been, by some unwarrantable means, led to pay a
visit here, and I cannot leave the house until I see
him.   If I should, my niece, Lady Euston, will be
highly alarmed (knowing you are at home,) for her
husband's safety.

Major Cyp. Sir George in this house! Ridiculous
supposition!

Mr Eus. Call her ladyship's woman—She deliver'd the message of invitation—I shall know her
again, for I saw her—and I saw Sir George soon
after follow her.

Major Cyp. Bloom! Bloom! Where's Bloom?

Enter BLOOM.

Pray were you at Sir George Euston's to-day, or
this evening?

Bloom. I!   At Sir George Euston's, sir!

Mr Eus. Yes: I saw you there.

Bloom. Oh! Oh! Oh! (*crying*) Oh dear!   I
was not there indeed, sir!

Major Cyp. You see she denies it, and confirms
the truth with her tears.

Mr Ant. I distrust them both—Both her truth
and her tears.

Major Cyp. Come, come, Mr Anthony Euston,
confess you were not brought hither to seek Sir
George—Clear yourself, in your turn, from the
suspicions I entertain of you.   But, if you dare to

avow yourself the contriver, or even abettor of the affront offered me at the masquerade—

Mr Eus. Major Cyprus! My brother Anthony knew no more of the appointment at the masquerade, than the child unborn. But, bless you, my niece and we meant you no ill by it; we only meant to have a joke at your and Sir Harry's expense—that was all.

Major Cyp. Then give me leave to tell you, Mr Euston, and you also Mr Anthony, that your present visit—

Mr Ant. We understand you, Sir—only assure us that Sir George Euston is safe, and we'll leave your house immediately—

Major Cyp. I! assure you that Sir George Euston is safe!

Mr Ant. You seem surprised—Let me then speak a word with Lady Harriet, whom the servants tell me is at home. Is she or not?

Major Cyp. (*To a servant without.*) Desire your lady to come hither. But have a care, gentlemen, how far you provoke me by your suspicions! For, by Heaven—

Mr Ant. I have no fears but for Sir George—nor will now your utmost rage induce me to quit the house till I am assured of his safety.

Major Cyp. And pray, sir, *who* in this house is to assure you of it?

Sir Geo. (*Bursting from the closet.*)—Himself!

Major Cyp. Confusion!

Mr Ant. You see, Sir, my intelligence was good.

Sir Geo. Strange as my concealment may appear, the cause was such as I can with honour reveal.

Major Cyp. Then, pray sir, with " honour re-" veal it."

Sir Geo. Why then I assure you, major—and I assure you all—upon my honour—and on the word

of a gentleman—that my being here—was—entirely
—owing—to—to—

Major Cyp. (*Warmly.*)   To what?   To what,
sir?

Col. Down. " I'll tell you what"—to " an un-
" describable something"—to be sure !

Major Cyp. Damnation !

Col. Down. Did not I tell you to keep the *key* of
the closet ?

Major Cyp. Colonel, I beg—this is not a time—

Enter BLOOM.

Bloom. (*To the Major.*)   The horns are ready,
sir—wou'd you choose to have them ?

Major Cyp. No.   (*In a fury.*)   [*Exit* BLOOM.

Enter LADY EUSTON, *and* LADY HARRIET, *at opposite doors.*

La. Eus. Where is Sir George ?

Mr Eus. Here, my dear—just stept out of the
closet.

La. Eus. What closet ?

Col. Down. That—that very *identical* closet.

Major Cyp. Heigh ho !

Mr Eus. Indeed, Lady Euston, you have cause
to reproach him.

La. Eus. I fear he will rather reproach me for
this abrupt intrusion—but my apprehensions for his
safety (hearing no tidings from his uncles) have
alone impell'd me to it.

La. Har. Had your ladyship not written this
letter to the amiable Sir Harry Harmless; (which I
unfortunately supposed intended for Major Cyprus,)
your ladyship's alarming " apprehensions" might
have been spared, as I sent for Sir George but to
shew him this letter.

Mr Eus. And that letter was only a joke—a scheme to mortify the Major and Sir Harry.

La. Eus. It was so—I own it. And the confusion the scheme has occasioned, Sir George, needs all your forgiveness.

Sir Geo. I sincerely pardon it—and hope the whole company will do me the justice to believe that my sole motive, for entering this house, was a compliance with, what I then thought, the dying request of that lady. And I now believe, that her ladyship's sole motive for wishing to see me was merely to shew me the letter of which she speaks— a copy of which, not without my knowledge, but against my opinion, was written by Lady Euston to Major Cyprus, appointing a fictitious interview, in return for his having dared to offend her with the profession of a licentious passion!

Major Cyp. Sir George, I am perfectly satisfied with this explanation. But, after what has happened, the world may despise me for being so, and therefore, Lady Harriet, from this moment we separate—And we had been wiser, as well as happier, if we had never met.

La. Har. Most willingly separate—Your unkind treatment—and my own constant inquietude—have long since taught a woman of the world too feelingly to acknowledge, " No lasting friendship is form'd on " vice."

Mr Ant. Preach this, my dear lady, to all your fair countrywomen—enforce your words by your future conduct, and they shall draw a veil over the frailty of your past life.

La. Har. Oh! Mr Anthony, cou'd I but retrieve my innocence, my honour, for ever lost !

Mr Ant. Yet, do not despair. You can still possess *one* inestimable good—that inborn virtue which *never perishes*—which never leaves us but to return.

For, when you think it extinguished, feel but due remorse, and it rises again in the soul.

Mr Eus. That's right, brother Anthony—comfort her—it is your duty. And we are all *relations*, you know—the whole company are related to one another. Though it is in an odd kind of a jumbled way—I wish some learned gentleman, of the law, would tell us *what* relations we all are—and what relation the child of a first husband is to his mother's second husband, while his own father is living.

Mr Ant. Brother, you think too deeply.

Mr Eus. Not at all, brother Anthony! And, for fear the gentlemen of the long robe shou'd not be able to find out the present company's *affinity*, let us apply to the *kindred ties* of each other's passions, weaknesses, and imperfections; and, thereupon, agree to part, this evening, not only *near relations*, but *good friends.*

SUCH THINGS ARE

SULTAN.—BEHOLD HIM IN THE SULTAN, AND ONCE MORE SEAL MY PARDON.
ACT V.   SCENE III.

PAINTED BY SINGLETON   PUBLISHED BY LONGMAN & CO   ENGRAVED BY WORTHINGTON
1806

Such Things Are

Act V, Scene III. Sultan: Behold him in the
Sultan. And once more seal my pardon.

SUCH THINGS ARE:

A PLAY,

IN FIVE ACTS;

BY MRS. INCHBALD,

AS PERFORMED AT THE

THEATRE ROYAL, COVENT-GARDEN.

PRINTED UNDER THE AUTHORITY OF THE MANAGERS
FROM THE PROMPT BOOK.

WITH REMARKS

BY THE AUTHOR.

———— ————

LONDON:

PRINTED FOR LONGMAN, HURST, REES, ORME, AND BROWN,
PATERNOSTER-ROW.

REMARKS.

THE writer of this play was, at the time of its production, but just admitted to the honours of an authoress, and wanted experience to behold her own danger, when she attempted the subject on which the work is founded. Her ignorance was her protection. Had her fears been greater, or proportioned to her task, her success had been still more hazardous. A bold enterprize requires bold execution; and, as skill does not always unite with courage, it is often advantageous, where cases are desperate, not to see with the eye of criticism : chance will sometimes do more for rash self-importance than that judgment which is the parent of timidity.

Such was the consequence on the first appearance of this comedy—its reception was favourable beyond the usual bounds of favour bestowed upon an admired play, and the pecuniary remuneration equally extraordinary.

There was novelty, locality and invention in "Such Things are ;" and the audience forgave, or, in their warmth of approbation, overlooked improbability in certain events, incorrectness of language, and meanness, bordering on vulgarity, in some of the characters,

As the scene is placed in the East Indies, where
the unpolished of the British nation so frequently re-
sort to make their fortune, perhaps the last mentioned
defect may be more descriptive of the manners of the
English inhabitants of that part of the globe, than had
elegance of dialogue, and delicacy of sentiment, been
given them. Nevertheless, a more elevated style of
conversation and manners in Sir Luke and Lady Tremor would not have been wholly improper, and would
assuredly have been much more pleasing, especially to
those who may now sit in judgment upon the work,
as readers, and cold admirers of that benevolence, no
longer the constant theme of enthusiastic praise, as
when this drama was first produced.

When this play was written, in 1786, Howard, the
hero of the piece, under the name of Haswell, was on
his philanthropic travels through Europe and parts of
Asia, to mitigate the sufferings of the prisoner. His
fame, the anxiety of his countrymen for the success
of his labours, and their pride in his beneficent character, suggested to the author a subject for the following pages. The scene chosen for its exhibition is
the island of Sumatra ; where the English settlement,
the system of government, modes snd habits of the
natives, the residents, and the visitors of the isle, may
well reconcile the fable and incidents of the drama to
an interesting degree of possibility.

As Haswell is the hero of the serious part of this
play, so is Twineall of the comic half. His charac-

ter and conduct is formed on the plan of Lord Ches-
terfield's finished gentleman. That nobleman's Letters to his Son excited, at least, the idea of Twineall
in the author's mind; and the public appeared to be
as well acquainted with his despicable reputation, as
with the highly honourable one of Howard.

Death having robbed the world of that good man's
active services, though the effect of his exertions will
ever remain, a short account of the virtuous tendency
of his inclinations, and success of his charitable pursuits, is at present requisite for some readers, as ex-
planatory of the following scenes.

John Howard, to whose revered memory a statue is
erected in St. Paul's Cathedral, with a suitable in-
scription, was born in 1726.

The life of Mr. Howard, till the year 1773, is of
little note, or has no reference whatever to his subsequent renown. At that period he was living on his
own estate at Cardington, near Bedford, a widower,
with one child. Here he served the office of sheriff
for the county, which, as he has declared, " brought
the distress of prisoners immediately under his notice,
and led him to form the design of visiting the gaols
through England, in order to devise means for alle-
viating the miseries of the sufferers."

In 1774, he was examined before the House of
Commons on the subject of prisons, and received the
thanks of the House.

He then extended his benevolent views to foreign

countries, making various excursions to all parts of Europe.

In 1789, he published an Account of the principal Lazarettos he had seen. In this work he signified his intention of revisiting Russia, Turkey, and of extending his route into the East.—" I am not insensible," he says, " of the dangers which must attend such a journey : Trusting, however, in the protection of that kind Providence which has hitherto preserved me, I calmly and cheerfully commit myself to the disposal of unerring wisdom. Should it please God to cut off my life in the prosecutien of this design, let not my conduct be uncandidly imputed to rashness or enthusiasm, but to a serious and deliberate conviction that I am pursuing the path of duty ; and to a sincere desire of being made an instrument of more extensive usefulness to my fellow creatures than could be expected in the narrower circle of a retired life."

He fell a sacrifice to his humanity ; for, visiting a sick patient at Cherson, who had a malignant fever, he caught the infection, and died January the 20th, 1790.

DRAMATIS PERSONÆ.

SULTAN	Mr. Farren.
LORD FLINT	Mr. Davies.
SIR LUKE TREMOR	Mr. Quick.
MR. TWINEALL	Mr. Lewis.
MR. HASWELL	Mr. Pope.
ELVIRUS	Mr. Holman.
MR. MEANRIGHT	Mr. Macready.
ZEDAN	Mr. Fearon.
FIRST KEEPER	Mr. Thompson.
SECOND KEEPER	Mr. Cubitt.
FIRST PRISONER	Mr. Helme.
SECOND PRISONER	Mr. Gardener.
GUARD	Mr. Blurton.
MESSENGER	Mr. Ledger.
LADY TREMOR	Mrs. Mattocks
AURELIA	Miss Wilkinson
FEMALE PRISONER	Mrs. Pope.

SCENE—*The Island of Sumatra, in the East Indies.*

Time of Representation—Twelve Hours.

SUCH THINGS ARE.

ACT THE FIRST.

SCENE I.

A parlour at SIR LUKE TREMOR's.

Enter SIR LUKE, *followed by* LADY TREMOR.

Sir Luke. I tell you, madam, you are two and thirty.

Lady. I tell you, sir, you are mistaken.

Sir Luke. Why, did not you come over from England exactly sixteen years ago?

Lady. Not so long.

Sir Luke. Have not we been married, the tenth of next April, sixteen years?

Lady. Not so long.

Sir Luke. Did you not come over the year of the great eclipse?—answer me that.

Lady. I don't remember it.

Sir Luke. But I do—and shall remember it as long as I live.—The first time I saw you was in the garden of the Dutch envoy: you were looking through a glass at the sun—I immediately began to make love to you, and the whole affair was settled while

the eclipse lasted—just one hour, eleven minutes, and
three seconds.

Lady. But what is all this to my age?

Sir Luke. Because I know you were at that time
near seventeen, and without one qualification except
your youth, and your fine clothes.

Lady. Sir Luke, Sir Luke, this is not to be borne!

Sir Luke. Oh! yes—I forgot—you had two letters
of recommendation from two great families in England.

Lady. Letters of recommendation!

Sir Luke. Yes ; your character——that you know,
is all the fortune we poor Englishmen, situated in
India, expect with a wife, who crosses the sea at the
hazard of her life, to make us happy.

Lady. And what but our characters would you
have us bring?—Do you suppose any lady ever came
to India, who brought along with her friends or fortune?

Sir Luke. No, my dear: and what is worse, she
seldom leaves them behind.

Lady. No matter, Sir Luke : but if I delivered to
you a good character——

Sir Luke. Yes, my dear, you did: and if you were
to ask me for it again, I can't say I could give it
you.

Lady. How uncivil! how unlike are your manners
to the manners of my Lord Flint !

Sir Luke. Ay, you are never so happy as when you
have an opportunity of expressing your admiration
of him.—A disagreeable, nay, a very dangerous man—
one is never sure of one's self in his presence—he
carries every thing he hears to the ministers of our
suspicious Sultan—and I feel my head shake whenever
I am in his company.

Lady. How different does his lordship appear to
me !—To me he is all *politesse.*

Sir Luke. Politesse ! how should you understand

what is real *politesse ?* You know your education was
very much confined.

Lady. And if it *was* confined?——I beg, Sir Luke,
you will cease these reflections : you know they are
what I can't bear !—[*Walks about in a passion*]—
Pray, does not his lordship continually assure me,
I might be taken for a countess, were it not for a
certain little grovelling toss I have caught with my
head, and a certain little confined hitch in my walk ;
both which I learnt of you—learnt by looking so much
at you.

Sir Luke. And now, if you don't take care, by looking so much at his lordship, you may catch some of
his defects.

Lady. I know of very few he has.

Sir Luke. I know of many—besides those he assumes.

Lady. Assumes.

Sir Luke. Yes : Do you suppose he is as forgetful
as he pretends to be ?—no, no ; but because he is a
favourite with the Sultan, and all our great men, he
thinks it genteel or convenient to have no memory ;
and yet, I'll answer for it, he has one of the best in
the universe.

Lady. I don't believe your charge.

Sir Luke. Why, though he forgets his appointments
with his tradesmen, did you ever hear of his forget-
ting to go to court when a place was to be disposed
of ? Did he ever make a blunder, and send a bribe to a
man out of power ? Did he ever forget to kneel before
the prince of this island, or to look in his highness's
presence like the statue of patient resignation, in humble expectation ?

Lady. Dear, Sir Luke——

Sir Luke. Sent from his own country in his very infancy, and brought up in the different courts of petty
arbitrary princes here in Asia, he is the slave of every
rich man, and the tyrant of every poor one.

Lady. " Petty princes !"—'tis well his highness, our Sultan, does not hear you.

Sir Luke. 'Tis well he does not—don't you repeat what I say : but you know how all this fine country is harassed and laid waste by a set of princes—Sultans, as they style themselves, and I know not what—who are for ever calling out to each other, " That's mine," and " That's mine ;"—and " You have no business here," and " You have no business there ;" —and " *I* have business every where. [*Strutting.*]— Then, " Give *me* this," and " Give *me* that ;"—and " Take this," and " Take that."

[*Makes signs of fighting.*

Lady. A very elegant description, truly.

Sir Luke. Why, you know 'tis all matter of fact : and Lord Flint, brought up from his youth among these people, has not one *trait* of an Englishman about him : he has imbibed all this country's cruelty ; and I dare say would mind no more seeing me hung up by my thumbs, or made to dance upon a red hot gridiron——

Lady. That is one of the tortures I never heard of ! —O ! I should like to see that of all things !

Sir Luke. Yes, by keeping this man's company, you'll soon be as cruel as he is : he will teach you every vice. A consequential, grave, dull——and yet with that degree of levity which dares to pay addresses to a woman, even before her husband's face.

Lady. Did not you declare, this minute, his lordship had not a *trait* of his own country about him ?

Sir Luke. Well, well—as you say, that last *is* a *trait* of his own country.

Enter SERVANT *and* LORD FLINT.

Serv. Lord Flint——   [*Exit* SERVANT

Lady. My lord, I am extremely glad to see you : we were just mentioning your name.

Lord. Were you, indeed, madam? You do me great honour.

Sir Luke. No, my lord—no great honour.

Lord. Pardon me, Sir Luke.

Sir Luke. But, I assure you, my lord, in what I said I did *myself* a great deal.

Lady. Yes, my lord; and I'll acquaint your lordship what it was.   [*Going up to him.*

Sir Luke. [*Pulling her aside.*] Why, you would not inform against me, sure! Do you know what would be the consequence? My head must answer it.

                           [*Frightened.*

Lord. Nay, Sir Luke, I insist upon knowing.

Sir Luke. [*To her.*] Hush! hush!——No, my lord, pray excuse me: your lordship, perhaps, may think what I said did not come from my heart; and I assure you, upon my honour, it did.

Lady. O, yes——that I am sure it did.

Lord. I am extremely obliged to you.   [*Bowing.*

Sir Luke. O, no, my lord, not at all—not at all. [*Aside to her.*] I'll be extremely obliged to *you*, if you will hold your tongue.—Pray, my lord, are you engaged out to dinner to-day? for her ladyship and I are.

Lady. Yes, my lord, and we should be happy to find your lordship of the party.

Lord. " Engaged out to dinner?"—Egad, very likely—very likely: but if I am, I have positively forgotten where.

Lady. We are going to——

Lord. No—I think, now you put me in mind of it—I think I have company to dine with me. I am either going out to dinner, or have company to dine with me; but I really can't tell which: however, my people know—but I can't recollect.

Sir Luke. Perhaps your lordship *has* dined: can you recollect that.

Lord. No, no—I have not dined———What's o'clock?

Lady. Perhaps, my lord, you have not breakfasted?

Lord. O, yes; I've breakfasted—I think so—but,
upon my word these things are very difficult to remember.

Sir Luke. They are, indeed, my lord—and I wish
all my family would entirely forget them.

Lord. What did your ladyship say was o'clock?

Lady. Exactly twelve, my lord.

Lord. Bless me! I ought to have been somewhere
else then—an absolute engagement.—I have broke
my word—a positive appointment.

Lady. Shall I send a servant?

Lord. No, no, no, no—by no means—it can't be
helped now; and they know my unfortunate failing:
besides, I'll beg their pardon, and I trust, that will be
ample satisfaction.

Lady. You are very good, my lord, not to leave us.

Lord. I could not think of leaving you so
soon—the happiness I enjoy in your society is so
extreme——

Sir Luke. That were your lordship to go away now,
you might never remember to come again.

Enter SERVANT.

Serv. A gentleman, sir, just landed from on board
an English vessel, says he has letters to present to
you.

Sir Luke. Show him in. [*Exit* SERVANT.]—*He*
has brought his character too, I suppose, and left it
behind, too, perhaps.

Enter MR. TWINEALL, *in a fashionable undress.*

Twi. Sir Luke, I have the honour of presenting to
you—[*Gives letters.*]—one from my Lord Cleland—
one from Sir Thomas Shoestring—one from Colonel
Fril.

Sir Luke, [*Aside.*] Who, in the name of wonder,

have my friends recommended?—[*Reads while* LORD FLINT *and the* LADY *talk apart.*]—No—as I live, he is a gentleman, and the son of a lord—[*Going to* LADY TREMOR.] My dear, that is a gentleman, notwithstanding his appearance.—Don't laugh; but let me introduce you to him.

Lady. A gentleman!—Certainly: I did not look at him before—but now I can perceive it.

Sir Luke. Mr. Twineall, give me leave to introduce Lady Tremor to you, and my Lord Flint—this, my lord, is the Honourable Mr. Twineall, from England, who will do me the favour to remain in my house till he is settled to his mind in some post here. [*They bow.*]—I beg your pardon, sir, for the somewhat cool reception Lady Tremor and I at first gave you—but I dare say her ladyship was under the same mistake as myself—and, I must own, I took you at first sight for something very different from the person you prove to be: for, really, no English ships having arrived in this harbour for these five years past, and the dress of English gentlemen being so much altered since that time——

Twi. But, I hope, Sir Luke, if it is, the alteration meets with your approbation.

Lady. Oh! it is extremely elegant and becoming.

Sir Luke. Yes, my dear, I don't doubt but you think so! for I remember you used to make your favourite monkey wear just such a jacket, when he went out a visiting.

Twi. Was he your favourite, madam?—Sir, you are very obliging.　　　　　[*Bowing to* SIR LUKE.

Sir Luke. My lord, if it were possible for your lordship to call to your *remembrance* such a trifle—

Lady. Dear Sir Luke——　　　　　[*Pulling him.*

Lord. Egad, I believe I do call to my remembrance—[*Gravely considering.*]—Not, I assure you, sir, that I perceive any great resemblance—or, if it was so—I dare say it is merely in the dress——which

I must own strikes me as most ridiculous—very ridiculous indeed.——

Twi. My lord!

Lord. I beg pardon, if I have said any thing that ——Lady Tremor, what did I say?——make my apology, if I have said any thing improper—you know my unhappy failing.   [*Goes up the stage.*

Lady. [*To* TWINEALL.] Sir, his lordship has made a mistake in the word " ridiculous," which I am sure he did not mean to say: but he is apt to make use of one word for another. His lordship has been so long out of England, that he may be said, in some measure, to have forgotten his native language.

[*His* LORDSHIP *all this time appears consequentially absent.*

Twi. You have perfectly explained, madam.—Indeed, I ought to have been convinced, without your explanation, that if his lordship made use of the word *ridiculous,* even intentionally, that the word had now changed its former sense, and was become a mode to express satisfaction—or he would not have used it, in the very forcible manner he did, to a perfect stranger.

Sir Luke. What, Mr. Twineall, have you new fashions for *words* too in England, as well as for dresses? and are you equally extravagant in their adoption?

Lady. I never heard, Sir Luke, but that the fashion of words varied, as well as the fashion of every thing else.

Twi. But what is most extraordinary, we have now a fashion, in England, of speaking without any words at all.

Lady. Pray, sir, how is that?

Sir Luke. Ay, do, Mr. Twineall, teach my wife to do without words, and I shall be very much obliged to you; it will be a great accomplishment.—Even you, my lord, ought to be attentive to this fashion.

Twi. Why, madam, for instance ; when a gentleman is asked a question which is either troublesome
or improper to answer, he does not say he *won't* answer it, even though he speaks to an inferior ; but he
says, " Really it appears to me o-e-e-e-e—[*Mutters
and shrugs.*]—that is—mo-mo-mo-mo-mo—[*Mutters.*]—if you see the thing—for my part—te-te-te-te
—and that's all I can tell about it at present."

Sir Luke. And you have told nothing.

Twi. Nothing upon earth.

Lady. But mayn't one guess what you mean ?

Twi. Oh, yes—perfectly at liberty to guess.

Sir Luke. Well, I'll be shot if I could guess.

Twi. And again—when an impertinent pedant asks
you a question which you know nothing about, and it
may not be convenient to say so—you answer boldly,
" Why really, sir, my opinion is, that the Greek poet
—he-he-he-he—[*Mutters.*]—we-we-we-we—you see
—if his ideas were—and if the Latin translator—
mis-mis-mis-mis—[*Shrugs.*]——that I should think
—in my humble opinion.—But the doctor may know
better than I."

Sir Luke. The Doctor must know very little else.

Twi. Or in case of a duel, where one does not care
to say who was right, or who was wrong—you answer—" *This*, sir, is the state of the matter—Mr. F.
—came first—te-te-te-te—on that—be-be-be-be—if
the other—in short—[*Whispers.*]—whis-whis-whis-
whis"——

Sir Luke. What ?

Twi. " There, now you have it—there it is : but
don't say a word about it—or if you do, don't say it
came from me."

Lady. Why, you have not told a word of the story !

Twi. But that your auditor must not say to you—
that's not the fashion—he never tells you that—he may
say—" You have not made yourself perfectly clear ;"
—or he may say—" He must have the matter more

particularly pointed out somewhere else ;"—but that
is all the auditor can say with good breeding.

Lady. A very pretty method indeed to satisfy curiosity !

Enter SERVANT.

Serv. Mr. Haswell.

Sir Luke. This is a countryman of ours, Mr. Twineall, and a very worthy man I assure you.

Enter MR. HASWELL.

Sir Luke. Mr. Haswell, how do you do? [*Warmly.*

Hasw. Sir Luke, I am glad to see you.——Lady
Tremor, how do you do ?   [*He bows to the rest.*

Lady. Oh, Mr. Haswell, I am extremely glad you
are come—here is a young adventurer just arrived
from England, who has been giving us such a strange
account of all that's going on there !

[*Introducing* TWINEALL.

Hasw. Sir, you are welcome to India.

[SIR LUKE *whispers* HASWELL.
Indeed !—*his* son.

Lady. Do, Mr. Haswell, talk to him—he can give
you great information.

Hasw. I am glad of it: I shall then hear many
things I am impatient to become acquainted with.
[*Goes up to* TWINEALL.] Mr. Twineall, I have
the honour of knowing your father extremely well
—he holds his seat in parliament still, I presume?

Twi. He does, sir.

Hasw. And your uncle, Sir Charles ?

Twi. Both, sir—both in parliament still.

Hasw. Pray, has any act in behalf of the poor clergy
taken place ?

Twi. In behalf of the poor clergy, sir ?—I'll tell you
—I'll tell you, sir.—As to that act—concerning—
[*Shrugs and mutters.*]—em-em-em-em—the Commit-
tee—em-em—ways and means—hee-hee—te-te-te—

[Sir Luke, Lady, *and* Lord Flint, *laugh.*] My father and my uncle both think so, I assure you.

Hasw. Think how, sir ?

Sir Luke. Nay, that's not good breeding—you must ask no more questions.

Hasw. Why not ?

Sir Luke. Because—we-we-we-we—[*Mimicks.*]—he knows nothing about the matter.

Hasw. What !—not know ?

Twi. Yes, sir, perfectly acquainted with every thing that passes in the House—but, I assure you, that when parliamentary business is reported——By the bye, Sir Luke, permit me, in my turn, to make a few inquiries concerning the state of this country.

> [Sir Luke *starts, and fixes his eyes*
> *suspiciously on* Lord Flint.

Sir Luke. Why, one does not like to speak much about the country one lives in.—But, Mr. Haswell, you have been visiting our encampments : you may tell us what is going on there.

Lady. Pray, Mr. Haswell, is it true that the Sultan cut off the head of one of his wives the other day because she said to him—" I won't ?"

Sir Luke. Do, my dear, be silent.

Lady. I won't.

Sir Luke. Oh, that the Sultan had you instead of me !

Lady. And with my head off, I suppose ?

Sir Luke. No, my dear ; in that state, I should have no objection to you myself.

Lady. [*Aside to* Sir Luke.] Now, I'll frighten you ten times more.—But, Mr. Haswell, I am told there are many persons suspected of disaffection to the present Sultan, who have been lately, by his orders, arrested, and sold to slavery—notwithstanding there was no proof against them produced.

Hasw. Proof ! in a state such as this, the charge is quite sufficient.

Sir Luke. [*In apparent agonies wishing to turn the discourse.*] Well, my lord, and how does your lordship find yourself this afternoon?—this morning, I mean. Bless my soul! why I begin to be as forgetful as your lordship.   [*Smiling and fawning.*

Lady. How I pity the poor creatures!

Sir Luke. [*Aside to* LADY.] Take care what you say before that tool of state : look at him, and tremble for your head.

Lady. Look at him, and tremble for your own.— And so, Mr. Haswell, all this is true?—and some persons of family too, I am told, dragged from their homes, and sent to slavery merely on suspicion?

Hasw. Yet, less do I pity those, than some, whom prisons and dungeons, crammed before, are yet prepared to receive.

Lord. Mr. Haswell, such is the Sultan's pleasure.

Sir Luke. Will your lordship take a turn in the garden? it looks from this door very pleasant. Does it, my lord?

Lady. But pray, Mr. Haswell, has not the Sultan sent for you to attend at his palace this morning?

Hasw. He has, madam.

Lady. There! I heard he had, but Sir Luke said not.—I am told he thinks himself under the greatest obligations to you.

Hasw. The report has flattered me: but if his highness *should* think himself under obligations, I can readily point a way by which he may acquit himself of them.

Lady. In the mean time, I am sure you feel for those poor sufferers.

Hasw. [*With stifled emotion.*] Sir Luke, good morning to you.—I called upon some trifling business, but I have out-staid my time, and therefore I'll call again in a couple of hours.—Lady Tremor, good morning —my lord—Mr. Twineall.   [*Bows, and exit.*

Twi. Sir Luke, your garden *does* look so divinely beautiful—

Sir Luke. Come, my lord, will you take a turn in it ?—Come, Mr. Twineall—come, my dear—[*Taking her hand.*] I can't think what business Mr. Haswell has to speak to me upon!—for my part I am quite a plain man, and busy myself about no one's affairs, except my own—but I dare say your lordship has forgotten all we have been talking about.

Lord. If you permit me, Sir Luke, I'll hand Lady Tremor.

Sir Luke. Certainly, my lord, if you please—Come, Mr. Twineall, and I'll conduct you. [*Exeunt.*

ACT THE SECOND.

SCENE I.

An apartment at SIR LUKE TREMOR'S.

Enter TWINEALL *and* MEANWRIGHT.

Twi. My dear friend, after so long a separation, how devilish unlucky that you should, on the very day of my arrival, be going to set sail for another part of the world! yet, before you go, I must beg a favour of you.—You know Sir Luke and his family perfectly well, I dare say ?

Mean. I think so—I have been in his house near six years.

Twi. The very person on earth I wanted!—Sir Luke has power here, I suppose?—a word from him might do a man some service perhaps? [*Significantly.*

Mean. Why, yes; I don't know a man who has more influence at a certain place.

Twi. And Lady Tremor seems a very clever gentlewoman.

Mean. Very.

Twi. And I have a notion they think me very clever.

Mean. I dare say they do.

Twi. Yes—but I mean *very* clever.

Mean. No doubt!

Twi. But, my dear friend, you must help me to make them think better of me still—and when my fortune is made, I'll make yours—for when I once become acquainted with people's dispositions, their little weaknesses, foibles, and faults, I can wind, twist, twine, and get into the corner of every one's heart, and lie so snug, they can't know I'm there till they want to pull me out, and find 'tis impossible.

Mean. Excellent talent!

Twi. Is not it?—And now, my dear friend, do you inform me of the secret dispositions and propensities of every one in this family, and that of all their connexions?—What lady values herself upon one qualification, and what lady upon another?—What gentleman will like to be told of his accomplishments, or what man would rather hear of his wife's or his daughter's?—or of his horses, or of his dogs?—Now, my dear Ned, acquaint me with all this; and, within a fortnight, I will become the most necessary rascal—not a creature shall know how to exist without me.

Mean. Why, such a man as you ought to have made your fortune in England.

Twi. No; there—my father and my three uncles

monopolized all the great men themselves, and would never introduce me where I was likely to become their rival.—This, this is the very spot for me to display my genius.—But then I must first penetrate the people, unless you will kindly save me that trouble.— Come, give me all their characters—all their little propensities—all their whims—in short, all I am to praise, and all I am to avoid praising, in order to endear myself to them. [*Takes out tablets.*] Come—begin with Sir Luke.

Mean. Sir Luke values himself more upon personal bravery, than upon any thing.

Twi. Thank you, my dear friend—thank you. [*Writes.*] Was he ever in the army?

Mean. Oh, yes, besieged a capital fortress a few years ago : and now the very name of a battle, or a great general tickles his vanity ; and he takes all the praises you can lavish upon the subject as compliments to himself.

Twi. Thank you—thank you, a thousand times. [*Writes.*] I'll mention a battle very soon.

Mean. Not directly.

Twi. Oh, no—let me alone for time and place.— Go on, my friend—go on—her ladyship—

Mean. Descended from the ancient kings of Scotland.

Twi. You don't say so !

Mean. And though she is so nicely scrupulous as never to mention the word genealogy, yet I have seen her agitation so great, when the advantages of high birth have been extolled, that she could scarcely withhold her sentiments of triumph ; which, in order to disguise, she has assumed a disdain for all " vain titles, empty sounds, and idle pomp."

Twi. Thank you—thank you : this is a most excellent *trait* of the lady's. [*Writes.*] " Pedigree of the kings of Scotland ?"—Oh, I have her at once.

Mean. Yet do it nicely;—oblique touches, rather than open explanations.

Twi. Let me alone for that.

Mean. She has, I know, in her possession—but I dare say she would not show it you; nay, on the contrary, would affect to be highly offended, were you to mention it;—and yet it certainly would flatter her to know you were acquainted with her having it.

Twi. What—what—what is it?

Mean. A large old-fashioned wig—which Malcolm the third or fourth, her great ancestor, wore when he was crowned at Scone, in the year—

Twi. I'll mention it.

Mean. Take care.

Twi. O, let me alone for the manner.

Mean. She'll pretend to be angry.

Twi. That I am prepared for.—Pray, who is my Lord Flint?

Mean. A deep man—and a great favourite at court.

Twi. Indeed!—how am I to please him?

Mean. By insinuations against the present Sultan.

Twi. Indeed!

Mean. With all his pretended attachment, his heart——

Twi. Are you sure of it?

Mean. Sure:—he blinds Sir Luke, who by the bye is no great politician—but I know his lordship; and if he thought he was certain of his ground—and he thinks, he shall be soon——then——

Twi. I'll insinuate myself, and join his party; but, in the mean time, preserve good terms with Sir Luke, in case any thing should fall in my way there.—Who is Mr. Haswell?

Mean. He pretends to be a man of principle and sentiment;—flatter him on that.

Twi. The easiest thing in the world—no characters love flattery better than such as those: they will bear

even to hear their vices praised.—I will myself, undertake to praise the vices of a man of sentiment, till he
shall think them so many virtues.—You have mentioned no ladies yet, but the lady of the house.

Mean. I know little about any other, except a pretty
girl who came over from England, about two years
ago, for a husband; and, not succeeding in a distant
part of the country, was recommended to this house;
and has been here three or four months.

Twi. Let me alone to please her;

Mean. Yes—I believe you are skilled.

Twi. In the art of flattery, no one more.

Mean. But, damn it, it is not a liberal art.

Twi. It is a great science, notwithstanding—and
studied, at present, by all wise men.—Zounds! I have
staid a long time—I can't attend to any more characters at present—Sir Luke and his lady will think
me inattentive, if I don't join them.—Shall I see you
again!—if not, I wish you a pleasant voyage—I'll
make the most of what you have told me—you'll hear
I'm a great man.—Heaven bless you!—good bye!—
you'll hear I'm a great man.   [*Exit.*

Mean. And, if I am not mistaken, I shall hear you
are turned out of this house before to-morrow morning. O, Twineall! exactly the reverse of every character have you now before you.—The greatest misfortune in the life of Sir Luke has been, flying from
his regiment in the midst of an engagement, and a
most humiliating degradation in consequence; which
makes him so feelingly alive on the subject of a battle,
that nothing but his want of courage can secure my
friend Twineall's life for venturing to name the subject. Then my Lord Flint, firmly attached to the
interest of the Sultan, will be all on fire when he hears
of open disaffection.—But most of all, Lady Tremor!
whose father was a grocer, and uncle a noted
advertising " Periwig-maker on a new construction."
She will run mad to hear of births, titles, and long

pedigrees.—Poor Twineall! little dost thou think what
is prepared for thee.—There is Mr. Haswell too!
but to him have I sent you to be reclaimed—to him,
who, free from faults, or even foibles, of his own,
has yet more potently received the blessing—of pity for
his neighbour's.   [*Exit.*

SCENE II.

The inside of a Prison.

Several PRISONERS *dispersed in different situations.*

Enter KEEPER *and* HASWELL, *with lights.*

Keep. This way, sir: the prisons this way are more
extensive still.—You seem to feel for those unthinking men; but they are a set of unruly people,
whom no severity can make such as they ought to
be.

Hasw. And would not gentleness, or mercy, do you
think, reclaim them?

Keep. That I can't say : we never make use of those
means in this part of the world.—That man, yonder,
suspected of disaffection, is sentenced to be here for
life, unless his friends can lay down a large sum by
way of penalty ; which he finds they cannot do, and
he is turned melancholy.

Hasw. [*After a pause.*] Who is that?
                              [*Pointing to another.*
Keep. He has been tried for heading an insurrec-
tion, and acquitted.

Hasw. What keeps him here?

Keep. Fees due to the court—a debt contracted
while he proved his innocence.

Hasw. Lead on, my friend—let us go to some other part. [*Putting his hand to his eyes.*

Keep. In the ward we are going to, are the prisoners who, by some small reserve of money, some little stock when they arrived, or by the bounty of some friends who visit them, or such like fortunate circumstance, are in a less dismal place.

Hasw. Lead on.

Keep. But stop—put on this cloak; for, before we arrive at the place I mention, we must pass a damp vault, which to those who are not used to it—[HAS-WELL *puts on the cloak.*] Or will you postpone your visit ?

Haw. No—go on.

Keep. Alas ! who would suppose you had been used to see such places!—you look concerned—grieved to see the people suffer.—I wonder you should come, when you seem to think so much about them.

Hasw. O, that, that is the very reason !

[*Exit, following the* KEEPER.

[ZEDAN, *a tawny Indian Prisoner, follows them, stealing out, as if intent on something secret.—Two* PRISONERS *walk slowly down the stage, looking after* HASWELL.

First Pris. Who is this man ?

Second Pris. From Britain—I have seen him once before.

First. Pris. He looks pale—he has no heart.

Second Pris. I believe, a pretty large one.

Re-enter ZEDAN.

Zedan. Brother, a word with you. [*To the* FIRST PRISONER—*the other retires.*] As the stranger and our keeper passed by the passage, a noxious vapour put out the light ; and, as they groped along, I purloined this from the stranger. [*Shows a pocket-book.*] See, it contains two notes will pay our ransom.

[*Showing the notes.*

First Pris. A treasure—our certain ransom !

Zedan. Liberty, our wives, our children, and our friends, will these papers purchase.

First Pris. What a bribe for our keeper !   He may rejoice too.

Zedan. And then the pleasure it will be to hear the stranger fret, and complain for his loss !—O, how my heart loves to see sorrow !—Misery, such as I have known, dealt to men who spurn me— who treat me as if, in my own island, I had no friends who loved me—no servants who paid me honour—no children who revered me.——Taskmasters, forgetful that I am a husband—a father—nay, a man.

First. Pris. Conceal your thoughts—conceal your treasure too—or the Briton's complaint—

Zedan. Will be in vain.—Our keeper will conclude the prize must come to him at last, and therefore make no great search for it.—Here in the corner of my belt, [*Puts up the pocket-book.*]—'twill be secure. —Come this way, and let us indulge our pleasant prospect.   [*They retire, and the scene closes.*

SCENE III.

Another part of the Prison.

A kind of sofa, with an OLD MAN *sleeping upon it—* ELVIRUS *sitting attentively by him.*

Enter KEEPER and HASWELL.

Keep. That young man, watching his aged father as he sleeps, by the help of fees gains his admission ; and he never quits the place, except to go and pur- chase cordials for the old man, who, though healthy and strong, when he was first a prisoner, is now become languid and ill.

Hasw. Are they from Europe ?

Keep. No—but descended from Europeans.   See how the youth holds his father's hand !—I have some-times caught him bathing it with tears.

Hasw. I'll speak to the young man. [*Going to him.*

Keep. He will speak as soon as he sees me—he has sent a petition to the Sultan, about his father, and never fails to inquire if a reply is come.

[*They approach—*Elvirus *starts, and comes forward.*

Elvir. [*To* Haswell.] Sir, do you come from court ?—Has the Sultan received my humble suppli-cation, can you tell ?—Softly !—let not my father hear you speak.

Hasw. I come but as a stranger, to see the prison.

Elvir. No answer yet, keeper ?

Keep. No—I told you it was in vain to implore : they never read petitions sent from prisons—their hearts are hardened to such worn-out tales of sorrow.

[Elvirus *turns towards his* Father, *and weeps.*

Hasw. Pardon me, sir—but what is the request you are thus denied ?

Elvir. Behold my father ! But three months has he been confined here ; and yet, unless he breathes a purer air—O, if you have influence at court, sir, pray represent what passes in this dreary prison—what passes in my heart.——My supplication is, to remain a prisoner here, while my father, released, shall retire to his paternal estate, and never more take arms against the present government, but at the peril of my life.—Or, if the Sultan would allow me to serve him as a soldier——

Hasw. You would fight against the party your fa-ther fought for ?

Elvir. [*Starting.*] No—but in the forests, or on the desert sands, amongst those slaves who are sent to battle with the wild Indians :—there I would go—and earn the boon I ask——Or in the mines——

c 2

Hasw. Give me your name : I will, at least, present your suit—and, perhaps—

Elvir. Sir! do you think it is likely?—Joyful hearing !

Hasw. Nay, be not too hasty in your hopes—I cannot answer for my success. [*Repeats.*] " Your father humbly implores to be released from prison ; and, in his stead, *you* take his chains : or, for the Sultan's service, fight as a slave, or dig in his mines ?"

Elvir. Exactly, sir—that is the petition—I thank you, sir.

Keep You don't know, young man, what *it is* to dig in mines—or fight against foes, who make their prisoners die by unheard-of tortures.

Elvir. You do not know, sir, what *it is*—to see a parent suffer.

Hasw. [*Writing.*] Your name, Sir ?

Elvir. Elvirus Casimir.

Hasw. Your father's ?

Elvio. The same—one who followed agriculture in the fields of Symria ; but, induced by the call of freedom——

Hasw. How!—have a care.

Elvir. I thank you—his son, by the call of nature, supplicates his freedom.

Keep. The rebel, you find, breaks out.

Elvir. [*Aside to the* KEEPER.] Silence ! silence ! he forgives it.—Don't remind him—don't undo my hopes.

Hasw. I will serve you, if I can.

Elvir. And I will merit it ; indeed I will.—You shall not complain of me—I will be—

Hasw. Retire—I trust you.

[ELVIRUS *bows lowly, and retires.*

Keep. Yonder cell contains a female prisoner.

Hasw. A female prisoner !

Keep. Without a friend or comforter, she has existed there these many years—nearly fifteen.

Hasw. Is it possible !

Keep. Would you wish to see her ?

Hasw. If it won't give her pain.

Keep. At least, she'll not resent it—for she seldom complains, except in moans to herself.—[*Goes to the cell.*] Lady, here is one come to visit all the prisoners —please to appear before him.

Hasw. I thank you—you speak with reverence and respect to her.

Keep. She has been of some note, though now totally unfriended—at least we think she has, from her gentle manners ; and our governor is in the daily expectation of some liberal ransom for her : this makes her imprisonment without hope of release, till that day arrives.—[*Going to the cell.*] Take my hand— you are weak.

[*He leads her from the cell—she appears faint, and as if the light affected her eyes.*—HASWELL *pulls off his hat, and after a pause—*

Hasw. I fear you are not in health, lady.

[*She looks at him solemnly for some time.*

Keep. Speak, madam—speak.

Pris. No—not very well.   [*Faintingly.*

Hasw. Where are your friends? When do you expect your ransom?

Pris. [*Shaking her head.*] Never.

Keep. She persists to say so; thinking, by that declaration, we shall release her without a ransom.

Hasw. Is that your motive ?

Pris. I know no motive for a falsehood.

Hasw. I was to blame—pardon me.

Keep. Your answers are somewhat more proud than usual.   [*He retires up the stage.*

Pris. They are.—[*To* HASWELL.] Forgive me— I am mild with all these people—but from a countenance like yours—I could not bear reproach.

Hasw. You flatter me.

Pris. Alas ! Sir, and what have I to hope from such a meanness ?—You do not come to ransom me.

Hasw. Perhaps I do.

Pris. Oh ! do not say so—unless—unless—I am not to be deceived. Pardon in your turn this suspicion : but when I have so much to hope for—when the sun, the air, fields, woods, and all that wondrous world wherein I have been so happy, is in prospect —forgive me, if the vast hope makes me fear.

Hasw. Unless your ransom is fixed at something beyond my power to give, I *will* release you.

Pris. Release me !—Benevolent !

Hasw. How shall I mark you down in my petition ? [*Takes out his book.*] What name ?

Pris. Tis almost blotted from my memory.

[*Weeping.*

Keep. It is of little note—a female prisoner, taken with the rebel party, and in these cells confined for fifteen years.

Pris. During which time I have demeaned myself with all humility to my governors : neither have I distracted my fellow-prisoners with a complaint that might recal to their memory their own unhappy fate. I have been obedient, patient ; and cherished hope to cheer me with vain dreams, while despair possessed my reason.

Hasw. Retire—I will present the picture you have given.

Pris. And be successful—or, never let me see you more.   [*She goes up the stage.*

Hasw. So it shall be.

Pris. [*Returns.*] Or, if you should miscarry in your views—for who forms plans that do not sometimes fail ?—I will not reproach you, even to myself.—— No—nor will I suffer much from the disappointment —merely that you may not have what I suffer, to account for.   [*Exit to her cell.*

Hasw. Excellent mind !

Keep. In this cell—   [*Going to another.*

Hasw. No—take me away: I have enough to do
for those I have seen—I dare not see more at present.

[*Exeunt.*

SCENE IV.

The former Prison Scene.

Enter ZEDAN.

Zedan. They are coming.—I'll stand here in his
sight, that, should he miss what I have taken, he may
not suspect me to be the robber, but suppose it is one
who has hid himself.

Enter KEEPER *and* HASWELL.

Keep. [*To* ZEDAN.] What makes you here ?—still
moping by yourself, and lamenting for your family ?
[*To* HASWELL.] That man, the most ferocious I ever
met with, laments, sometimes even with tears, the separation from his wife and children.

Hasw. [*Going to him.*] I am sorry for you, friend :
[ZEDAN *looks sullen and morose.*] I pity you.

Keep. Yes, he had a pleasant hamlet on the neigh-
bouring island : plenty of fruits, clear springs, and
wholesome roots, and now complains bitterly of his
repasts—sour rice, and muddy water.   [*Exit* KEEPER.

Hasw. Poor man ! bear your sorrows nobly.—And,
as we are alone, no miserable eye to grudge the favour
—[*Looking round.*] take this trifle—[*Gives money.*] it
will, at least, make your meals better for a few short
weeks, till Heaven may please to favour you with a

less sharp remembrance of the happiness you have
lost.—Farewell.   [*Going.*
  [ZEDAN *catches hold of him, and taking the*
    pocket-book from his belt, puts it into
    HASWELL's *hand.*

Hasw. What's this ?

Zedan. I meant to gain my liberty with it—but
I will not vex you.

Hasw. How came you by it ?

Zedan. Stole it—and would have stabb'd you, too,
had you been alone—but I am glad I did not—Oh, I
am glad I did not?

Hasw. You like me then?

Zedan. [*Shakes his head, and holds his heart.*] 'Tis
something that I never felt before—it makes me like
not only you, but all the world besides.—The love of
my family was confined to them alone—but this sensation makes me love even my enemies.

Hasw. O, nature! grateful! mild ! gentle ! and for-
giving !—worst of tyrants they, who, by hard usage,
drive you to be cruel.

Re-enter KEEPER.

Keep. The lights are ready, sir, through the dark
passage. [*To* ZEDAN.] Go to your fellows.

Hasw. [*To* ZEDAN.] Farewell—we will meet again.
  [ZEDAN *exit on one side ;* HASWELL *and* KEEPER
   exeunt on the other.

ACT THE THIRD.

SCENE I.

An apartment at Sir Luke Tremor's.

Enter Sir Luke *and* Aurelia.

Sir Luke. Why, then, Aurelia, (though I never mentioned it to my Lady Tremor) my friend wrote me word he had reason to suppose your affections were improperly fixed upon a young gentleman in that neighbourhood; and this was his reason for wishing you to leave that place to come hither; and this continual dejection convinces me my friend was not mistaken.—Answer me—can you say he was?

Aure. Sir Luke, candidly to confess—

Sir Luke. Nay, no tears—why in tears? for a husband?—be comforted—we'll get you one ere long, I warrant.

Aure. Dear, Sir Luke, how can you imagine I am in tears because I have not a husband, while you see Lady Tremor every day in tears for the very opposite cause?

Sir Luke. No matter; women like to have a husband through pride; and I have known a woman marry, from that very motive, even a man she has been ashamed of.

Aure. Perhaps Lady Tremor married from pride.

Sir Luke. Yes—and I'll let her know that pride is painful.

Aure. But, sir, her ladyship's philosophy—

Sir Luke. She has no philosophy

Enter LADY TREMOR *and* TWINEALL.

Sir Luke. Where is my Lord Flint? What have you done with him?

Lady. He's speaking a word to Mr. Meanright, about his passport to England—Did you mean me, Sir Luke, who has no philosophy?—I protest, I have a great deal.

Sir Luke. When did you show it?

Lady. When the servant at my Lady Grissel's threw a whole urn of boiling water upon your legs.—Did I then give any proofs of female weakness? did I faint, scream, or even shed a tear?

Sir Luke. No, very true; and while I lay sprawling on the carpet, I could see you holding a smelling-bottle to the lady of the house, begging of her not to make herself uneasy, " for that the accident was of no manner of consequence."

Aure. Dear sir, don't be angry: I am sure her ladyship spoke as she thought.

Sir Luke. I suppose she did, Miss.

Aure. I mean—she thought the accident might be easily——She thought you might be easily recovered.

Lady. No, indeed, I did not: but I thought Sir Luke had frequently charged me with the want of patience; and, that moment, the very ' thing in the world I could have wish'd occurred, on purpose to give me an opportunity to prove his accusation false.

Sir Luke. Very well, madam—but did not the whole company censure your behaviour? did not they say, it was not the conduct of a wife?

Lady. Only our particular acquaintance could say so; for the rest of the company, I am sure, did not take me to be your wife.—Thank Heaven, our appearance never betrays that secret. Do you think we look like the same flesh and blood?

Sir Luke. That day, in particular, we did not; for I remember you had been no less than three hours at your toilet.

Lady. And indeed, Sir Luke, if you were to use milk of roses, and several other things of the same kind, you can't think how much more like a fine gentleman you would look.—Such things as those make, almost, all the difference between you and such a man as Mr. Twineall.

Twi. No, pardon me, madam—a face like mine may use those things ; but in Sir Luke's they would entirely destroy that fine martial appearance—[SIR LUKE *looks confounded*]—which women, as well as men admire—for, as valour is the first ornament of our sex——

Lady. What are you saying, Mr. Twineall?— [*Aside.*] I'll keep on this subject if I can.

Twi. I was going to observe, madam, that the reputation of a general—which puts me in mind, Sir Luke, of an account I read of a battle——

> [*He crosses over to* SIR LUKE, *who turns up the stage, in the utmost confusion, and steals out of the room.*

Lady. Well, sir—go on, go on—you were going to introduce——

Twi. A battle, madam—but Sir Luke is gone !

Lady. Never mind that, sir : he generally runs away on these occasions.

Sir Luke. [*Coming back.*] What were you saying, Aurelia, about a husband ?

Lady. She did not speak.

Sir Luke. To be sure, ladies in India do get husbands very soon.

Twi. Not always, I am told, Sir Luke——Women of family, [*Fixing his eyes stedfastly on* LADY TREMOR,] indeed, may soon enter into the matrimonial state—but the rich men in India, we are told in England, are grown of late very cautious with whom they

marry; and there is not a man of any repute that
will now look upon a woman as a wife, unless she is
descended from a good family.

> [*Looking at* Lady Tremor, *who walks up
> the stage, and steals out of the room, just
> as* Sir Luke *had done before.*

Sir Luke. I am very sorry—very sorry to say, Mr.
Twineall, that has not been always the case.

Twi. Then I am very sorry too, Sir Luke; for it is
as much impossible that a woman, who is not born
of an ancient family, can be——

> [Lady Tremor *returns.*

Sir Luke. That is just what I say—they *cannot*
be——

Lady. Sir Luke, let me tell you——

Sir Luke. It does not signify telling, my dear—you
have proved it.

Lady. [*To* Twineall.] Sir, let me tell *you.*

Twi. O! O! my dear madam, 'tis all in vain—
there is no such thing—it can't be—there is no pleading against conviction—a person of low birth must,
in every particular, be a terrible creature.

Sir Luke. [*Going to her.*] A terrible creature! a
terrible creature!

Lady. Here comes my Lord Flint—I'll appeal to
him.

Enter Lord Flint.

Sir Luke. [*Going to him.*] My lord, I was saying,
as a proof that our great Sultan, who now fills this
throne, is no impostor, as the rebel party would insinuate, no low-born man, but of the royal stock, his
conduct palpably evinces—for, had he not been
nobly born, we should have beheld the plebeian
bursting forth upon all occasions—[*Looking at* Lady
Tremor.]—and plebeian manners who can support?

Lady. Provoking!   [*Goes up the stage.*

Lord. Sir Luke, is there a doubt of the Emperor's

birth and title? he is the real Sultan, depend upon it : it surprises me to hear you talk with the smallest uncertainty.

Twi. Indeed, Sir Luke, I wonder at it too : [*Aside to* LORD FLINT.] and yet, damn me, my lord, if I have not my doubts.   [LORD FLINT *starts.*

Sir Luke. I, my lord? far be it from me! I was only saying what other people have said ; for my part, I never harboured a doubt of the kind.— [*Aside.*] My head begins to nod, only for that word— Pray Heaven, I may die with it on!—I should not like to lose my head ; nor should I like to die by a bullet—nor by a sword ; and a cannon-ball would be as disagreeable as any thing I know.—It is very strange that I never yet could make up my mind in what manner I should like to go out of the world. [*During this speech,* TWINEALL *is paying court to* LORD FLINT—*they come forward, and* SIR LUKE *retires.*

Lord. Your temerity astonishes me!

Twi. I must own, my lord, I feel somewhat awkward in saying it to your lordship—but my own heart, my own conscience, my own sentiments—they *are* my own ; and they are dear to me.—So it is—the Sultan does not appear to me—[*With significance*]— that great man some people think him.

Lord. Sir, you astonish me—Pray, what is your name? I have forgotten it.

Twi. Twineall, my lord—the Honourable Henry Twineall—your lordship does me great honour to ask.—Landed this morning from England, as your lordship may remember, in the ship Mercury, my lord ; and all the officers on board speaking with the highest admiration and warmest terms of your lordship's official character.

Lord. Why, then, Mr. Twineall, I am very sorry—

Twi. And so am I, my lord, that your sentiments

and mine should so far disagree, as I know they do.—
I am not unacquainted with your firm adherence to
the Sultan, but I am unused to disguise my thoughts—
I could not, if I would. I have no little views, no
sinister motives, no plots, no intrigues, no schemes
of preferment ; and I verily believe, that, if a pistol
was now directed to my heart, or a large pension
directed to my pocket (in the first case at least), I
should speak my mind.

Lord. [*Aside.*] A dangerous young man this! and
I may make something of the discovery.

Twi. [*Aside.*] It tickles him to the soul I find.—
My lord, now I begin to be warm on the subject, I
feel myself quite agitated ; and, from the intelligence
which I have heard, even when I was in England—
there is every reason to suppose——exm—exm—
exm—   [*Mutters.*

Lord. What, sir ? what ?

Twi. You understand me.

Lord. No—explain.

Twi. Why, then, there is every reason to suppose—
some people are not what they should be—pardon
my suspicions, if they are wrong.

Lord. I *do* pardon your thoughts, with all my
heart—but your words young man, you must answer for. [*Aside.*]—Lady Tremor, good morning.

Twi. [*Aside.*] He is going to ruminate on my sentiments, I dare say.

Lady. Shall we have your lordship's company in
the evening. Mr. Haswell will be here ; if your
lordship has no objection.

Sir Luke. How do you know Mr. Haswell will be
here ?

Lady. Because he has just called in his way to the
palace and said so : and he has been telling us some
of the most interesting stories.

Sir Luke. Of his morning visits, I suppose—I heard
Meanright say, he saw him very busy.

Lady. Sir Luke and I dine out, my lord ; but we shall return early in the evening.

Lord. I will be here, without fail.—Sir Luke, a word with you, if you please—[*They come forward.*]—Mr. Twineall has taken some very improper liberties with the Sultan's name, and I must insist on making him accountable for them.

Sir Luke. My lord, you are extremely welcome—[*Trembling,*]—to do whatever your lordship pleases with any one belonging to me, or to my house—but I hope your lordship will pay some regard to the master of it.

Lord. O ! great regard to the master—and to the mistress also.—But for that gentleman——

Sir Luke. Do what your lordship pleases.

Lord. I will—and I will make him —

Sir Luke. If your lordship does not forget it.

Lord. I shan't forget it, Sir Luke—I have a very good memory when I please.

Sir Luke. I don't in the least doubt it, my lord—I never did doubt it.

Lord. And I can be very severe, Sir Luke, when I please.

Sir Luke. I don't in the least doubt it, my lord—I never did doubt it.

Lord. You may depend upon seeing me here in the evening ; and then you shall find I have not threatened more than I mean to perform—Good morning.

Sir Luke. Good morning, my lord—I don't in the least doubt it.   [*Exit* LORD FLINT.

Lady. [*Coming forward with* TWINEALL.] For Heaven's sake, Mr. Twineall, what has birth to do with——

Twi. It has to do with every thing,—even with beauty ;—and I wish I may suffer death, if a woman, with all the mental and personal accomplishments of

D 2

the finest creature in the world, would, to me, be of
the least value, if lowly born.

Sir Luke. I sincerely wish every man who visits
me was of the same opinion.

Aure. For shame, Mr. Twineall! persons of mean
birth ought not to be despised for what it was not in
their power to prevent: and, if it is a misfortune, you
should consider them only as objects of pity.

Twi. And so I do pity them—and so I do—most
sincerely—Poor creatures!

[*Looking on* LADY TREMOR.

Sir Luke. Aye, now he has atoned most properly.

Lady. Mr. Twineall, let me tell you——

Sir Luke. My dear Lady Tremor—[*Taking her
aside.*]—let him alone—let him go on—there is something preparing for him he little expects—so let the
poor man say and do what he pleases for the present
—it won't last long, for he has offended my Lord
Flint; and I dare say his lordship will be able, upon
some account, or another, to get him imprisoned for
life.

Lady. Imprisoned!—Why not take off his head at
once?

Sir Luke. Well, my dear, I am sure I have no objection; and I dare say my lord will have it done, to
oblige you.—Egad, I must make friends with her to
keep mine safe.   [*Aside.*

Lady. Do you mean to take him out to dinner
with us?

Sir Luke. Yes, my dear, if you approve of it—not
else.

Lady. You are become extremely polite.

Sir Luke. Yes, my dear, his lordship has taught
me how to be polite.——Mr. Twineall, Lady Tremor,
and I, are going to prepare for our visit, and I will
send a servant to show you to your apartment, to
dress; for you will favour us with your company, I hope?

Twi. Certainly, Sir Luke, I shall do myself the honour.

Lady. Come this way, Aurelia ; I can't bear to look at him.   [*Exit with* AURELIA.

Sir Luke. Nor I to think of him.   [*Exit.*

Twi. If I have not settled my business in this family, I am mistaken : they seem to be but of one opinion about me.—Devilish clever fellow !—egad I am the man to send into the world—such a volatile, good-looking scoundrel too, that no one suspects me. —To be sure, I am under some few obligations to my friend for letting me into the different characters of the family ; and yet I don't know whether I am obliged to him or not ; for if he had not made me acquainted with them, I should soon have had the skill to find them out myself.—No : I will not think myself under any obligation to him—it is very inconvenient for a gentleman to be under obligations.   [*Exit.*

SCENE II.

The Palace.

The SULTAN *discovered, with* GUARDS *and* OFFICERS *attending.*

HASWELL *is conducted in by an* OFFICER.

Sult. Sir, you were invited hither to receive public thanks for our troops restored to health by your prescriptions.—Ask a reward adequate to your services.

Hasw. Sultan, the reward I ask, is to preserve more of your people still.

Sult. How ! more ! my subjects are in health : no contagion visits them.

Hasw. The prisoner is your subject. There, misery,

more contagious than disease, preys on the lives of
hundreds : sentenced but to confinement, their doom
is death. Immured in damp and dreary vaults, they
daily perish ; and who can tell but that, among these
many hapless sufferers, there may be hearts bent down
with penitence to heaven and you for every slight
offence—there may be some, among the wretched mul-
titude, even innocent victims. Let me seek them out
—let me save them and you.

Sult. Amazement ! retract your application : curb
this weak pity ; and receive our thanks.

Hasw. Restrain my pity!—and what can I receive
in recompense for that soft bond which links me to
the wretched? and, while it soothes their sorrow, re-
pays me more than all the gifts an empire could bestow.——But, if repugnant to your plan of government, I apply not in the name of pity, but of justice.

Sult. Justice!

Hasw. The justice which forbids all, but the worst
of criminals, to be denied that wholesome air the very
brute creation freely takes.

Sult. Consider for whom you plead—for men (if
not base culprits,) so misled, so depraved, they
are dangerous to our state, and deserve none of its
blessings.

Hasw. If not upon the undeserving—if not upon
the hapless wanderer from the paths of rectitude,—
where shall the sun diffuse his light, or the clouds dis-
til their dew ? Where shall spring breathe fragrance, or
autumn pour its plenty

Sult, Sir, your sentiments, still more your character, excite my curiosity. They tell me, that in our
camps you visited each sick man's bed, administered
yourself the healing draught, encouraged our savages
with the hope of life, or pointed out their better hope
in death.——The widow speaks your charities, the
orphan lisps your bounties, and the rough Indian melts
in tears to bless you.—I wish to ask why you have

done all this ?—What is it which prompts you thus to
befriend the wretched and forlorn ?

Hasw. In vain for me to explain :—the time it would
take to reveal to you—

Sult. Satisfy my curiosity in writing then.

Hasw. Nay, if you will read, I'll send a book in
which is already written why I act thus.

Sult. What book ?—What is it called ?

Hasw. " The Christian Doctrine." [HASWELL
bows here with the utmost reverence.] There you will
find—all I have done was but my duty.

Sult. [*To the* GUARDS.] Retire, and leave me
alone with the stranger. [*All retire except* HASWELL
and the SULTAN—*They come forward.*] Your words
recal reflections that distract me ; nor can I bear the
pressure on my mind, without confessing—I am a
Christian.

Hasw. A Christian !—What makes you thus assume
the apostate ?

Sult. Misery and despair.

Hasw. What made you a Christian ?

Sult. My Arabella, a lovely European, sent hither
in her youth, by her mercenary parents, to sell herself to the prince of all these territories.   But 'twas
my happy lot, in humble life, to win her love, snatch
her from his expecting arms, and bear her far away ;
where, in peaceful solitude we lived, till, in the heat
of the rebellion against the late Sultan, I was forced
from my happy home to take a part.—I chose the
imputed rebels' side, and fought for the young aspirer.
—An arrow, in the midst of the engagement, pierced
his heart ; and his officers, alarmed at the terror this
stroke of fate might cause among their troops, urged
me (as I bore a strong resemblance to him,) to
counterfeit a greater still, and show myself to the
soldiers as their king recovered.   I yielded to their
suit, because it gave me ample power to avenge
the loss of my Arabella, who had been taken from

her home by the merciless foe, and barbarously murdered.

Hasw. Murdered!

Sult. I learnt so, and my fruitless search to find
her has confirmed the intelligence. Frantic for her
loss, I joyfully embraced a scheme which promised
vengeance on the enemy :—it prospered ; and I re-
venged my wrongs and hers with such unsparing
justice on the opposite army and their king, that
even the men, who made me what I am, trembled to
reveal their imposition ; and for their interest still continue it.

Hasw. Amazement!

Sult. Nay, they fill my prisons every day with
wretches, who but whisper I am not their real Sultan.
The secret, therefore, I myself boldly relate in private :
the danger is to him who speaks it again ; and, with
this caution, I trust it is safe with you.

Hasw. It was, without that caution.—Now hear my
answer to your tale :—Involved in deeds, in cruelties,
at which your better thoughts revolt, the meanest
wretch your camps or prisons hold, claims not half the
compassion *you* have excited. Permit me, then, to be
your comforter.

Sult. Impossible!

Hasw. In the most fatal symptoms, I have undertaken the body's cure. The mind's disease, perhaps,
I am not less a stranger to. Oh! trust the noble
patient to my care.

Sult. What medicine will you apply?

Hasw. Lead you to behold the wretched in their
misery, and 'then show you yourself in their de-
liverer.——I have your promise for a boon—'tis
this :—give me the liberty of six whom I shall name,
now in confinement, and be yourself a witness
of their enlargement.——See joy lighted in the
countenance where sorrow still has left its rough
remains—behold the tear of rapture chase away

that of anguish—hear the faultering voice, long
used to lamentation, in broken accents, utter thanks
and blessings!—Behold this scene, and if you find
the prescription ineffectual, dishonour your physician.

Sult. I will make trial of it.

Hasw. Come, then, to the governor's house this
very night,—into that council-room so often perverted
to the use of the torture; and there (unknown to
those, I shall release, as their king,) you will be witness to all the grateful heart can dictate, and feel all
that benevolence can taste.

Sult. I will meet you there.

Hasw. In the evening?

Sult. At ten precisely.—Guards, conduct the stranger
from the palace.   [*Exit* SULTAN.

Hasw. Thus far advanced, what changes may not
be hoped for!   [*Exit.*

ACT THE FOURTH.

SCENE I.

An apartment at SIR LUKE TREMOR'S.

Enter ELVIRUS *and* AURELIA.

Elvir. Oh! my Aurelia, since the time I first
saw you—since you left the pleasant spot where I
first beheld you—what distress, what anguish have we
known!

Aure. Your family ?

Elvir. Yes; and that caused the silence which I hope you have lamented. I could not wound you with the recital of our misfortunes : and now, only with the sad idea that I shall never see you more, am I come to take my last farewell.

Aure. Is there a chance that we may never meet again ?

Elvir. There is; and I sincerely hope it may prove so.—To see you again, would be again to behold my father pining in misery.

Aure. Explain—[*A loud rapping at the door.*] That is Sir Luke and Lady Tremor.—What shall I say, should they come into this room ?—They suspect I correspond with some person in the country.—Who shall I tell them you are? upon what business can I say you are come?

Elvir. To avoid all suspicion of my real situation, and to ensure admittance, I put on this habit, and told the servant, when I inquired for you, I was just arrived from England.—[*She starts.*]—Nay, it was but necessary I should conceal who I was in this suspicious place, or I might plunge a whole family in the imputed guilt of mine.

Aure. Good heaven !

Elvir. I feared, besides, there was no other means, no likelihood, to gain admission ; and what, what would I not have sacrificed, rather than have left you for ever without a last farewell ? Think on these weighty causes, and pardon the deception.

Aure. But if I should be asked——

Elvir. Say as I have done.—My stay must be so short, it is impossible they should detect me—for I must be back—

Aure. Where ?

Elvir. No matter where—I must be back before the evening—and wish never to see you more.—I love you,

Aurelia—O, how truly !—and yet there is a love more dear, more sacred still.

Aure. You torture me with suspense—Sir Luke is coming this way—What name shall I say if he asks me ?

Elvir. Glanmore—I announced that name to the servant.

Aure. You tremble.

Elvir. The imposition hurts me ; and I feel as if I dreaded a detection, though 'tis scarce possible. Sorrows have made a coward of me : even the servant, I thought, looked at me with suspicion, and I was both confounded and enraged.

Aure. Go into this apartment : I'll follow you.

[*Exit* ELVIRUS *at a door.*

Sir Luke. [*Without.*] Abominable ! provoking ! impertinent ! not to be borne !

Aure. [*Listening.*] Thank heaven, Sir Luke is so perplexed with some affairs of his own, he may not think of mine.   [*Exit to* ELVIRUS.

Enter SIR LUKE, *followed by* LADY TREMOR.

Sir Luke. I am out of all patience, and all temper—did you ever hear of such a complete impertinent coxcomb ? Talk, talk, talk, continually ! and referring to me on all occasions ! " Such a man was a brave general—another a great admiral ;" and then he must tell a long story about a siege, and ask me if it did not make my bosom glow !

Lady. It had not that effect upon your face, for you were as white as ashes.

Sir Luke. But you did not see yourself while he was talking of grandfathers and great grandfathers ;— If you had—

Lady. I was not white, I protest.

Sir Luke. No—but you were as red as scarlet.

Lady. And you ought to have resented the insult,

E

if you saw me affected by it.—Oh! some men would
have given him such a dressing!

Sir Luke. Yes, my dear, if your uncle the frisseur
had been alive, he would have given him a dressing, I
dare say.

Lady. Sir Luke, none of your impertinence : you
know I can't, I won't bear it—neither will I wait for
Lord Flint's resentment on Mr. Twineall.—No, I
desire you will tell him to quit this roof immediately.

Sir Luke. My dear, you must excuse me—I can't
think of quarrelling with a gentleman in my own
house.

Lady. Was it your own house to-day at dinner when
he insulted us ? and would you quarrel then ?

Sir Luke. No ; that was a friend's house—and I
make it a rule never to quarrel in my own house, a
friend's house, in a tavern, or in the streets.

Lady. Well, then, I would quarrel in my own
house, a friend's house, a tavern, or in the street, if
any one offended me.

Sir Luke. O, my dear, I have no doubt of it—no
doubt, in the least.

Lady. But, at present, it shall be in my own house :
and I will desire Mr. Twineall to quit it immediately.

Sir Luke. Very well, my dear—pray do.

Lady. I suppose, however, I may tell him, I have
your authority to bid him go ?

Sir Luke. Tell him I have no authority—none in
the world over you—but that you will do as you
please.

Lady. I can t tell him so—he won't believe it.

Sir Luke. Why not ?—You tell me so, and make
me believe it too.

Lady. Here the gentleman comes—Go away for a
moment.

Sir Luke. With all my heart, my dear.

                           [*Going in a hurry.*

Lady. I'll give him a few hints, that he must either change his mode of behaviour, or leave us.

Sir Luke. That's right—but don't be too warm : or if he should be very impertinent, or insolent— I hear Aurelia's voice in the next room—call *her,* and I dare say she'll come and take your part.

[*Exit* SIR LUKE.

Enter TWINEALL.

Twi. I positively could pass a whole day upon that stair-case—those reverend faces !—I presume they are the portraits of some of your ladyship's illustrious ancestors ?

Lady. Sir ! Mr. Twineall—give me leave to tell you—   [*In a violent passion.*

Twi. The word illustrious, I find, displeases you. Pardon me—I did not mean to make use of so forcible an epithet. I know the delicacy of sentiment, which cannot bear the reflection that a few centuries only should reduce from royalty, one whose dignified deportment seems to have been formed for that resplendent station.

Lady. The man is certainly mad !——Mr. Twineall——

Twi. Pardon me, madam ; I own I am an enthusiast on these occasions. The dignity of blood—

Lady. You have too much, I am sure—do have a little taken from you.

Twi. Gladly would I lose every drop that fills these plebeian veins, to be ennobled by the smallest—

Lady. Pray, sir, take up your abode in some other place.

Twi. Madam ?   [*Surprised.*

Lady. Your behaviour, sir—

Twi. If my friend had not given me the hint, damn me if I should not think her downright angry. [*Aside.*

Lady. I can scarcely contain my rage at being so laugh'd at.   [*Aside.*

Twi. I'll mention the wig : this is the time—
[*Aside.*]—Perhaps you may resent it, madam : but
there is a favour—

Lady. A favour, sir ! is this a time to ask a favour?

Twi. To an admirer of antiquity, as I am—

Lady. Antiquity again !

Twi. I beg pardon——but——a wig—

Lady. A what ?   [*Petrified.*

Twi. A wig.   [*Bowing.*

Lady. Oh ! oh ! oh ! [*Choking.*] this is not to be
borne—this is too much—ah ! ah ! [*Sitting down
and going into fits.*] a direct, plain, palpable, and un-
equivocal attack upon my family, without evasion or
palliative.—I can't bear it any longer.—Oh ! oh !—
                                          [*Shrieking.*

Twi. Bless my soul, what shall I do?—what's the
matter ?

Sir Luke. [*Without.*] Maids ! maids ! go to your
mistress—that good-for-nothing man is doing her a
mischief.

Enter AURELIA.

Aure. Dear madam, what is the matter ?

Enter SIR LUKE, *and stands close to the scenes.*

Lady. Oh ! oh !   [*Crying.*

Sir Luke. How do you do now, my dear ?

Twi. Upon my word, Sir Luke—

Sir Luke. O, sir, no apology—it does not signify—
never mind it—I beg you won't put yourself to
the trouble of an apology—it is of no kind of consequence.

Lady. What do you mean, Sir Luke ? [*Recovered.*

Sir Luke. To shew proper philosophy, my dear,
under the affliction I feel for your distress.

Lady. [*To* AURELIA.] Take Twineall out of the
room.

Aure. Mr. Twineall, her ladyship begs you'll leave the room till she is a little recovered.

Twi. Certainly.

[*Bows respectfully to* LADY TREMOR, *and exit with* AURELIA.

Sir Luke. I thought what you would get by quarrelling,—fits—and tears.

Lady. And you know, Sir Luke, if you had quarrelled, you would have been in the same situation. [*Rising from her seat.*] But, Sir Luke, my dear Sir Luke, show yourself a man of courage but on this occasion.

Sir Luke. My dear, I would do as much for you as I would for my own life—but damn me if I think I could fight to save that.

Enter LORD FLINT.

Lord. Lady Tremor, did the servant say you were very well, or very ill?

Lady. O, my lord, that insolent coxcomb, the Honourable Mr. Twineall—

Lord. I am very glad you put me in mind of him —I dare say I should have forgot else, notwithstanding I came on purpose.

Lady. Forgot what?

Lord. A little piece of paper here : [*Pulling out a parchment.*] but it will do a great deal.—Has he offended you?

Lady. Beyond bearing.

Lord. I am glad of it, because it gives double pleasure to my vengeance.—He is a disaffected person— boldly told me he doubted the Sultan's right to the throne.—I have informed against him ; and his punishment is left to my discretion. I may have him imprisoned, shot, sent to the gallies, or his head cut off— but which does your ladyship choose?—Which ever you choose is at your service.   [*Bowing.*

E 2

Lady. [*Curtsying.*] O, they are all alike to me : which ever you please, my lord.

Sir Luke. What a deal of ceremony ! how cool they are upon the subject !

Lord. And why not cool, sir ? why not cool ?

Sir Luke. O, very true—I am sure it has frozen me.

Lord. I will go instantly, for fear it should slip my memory, and put this paper into the hands of proper officers. In the mean time, Sir Luke, if you can talk with your visitor, Mr. Twineall, do.—Inquire his opinion of the Sultan's rights—ask his thoughts, as if you were commissioned by me—and, while he is revealing them to you, the officers shall be in ambush, surprise him in the midst of his sentiments, and bear him away to—   [TWINEALL *looking in.*

Twi. May I presume to inquire how your ladyship does ?

Lady. O, yes—and pray walk in—I am quite recovered.

Lord. Lady Tremor, I bid you good day for the present.

Sir Luke. [*Following him to the door.*] Your lordship won't forget ?

Lord. No—depend upon it, I shall remember.

Sir Luke. Yes—and make some other people remember too.   [*Exit* LORD FLINT.

Twi. Is his lordship gone ? I am very sorry.

Sir Luke. No—don't be uneasy, he'll soon come back.

Enter HASWELL.

Sir Luke. Mr. Haswell, I am glad to see you !

Hasw. I told Lady Tremor I would call in the evening, Sir Luke ; and I have kept my word—I hoped to meet my Lord Flint here, as I have some business on which I want to speak to him; but he passed me at the door in such great haste he would hardly allow me to ask him how he did—I hope your ladyship is well this afternoon.

[*Bows to* TWINEALL—SIR LUKE *exit at the door to* AURELIA *and* ELVIRUS.]

Twi. Pardon me, Mr. Haswell, but I almost suspect you heard of her ladyship's indisposition, and therefore paid this visit ; for I am perfectly acquainted with your care and attention to all under affliction.

Hasw. [*Bows gravely.*] Has your ladyship been indisposed ?

Lady. A little—but I am much better.

Twi. Surely, of all virtues, charity is the first ! it so protects our neighbour !

Hasw. Do not you think, sir, that *patience* frequently protects him as much ?

Twi. Dear sir—pity for the poor and miserable—

Hasw. Is oftener excited than the poor and miserable are aware of.   [*Looking significantly at him.*

Sir Luke. [*From the room where* AURELIA *and* ELVIRUS *are.*] Nay, sir, I beg you will walk into this apartment.—Aurelia, introduce the gentleman to Lady Tremor.

Lady. Who has she with her ?

Hasw. Aurelia!—oh ! I have not seen her I know not when : and, besides my acquaintance with her relations in England, there is a frank simplicity in her manners that has won my friendship.

Enter SIR LUKE, AURELIA, *and* ELVIRUS.

Sir Luke. You should have introduced Mr. Glanmore before.—I assure you, sir, [*To* ELVIRUS.] I did not know, nor should I have known, if I had not accidentally come into that room——

[HASWELL *starts, on seeing* ELVIRUS.

Sir Luke. [*To* LADY TREMOR.] A relation of Aurelia's—a Mr. Glanmore, my dear, just arrived from England; who has call'd to pass a few minutes with

us before he sets off to the part of India he is to reside
in.   [ELVIRUS *and* AURELIA *appear in confusion.*

Lady. I hope, sir, your stay with us will not be so
short as Sir Luke has mentioned ?

Elvir. Pardon me, madam, it must.—The caravan,
with which I travel, goes off this evening, and I must
accompany it.

Hasw. [*Aside.*] I doubted my eyes : but his voice
confirms me.   [*Looking on* ELVIRUS.

Lady. Why, if you only arrived this morning, Mr.
Glanmore, you came passenger in the same ship with
Mr. Twineall ?

Twi. No, madam.—Sir, I am very sorry we had
not the pleasure of your company on board of us.

[*To* ELVIRUS.

Sir Luke. You had : Mr. Glanmore came over in
the Mercury.—Did not you tell me so, sir ?

[ELVIRUS *bows.*

Twi. Bless my soul, sir! I beg your pardon : but
surely that cannot be—I got acquainted with every
soul on board of us—every creature—all their connexions—and I can scarcely suppose you were of the
number.

Sir Luke. [*Aside.*] How impertinent he is to every
body! O, that I had but courage to knock him
down !

Elvir. [*To* TWINEALL.] Perhaps, sir—

Aure. Yes, I dare say, that was the case.

Twi. What was the case, madam ?

Sir Luke. Wha—wha—wha—[*Mimicks.*] that is
not good breeding.

Hasw. Why do you blush, Aurelia ?

Aure. Because [*Hesitating*]—this gentleman——
came over in the same ship with Mr. Twineall.

Sir Luke. And I can't say I wonder at your blush-
ing.

Twi. Why then positively, sir, I thought I had
known every passenger—and surely—

Lady. Mr. Twineall, your behaviour puts me out of all patience.—Did you not hear Mr. Glanmore say he came in the same vessel; and is not that sufficient?

Twi. Perfectly, madam—perfectly : but I thought there might be some mistake.

Elvir. And there is, sir : you find *you* are mistaken.

Lady. I thought so.—

Hasw. [*To* ELVIRUS.] And you *did* come in the same vessel?

Elvir. Sir, do you doubt it?

Hasw. Doubt it!

Elvir. Dare not doubt it.—[*Trembling and confused.*]

Hasw. Dare not!

Elvir. No, sir; dare not.   [*Violently.*

Aure. Oh, heavens!

Sir Luke. [*To* AURELIA.] Come, my dear, you and I will get out of the way.   [*Retiring with her.*

Lady. O dear!—for heaven's sake!—Mr. Twineall, this is your doing.

Twi. Me, madam!——

Hasw. I beg the company's pardon—but [*To* ELVIRUS.] a single word with you, sir, if you please.

Lady. Dear Mr. Haswell—

Hasw. Trust my prudence and forbearance, madam —I will but speak a word in private to this gentleman.

  [HASWELL *takes* ELVIRUS *down to the bottom of
      the Stage—the rest retire.*

Hasw. Are you, or are you not, an impostor?

Elvir. I am—I am—but do not you repeat my words.—Do not *you* say it.   [*Threatening.*

Hasw. What am I to fear?

Elvir. Fear *me*—I cannot lie with fortitude; but I can——Beware of me.

Hasw. I *will* beware of you, and so shall all my friends.

Elvir. Insolent, insulting man!—
        [*With the utmost contempt.*

LADY TREMOR *and the rest come forward.*

Lady. Come, come, gentlemen, I hope you are now
perfectly satisfied concerning this little misunderstand-
ing—let us change the subject.—Mr. Haswell, have
you been successful before the Sultan for any of those
poor prisoners you visited this morning?

Sir Luke. Aye; Meanright told me he saw you
coming from them wrapt up in your long cloak; and
he said he should not have known you, if somebody
had not said it was you.

[ELVIRUS *looks with surprize, confusion, and re-
        pentance.*

Lady. But what success with the Sultan?

Hasw. He has granted me the pardon and freedom
of any six whom I shall present as objects of his
mercy.

Lady. I sincerely rejoice:—Then the youth and
his father, whom you felt so much for, I am sure will
be in the number of those who are to share your inter-
cession.

[HASWELL *makes no reply; and, after a pause—*

Elvir. [*With the most supplicatory tone and manner.*] Sir—Mr. Haswell—O heavens! I did not know
you.

Sir Luke. Come, Mr. Haswell, this young man
seems sorry he has offended you—forgive him.

Lady. Aye, do, Mr. Haswell.—Are you sorry, sir?

Elvir. Wounded to the heart— and, without his pardon, see nothing but despair.

Lady. Good heavens!

Hasw. Sir Luke, my Lord Flint told me he was
coming back directly. Pray inform him I had business elsewhere, and could wait no longer.   [*Exit.*

Elvir. O! I'm undone.

Lady. Follow him if you have any thing to say.

Elvir. I dare not—I feel the terror of his just reproach.

Lady. Did you know him in England?

Aure. Dear madam, will you suffer me to speak a few words——

Sir Luke. [*Aside to* LADY TREMOR.] Leave her and her relation together, and let us take a turn in the garden with Mr. Twineall.—I'm afraid his lordship will be back before we have drawn him to say any more .on the subject, for which he is to be arrested.

Lady. You are right.

Sir Luke. Mr. Twineall, will you walk this way? —that young lady and gentleman wish to have a little private conversation.

Twi. O, certainly, Sir Luke, by all means. [*Exeunt* SIR LUKE *and* LADY.]—[*To* ELVIRUS.] I am extremely sorry, sir, that you kept your bed during the voyage : I should else have been most prodigiously happy in such good company.   [*Exit.*

Aure. Why are you thus agitated? It was wrong to be so impetuous—but such regret as this is too much.

Elvir. Hear the secret I refused to tell you before— my father is a prisoner for life.

Aure. Oh, heavens ! then Mr. Haswell was the only man——

Elvir. And he had promised me—promised me, with benevolence, his patronage : but the disguise he wore, when I first saw him, led me to mistake his figure and appearance—has made me expose my falsehood, my infamy, and treat his honour'd person with abuse.

Aure. Yes, let his virtues make you thus repent : but let them also make you hope for pardon.

Elvir. Nay, he is just as well as compassionate; and for detected falsehood——

Aure. You make me tremble.

Elvir. Yet he shall hear my story—I'll follow him, and obtain his pity, if not his forgiveness.

Aure. And do not blush, or feel yourself degraded
to *kneel* to him, for *he* would scorn that pride which
triumphs over the humbled.   [*Exeunt.*

SCENE II.

The Garden.

Enter SIR LUKE, TWINEALL, *and* LADY TREMOR.

Twi. Why, really, Sir Luke, as my lord has given
you charge to sound my principles, I must own they
are just such as I delivered them to him.

Sir Luke. Mr. Twineall, I only wish you to be a
little more circumstantial—we will suppose the present Sultan no impostor—yet what pretensions do you
think the other family possessed?

Twi. That I'll make clear to you at once—or if
my reasons are not very clear, they are at least very
positive, and that you know is the same thing:—this
family—no—that family—the family that reigned before this—this came after that—that came before this.
Now every one agrees that this family was always
—so and so—[*Whispering.*]—and that the other was
always—so and so—[*Whispering.*]—in short, every
body knows that one of them had always a very suspicious—you know what.

Sir Luke. No, I don't.

Twi. Pshaw—pshaw—every body conjectures what
—and though it was never said in so many words,
yet it was always supposed—and though there never
has been any proof, yet there have been things much
more strong than proof—and for that very reason,
Sir William—(Sir Luke, I mean—I beg your pardon)
for that very reason—I can't think what made

me call you Sir William—for that very reason—
(O, I was thinking of Sir William Tiffany)—for
that very reason, let people say what they will—
that, that must be their opinion.—But then where
is the man who will speak his thoughts freely, as I
have done?

Enter GUARDS, *who had been listening at a distance,
during this speech.*

Sir Luke. [*Starting.*] Bless my soul, gentlemen,
you make my heart leap to my very lips.

Guards. [*To* TWINEALL.] Sir, you are our prisoner, and must go with us.

Twi. Gentlemen, you are mistaken—I had all my
clothes made in England, and 'tis impossible the bill
can have followed me already.

Guard. You are charged with treason against the
state.

Twi. Treason against the state—You are mistaken : it cannot be me.

Guard. No—there is no mistake. [*Pulling out a
paper.*] You are here called Henry Twineall.

Twi. But if they have left out *honourable*, it can't
be me——I am the Honourable Henry Twineall.

Sir Luke. That you are to prove before your
judges.

Guard. Yes, sir ; and we are witnesses of the long
speech you have just now been making.

Twi. And pray, gentlemen, did you know what I
meant by it?

Guard. Certainly.

Twi. Why, then, upon my soul, it is more than
I did—I wish I may be sacrificed——

Sir Luke. Well, well, you are going to be sacrificed
—Don't be impatient.

Twi. But, gentlemen—Sir Luke !
[*The* GUARDS *seize him.*

Lady. Dear Mr. Twineall, I am afraid you will have

occasion for the dignity of all my ancestors to support you under this trial.

Sir Luke. And have occasion for all my courage too.

Twi. But, sir—but, gentlemen——

Sir Luke. Oh, I would not be in your coat, fashionable as it is, for all the Sultan's dominions.

[*Exeunt* SIR LUKE *and* LADY *on one side—* TWINEALL *and* GUARDS *on the other.*

ACT THE FIFTH.

SCENE I.

The Prison.

HASWELL *and the* FEMALE PRISONER *discovered.*

Hasw. Rather remain in this loathsome prison!— refuse the blessing offered you!—the blessing your pleased fancy formed so precious, that you durst not even trust its reality?

Pris. While my pleased fancy only saw the prospect, I own it was delightful: but now reason beholds it, the view is changed; and what, in the gay dream of fond delirium, seemed a blessing, in my waking hours of sad reflexion, would prove the most severe of punishments.

Hasw. Explain—what is the cause that makes you think thus?

Pris. A cause, that has alone for fourteen years made me resigned to a fate like this.—When you first mentioned my release from this dark dreary place, my wild ideas included, with the light, all that had ever made the light a blessing.—'Twas not the sun I saw in my mad transport, but a lost husband filled my imagination—'twas his idea, that gave the colours of the world their beauty, and made me fondly hope to be cheered by its brightness.

Hasw. A husband!

Pris. But the world that I was wont to enjoy with him—to see again without him; every well-known object would wound my mind with dear delights for ever lost, and make my freedom torture.

Hasw. But yet——

Pris. Oh! on my knees a thousand times I have thanked Heaven that he partook not of this dire abode—that he shared not with me my hard bondage; a greater blessing I possess'd from that reflection, than all his loved society could have given.—But in a happy world, where smiling nature pours her boundless gifts! oh! there his loss would be insupportable.

Hasw. Do you lament him dead?

Pris. Yes—or, like me, a prisoner—else he would have sought me out—have sought his Arabella!— [HASWELL *starts.*] Why do you start?

Hasw. Are you a Christian? an European?

Arabella. I am.

Hasw. The name made me suppose it.—I am shocked that—the Christian's sufferings—[*Trying to conceal his suprise.*] But were you made a prisoner in the present Sultan's reign?

Arab. I was—or I had been set free on his ascent to the throne; for he of course gave pardon to all the enemies of the slain monarch, among whom I and my husband were reckoned: but I was taken in a vessel, where I was hurried in the heat of the battle with a party of the late emperor's friends; and all these prisoners were, by the officers of the present Sultan, sent to slavery, or confined, as I have been, in hopes of ransom.

Hasw. And did never intelligence or inquiry reach you from your husband?

Arab. Never.

Hasw. Never?

Arab. I was once informed of a large reward offered for the discovery of a female Christian, and, with boundless hopes, I asked an interview with the messenger,—but found, on questioning him, *I* could not answer his description; as he secretly informed me, it was the Sultan who had caused the search, for one, *himself* had known, and dearly loved.

Hasw. Good Heaven! [*Aside.*] You then conclude your husband dead?

Arab. I do; or, like me, by some mischance, taken with the other party: and having no friend to plead his cause before the emperor whom he served——

Hasw. I will plead it, should I ever chance to find him: but, ere we can hope for other kindness, you must appear before the Sultan, to thank him for the favour which you now decline, and to tell the cause why you cannot accept it.

Aarb. Alas! almost worn out with sorrow—an object of affliction as I am—in pity excuse me. Present my acknowledgements—my humble gratitude—but pardon my attendance.

Hasw. Nay; you must go—it is necessary. I will accompany you to his presence.—Retire a moment; but when I send, be ready.

Arab. I shall obey. [*She bows obediently, and exit.*

[*As* HASWELL *comes down,* ELVIRUS *places himself in his path—*HASWELL *stops, looks at him with an austere earnestness, which* ELVIRUS *observing, turns away his face.*

Elvir. Nay, reproach me —I can bear your anger, but do not let me meet your eye.—Oh ! it is more awful, now I know who you are, than if you had kingdoms to dispense, or could deal instant death.— [HASWELL *looks on him with a manly firmness, and then walks on,* ELVIRUS *following him.*]—I do not plead for my father now.—Since what has passed, I only ask forgiveness.

Hasw. Do you forgive yourself ?

Elvir. I never will.

Enter KEEPER.

Keep. One of our prisoners, who, in his cell, makes the most piteous moans, has sent to entreat that Mr. Haswell will not leave this place till he has heard his complaints and supplications.

Hasw. Bring me to him.   [*Going.*

Elvir. Nay, leave me not thus—perhaps never to see you more !

Hasw. You shall see me again : in the mean time, reflect on what you merit.   [*Exit with* KEEPER.

Elvir. And what is that ?—Confusion !—and yet, he says, I am to see him again—speak with him, perhaps.—Oh ! there's a blessing the most abandoned feel, a divine propensity, they know not why, to commune with the virtuous.   [*Exit.*

SCENE II.

The First Prison Scene.

Enter SECOND KEEPER, HASWELL *following.*

Hasw. Where is the poor unfortunate ?

Second Keep. Here, sir.

Hasw. Am I to behold greater misery still ?—a still greater object of compassion ?

[SECOND KEEPER *opens a door, and*

TWINEALL *enters a prisoner, in one of the prison dresses.*

Hasw. What have we here ?

Twi. Don't you know me, Mr. Haswell ?

Hasw. I beg your pardon—I beg your pardon——but is it—is it——

Twi. Why, Mr. Haswell, if you don't know me, or won't know me, I shall certainly lose my senses.

Hasw. O, I know you—know you very well.

Twi. What, notwithstanding the alteration in my dress ?—there was a cruel plunder !

Hasw. O, I'll procure you that again ; and, for all things else, I'm sure you will have patience.

Twi. O, no, I can't—upon my soul, I can't.—I want a little lavender water—My hair is in such a trim too !—no powder—no brushes——

Hasw. I will provide you with them all.

Twi. But who will you provide to look at me, when I am dress'd ?

Hasw. I'll bring all your acquaintance.

Twi. I had rather you would take me to see them.

Hasw. Pardon me.

Twi. Dear Mr. Haswell !—Dear sir !—Dear friend !—What shall I call you ?—Only say what title you like best, and I'll call you by it directly.—I always did love to please every body ; and I am sure, at this time, I am more in need of a friend than ever I was in my life.

Hasw. What has brought you here ?

Twi. Trying to get a place.

Hasw. A place ?

Twi. Yes ; and you see I have got one—and a very bad place it is—in short, sir, my crime is said to be an offence against the state ; and they tell me, no man on earth but you can get that remitted.

Hasw. Upon my word the pardons I have obtained are but for few persons, and those already promised.

Twi. O, I know I am no favourite of yours : you think me an impertinent, silly, troublesome fellow,— .nd that my conduct in life will be neither of use to .ny country, nor of benefit to society.

Hasw. You mistake me, sir ; I think such glaring imperfections as yours are, will not be of so much disadvantage to society, as those of a less faulty man. In beholding your conduct, thousands shall turn from the paths of folly to which fashion impels them : therefore, Mr. Twineall, if not pity for your failings, yet a concern for the good effect they may have upon the world (should you be admitted there again) will urge me to solicit your release.

Twi. Sir, you have such powers of oratory—such eloquence !—and I doubt not but that you are admired by the world equally for those advantages——

Enter MESSENGER *to* HASWELL,

Mess. Sir, the Sultan is arrived in the council chamber, and has sent me——   [*Whispers.*

Hasw. I come—Mr. Twineall, farewell for the present.   [*Exit with* MESSENGER.

Twi. Now, what was that whisper about ?—Oh, Heavens ! perhaps my death in agitation !—I ˙have brought myself into a fine situation !—done it by wheedling too !

Second Keep. Come, your business with Mr. Haswell being ended, return to your cell.   [*Roughly.*

Twi. Certainly, sir—certainly !—O, yes ! —How

happy is this prison in having such a keeper as you!
—so mild, so gentle—there is something about you—
I said, and I thought the moment I had the happiness
of meeting you here, Dear me! said I—what would
one give for such a gentleman as him in England!—
You would be of infinite service to some of our young
bucks, sir.

Second Keep. Go to your cell—go to your cell.
                                    [*Roughly.*
Twi. This world would be nothing without elegant manners, and elegant people in all stations of
life.——

Enter MESSENGER, *who whispers* SECOND KEEPER.

Another whisper!   [*Terrified.*
Second Keep. No; come this way.—The judges
are now sitting in the hall, and you must come before
them.

Twi. Before the judges, sir—O, dear sir!—what, in
this deshabille?—in this coat?—Dear me!—but to
be sure one must conform to customs—to the custom
of the country where one resides. [*He goes to the
door, and then stops.*] I beg your pardon, sir—would
not you choose to go first?

Second Keep. No.
Twi. O!   [*Exeunt*

SCENE III.

The Council Chamber.

Enter SULTAN, HASWELL, *and* GUARDS.

Hasw. Sultan, I have gone beyond the limits of
your bounty in my promises; and for one poor un-

happy female, I have still to implore your clemency.

Sult. No—you named yourself the number to release, and it is fixed—I'll not increase it.

Hasw. A poor miserable female——

Sult. Am I less miserable than she is?—And who
shall relieve me of my sorrows?

Hasw. Then let me tell you, Sultan, she is above
your power to oblige, or to punish.—Ten years, nay,
more, confinement in a dreary cell, has been no greater
punishment to her, than had she lived in a pleasant
world without the man she loved.

Sult. Ha!

Hasw. And freedom, which I offered, she rejects
with scorn, because he is not included in the blessing.

Sult. You talk of prodigies!—[*He makes a sign for
the* GUARDS *to retire, and they withdraw.*] And yet I
once knew a heart equal to this description.

Hasw. Nay, will you see her, witness yourself the
fact?

Sult. I will.—Why do I tremble!—My busy fancy
presents an image——

Hasw. Yes, tremble!   [*Threatening.*

Sult. Ha! have a care—what tortures are you preparing for me?—My mind shrinks at the thought.

Hasw. Your wife you will behold—whom you have
kept in want, in wretchedness, in a damp dungeon,
for these fourteen years, because you would not listen
to the voice of pity.——Dread her look—her frown—
not for herself alone, but for hundreds of her fellow-
sufferers: for while your selfish fancy was searching
with wild anxiety for her *you* loved—unpitying you
forgot—others might love like you.

Sult. O! do not bring me to a trial which I have
not courage to support.

Hasw. She attends without.—I sent for her to thank
you for the favour she declines.—Nay, be composed

—she knows you not—cannot, thus disguised as the
Sultan.   [*Exit* HASWELL.

Sult. O, my Arabella! could I have thought that
your approach would ever impress my mind with
horror!—or that, instead of flying to your arms with
all the love I bear you, terror and shame should fix me
a statue of remorse!

Enter HASWELL, *leading* ARABELLA.

Hasw. Here kneel, and return your thanks.
Sult. My Arabella! worn with grief and anguish .
                                      [*Aside.*
Arab. [*Kneeling to the* SULTAN.] Sultan, the favour you would bestow, I own and humbly thank
you for.
Sult. Gracious heaven!   [*In much agitation.*
Arab. But as I am now accustomed to confinement,
and the brightest prospect of all the world can give,
cannot inspire a wish that warms my heart to the enjoyment—I supplicate permission to transfer the blessing you have offered, to one of those who may have
friends to welcome their return from bondage, and so
make freedom precious.—I have none to rejoice at *my*
release—none to lament my destiny while a prisoner.
—And were I free in this vast world, forlorn and friendless, 'tis but a prison still.
Sult. What have I done!
      [*Throwing himself on a sofa, with the greatest
      emotion.*]
Hasw. Speak to him again : he repents of the severity with which he has caused his fellow-creatures to be
used. Tell him you forgive him.
Arab. [*Going to him.*] Believe me, emperor, I forgive all who have ever wronged me—all who have
ever caused my sufferings.——Pardon *you.*—Alas!
I have pardoned even those who tore me from my
husband!—Oh, Sultan! all the tortures you have
made me suffer, compared to such a pang as that was

—did I say I had forgiven those enemies of my peace?
—Oh! I am afraid—afraid I have not yet.

Sult. Forgive them now, then,—for he is restored.
—[*Taking off his turban.*]—Behold him in the Sultan,
and once more seal my pardon.—[*She faints on* HAS-
WELL.]—Nay, pronounce it quickly, or my remorse
for what you have endured will make my present tortures greater—than any my cruelties have yet inflicted.

Arab. [*Recovering.*] Is this the light you promised?
—[*To* HASWELL.]—Dear precious light!—Is this
my freedom? to which I bind myself a slave for ever
—[*Embracing the* SULTAN.]—Was I *your* captive?—
Sweet captivity! more precious than an age of
liberty!

Sult. Oh! my Arabella! through the amazing
changes of my fate (which I will soon disclose,) think
not, but I have search'd for *thee* with unceasing care:
but the blessing to behold you once again was left
for my kind monitor alone to bestow.——Oh, Haswell! had I, like you, made others' miseries my concern, like you sought out the wretched, how many
days of sorrow had I spared myself, as well as her I
love!—for I long since had found my Arabella.

Arab. Oh, heaven! that weighest our sufferings
with our joys, and as our lives decline seest in the
balance thy blessings far more ponderous than thy
judgments—be witness, I complain no more of what
I have endured, but find an ample recompense this
moment.

Hasw. I told you, sir, how you might be happy.

Sult. ——Take your reward—(to a heart like
yours, more valuable than treasure from my coffers)
—this signet, with power to redress the wrongs of all
my injured subjects.

Hasw. Valuable indeed!——

Arab. [*To* HASWELL.] Oh, virtuous man!—to reward thee are we made happy—to give thy pitying

bosom the joy to see us so, heaven has remitted its intended punishment of continual separation.

Sult. Come, my beloved wife! come to my palace: there, equally, my dearest blessing, as when the cottage gave its fewer joys.—And in him [*To* HAS-WELL.] we not only find our present happiness, but dwell securely on our future hopes—for here I vow, before he leaves our shores, I will adopt every measure he shall point out; and those acts of my life whereon he shall lay his censure, these will I make the subject of repentance.

[*Exeunt* SULTAN *and* ARABELLA.—HASWELL *bows to heaven in silent thanks.*

Enter KEEPER.

Keep. An English prisoner, just now condemned to lose his head, one Henry Twineall, humbly begs permission to speak a few short sentences, his last dying words, to Mr. Haswell.

Hasw. Condemned to lose his head!—Lead me to him.

Keep. O, sir, you need not hurry yourself: for it is off by this time, I dare say.

Hasw. Off!

Keep. Yes, sir: we don't stand long about these things in this country—I dare say it is off.

Hasw. [*Impatiently.*] Lead me to him instantly.

Keep. O! 'tis of consequence, is it, sir?—if that is the case—   [*Exit* KEEPER *followed by* HASWELL.

SCENE IV.

An archway at the top of the stage;

Through which several GUARDS *enter.*—TWINEALL
*in the middle, dressed for execution, with a large
book in his hand.*

Twi. One more stave, gentlemen, if you please.

Offi. The time is expired.

Twi. One more, gentlemen, if you please.

Offi. The time is expired.

Enter HASWELL.

Twi. Oh! my dear Mr. Haswell!

[*Bursting into tears.*

Hasw. What, in tears at parting with me?—This is
a compliment indeed!

Twi. I hope you take it as such—I am sure I mean
it as such.—It kills me to leave *you*—it breaks my
heart; and I once flattered myself such a charitable,
good, feeling, humane heart, as you——

Hasw. Hold! hold!—This, Mr. Twineall, is the
vice which has driven you to the fatal precipice
whereon you stand; and in death will you not re-
linquish it?

Twi. What vice, sir, do you mean?

Hasw. Flattery!—a vice that renders you not only
despicable, but odious.

Twi. But how has flattery been the cause?

Hasw. Your English friend, before he left the island,
told me what information you had asked from him;
and that he had given you the direct *reverse* of every
person's character, as a just punishment for your mean
premeditation and designs.

G

Twi. I never imagined that amiable friend had sense enough to impose upon any body !

Hasw. And, I presume, he could not suppose that fate would carry resentment to a length like this.

Twi. Oh ! could fate be arrested in its course !

Hasw. You would reform your conduct ?

Twi. I would—I would never say another civil thing to any body—never—never again make myself agreeable.

Hasw. Release him—here is the Sultan's signet.

[*They release him.*

Twi. Oh ! my dear Mr. Haswell ! never was compassion !—never benevolence !—never such a heart as yours !

Hasw. Seize him—he has broken his contract already.

Twi. No, sir—No, sir—I protest you are an ill-natured, surly, crabbed fellow. I always thought so, upon my word, whatever I may have said.

Hasw. And, I'll forgive *that* language sooner than the other—utter any thing but flattery.—Oh ! never let the honest, plain, *blunt*, English name become a proverb for so base a vice.

Lady Tremor. [*Without.*] Where is the poor creature ?

Enter LADY TREMOR.

Lady. Oh ! if his head be off, pray let me *look* at it.

Twi. No, madam, it is on—and I am very happy to tell you so.

Lady. Dear heaven !—I expected to have seen it off !—but no matter. As it is on, I am come that it may be kept on ; and have brought my Lord Flint, and Sir Luke, as witnesses.

Enter LORD FLINT, AURELIA, *and* SIR LUKE.

Hasw. And what have they to say ?

Sir Luke. Who are we to tell our story to?—There does not seem to be any one sitting in judgment.

Hasw. Tell it to me, sir: I will report it.

Sir Luke. Why then, Mr. Haswell, as ghosts sometimes walk, and as one's conscience is sometimes troublesome, I think Mr. Twineall has done nothing to merit death; and the charge which his lordship sent in against him we begin to think was too hastily made: but, if there was any false statement——

Lord. It was the fault of my not charging my memory.—Any error I have been guilty of must be laid to the fault of my total want of memory.

Hasw. And what do you hope from this confession?

Sir Luke. To have the prisoner's punishment of death remitted for some more favourable sentence.

Lord. Yes—for ten or twelve years imprisonment —or the gallies for fourteen years—or—

Sir Luke. Ay, ay, something in that mild way.

Hasw. For shame, for shame, gentlemen!—the extreme rigour you show in punishing a dissention from your opinion, or a satire upon your folly, proves, to conviction, what reward you had bestowed upon the *skilful* flatterer.

Twi. Gentlemen and ladies, pray, why would you wish me requited with such extreme severity, merely for my humble endeavours to make myself agreeable? —Lady Tremor, upon my honour, I was credibly informed your ancestors were Kings of Scotland.

Lady. Impossible!—you might as well say that you heard Sir Luke had distinguished himself at the battle of——

Twi. And I *did* hear so.

Lady. And he *did* distinguish himself; for he was the only one who ran away.

Twi. Could it happen?

Lady. Yes, sir, it did happen.

Sir Luke. And go *you*, Mr. Twineall, into a field of battle, and I think it is very likely to happen again.

Lord. If Mr. Haswell has obtained your pardon, sir, it is all very well : but let me advise you to conceal your sentiments on politics for the future, as you value your head.

Twi. I thank you, sir—I do value it.

Enter ELVIRUS

Hasw. [*Going to him.*] Aurelia, in this letter to me, has explained your story with so much compassion, that, I must pity it too.—With freedom to your father and yourself, the Sultan restores his forfeited lands—and might I plead, Sir Luke, for your interest with Aurelia's friends, this young man's filial love should be repaid by conjugal affection.

Sir Luke. As for that, Mr. Haswell, you have so much interest at court, that your taking the young man under your protection is at once making his fortune ; and as Aurelia was sent hither merely to get a husband, I don't see——

Aure. True, Sir Luke—and I am afraid my father and mother will begin to be uneasy that I have not procured one yet ; and I should be very sorry to grieve them.

Elvir. No—say rather, sorry to make me wretched
[*Taking her hand*

Enter ZEDAN.

Hasw. My Indian friend, have you received your freedom ?

Zedan. Yes—and come to bid you farewell—which I would *never* do, had I not a family in sorrow till my return—for you should be my master, and I *would* be your slave.

Hasw. I thank you—may you meet at home every comfort !

Zedan. May you—may you—what shall I say ?—
May you once in your life be a prisoner—then released—to feel such joy as I feel now !

Hasw. I thank you for a wish that tells me most
emphatically, how much you think I have served
you.

Twi And, my dear lord, I sincerely wish you may
once in your life have your head chopped off—just to
know what I should have felt in that situation.

Zedan. [*Pointing to* HASWELL.] Are all his countrymen as good as he ?

Sir Luke. No-no-no-no—not all—but the worst of
them are good enough to admire him.

Twi. Pray, Mr. Haswell, will you suffer all these
encomiums ?

Elvir. He *must* suffer them.—There are virtues
which praise cannot taint—such are Mr. Haswell's
—for they are the offspring of a mind superior even
to the love of fame.   Neither can he, through malice,
suffer by applause ; for his character is too sacred to
incite envy, and conciliates the respect, the love, and
the admiration of all mankind.

THE END.

Printed by Augustus Applegath and Edward Cowper,
24, Nelson-Square, Great Surrey-Street.

Every One Has His Fault
Act V, Scene I. Lady Eleanor: You love me.
It's in vain to say you do not.
You love my child,

EVERY ONE HAS HIS FAULT;

A COMEDY,

IN FIVE ACTS;

BY MRS INCHBALD.

AS PERFORMED AT THE

THEATRE ROYAL, COVENT-GARDEN.

PRINTED UNDER THE AUTHORITY OF THE MANAGERS

FROM THE PROMPT BOOK.

WITH REMARKS

BY THE AUTHOR.

LONDON:

PRINTED FOR LONGMAN, HURST, REES, ORME, AND BROWN,
PATERNOSTER-ROW.

EDINBURGH:
Printed by James Ballantyne and Co.

REMARKS.

There is at present an opinion prevailing, in regard to dramatic works, which, if just, is wholly contradictory to every proof of *cause and effect*, which has been applied to the rise and fall of other arts and sciences.

It is said, that modern dramas are the worst that ever appeared on the English stage,—yet it is well known, that the English theatres never flourished as they do at present.

When it is enquired, why painting, poetry, and sculpture, decline in England ? " Want of encouragement" is the sure reply—but this reply cannot be given to the question, " Why dramatic literature fails ?" for never was there such high remuneration conferred upon every person, and every work, belonging to the drama.

A new play, which, from a reputed wit of former times, would not, with success, bring him a hundred pounds, a manager will now purchase, from a reputed blockhead, at the price of near a thousand; and sustain all risk whether it be condemned or not.

Great must be the attraction of modern plays to repay such speculation.

It follows, then, if the stage be really sunk so low as it is said to be, that patronage and reward have ruined, instead of having advanced, genius. Or, is it not more likely, that public favour has incited the envious to rail; or, at best, raised up minute enquirers into the excellence of that amusement, which charms a whole nation; and criticism sees faults, as fear sees ghosts—whenever they are looked for.

It is a consolation to the dramatist of the present age, that, while his plays are more attractive than ever those of former writers were, those authors had their contemporary critics as well as he, though less acute and less severe, indeed, than the present race. As a testimony—they often had not satire sharp enough to avert that bitterest punishment to an ambitious author—neglect.

Of this play, " Every One has his Fault," nothing, in modesty, can be said, beyond mere matter of fact. It has been productive both to the manager and the writer, having, on its first appearance, run, in the theatrical term, near thirty nights; during which, some of the audience were heard to laugh, and some were seen to weep—it may likewise with truth be added, that, whatever critics may please to say against the production, they cannot think more humbly of its worth, than

THE AUTHOR.

DRAMATIS PERSONÆ.

LORD NORLAND	*Mr Farren*
SIR ROBERT RAMBLE	*Mr Lewis.*
MR SOLUS	*Mr Quick.*
MR HARMONY	*Mr Munden.*
MR PLACID	*Mr Fawcett.*
MR IRWIN	*Mr Pope.*
HAMMOND	*Mr Powell.*
PORTER	*Mr Thompson.*
EDWARD	*Miss Grist.*
LADY ELEANOR IRWIN	*Mrs Pope.*
MRS PLACID	*Mrs Mattocks.*
MISS SPINSTER	*Mrs Webb.*
MISS WOOBURN	*Mrs Esten.*

SERVANTS, &c.

SCENE—London.

EVERY ONE HAS HIS FAULT.

ACT THE FIRST.

SCENE I.

An Apartment at Mr Placid's.

Enter Mr Placid *and* Mr Solus.

Plac. You are to blame.

Sol. I say the same by you.

Plac. And yet your singularity pleases me ; for you are the first elderly bachelor I ever knew, who did not hug himself in the reflection, that he was not in the trammels of wedlock.

Sol. No ; I am only the first elderly bachelor who has truth and courage enough to confess his dissatisfaction.

Plac. And you really wish you were married ?

Sol I do. I wish still more, that I had been married thirty years ago. Oh ! I wish that a wife and half a score children would now start up around me, and bring along with them all that affection, which we should have had for each other by being earlier acquainted. But as it is, in my present state, there is not a person in the world I care a straw for ;—and the

6

world is pretty even with me, for I don't believe there
is a creature in it who cares a straw for me.

Plac. Pshaw! You have in your time been a man
of gallantry; and, consequently, must have made
many attachments.

Sol. Yes, such as men of gallantry usually make.
I have been attached to women, who have purloined
my fortune, and to men, who have partaken of the
theft: I have been in as much fear of my mistress
as you are of your wife.

Plac. Is that possible?

Sol. Yes; and without having one of those tender,
delicate ties of a husband, an excuse for my apprehension.—I have maintained children——

Plac. Then why do you complain for the want of
a family?

Sol. I did not say, I ever had any children; I said,
I had maintained them; but I never believed they
were mine; for I could have no dependence upon
the principles of their mother—and never did I take
one of those tender infants in my arms, that the forehead of my valet, the squint eye of my apothecary,
or the double chin of my chaplain, did not stare me
in the face, and damp all the fine feelings of the parent, which I had just called up.

Plac. But those are accidents, which may occur in
the marriage state.

Sol. In that case, a man is pitied—in mine, he is
only laughed at.

Plac. I wish to heaven I could exchange the pity
which my friends bestow on me, for the merriment
which your ill fate excites.

Sol. You want but courage to be envied.

Plac. Does any one doubt my courage?

Sol. No; if a prince were to offend you, you would
challenge him——

Plac. But if my wife offend me, I am obliged to

make an apology.—Was not that her voice ? I hope she has not overheard our conversation.

Sol. If she have, she'll be in an ill humour.

Plac. That she will be, whether she have heard it or not.

Sol. Well, good day. I don't like to be driven from my fixed plan of wedlock; and, therefore, I won't be a spectator of your mutual discontent.

[*Going.*

Plac. But before you go, Mr Solus, permit me to remind you of a certain concern, that, I think, would afford you much more delight than all you can, at this time of life, propose to yourself in marriage. Make happy, by your beneficence, a near relation, whom the truest affection has drawn into that state, but who is denied the blessing of competency, to make the state supportable.

Sol. You mean my nephew, Irwin? But do not you acknowledge he has a wife and children? Did not he marry the woman he loved, and has he not at this moment a large family, by whom he is beloved? And is he not, therefore, with all his poverty, much happier than I am ? He has often told me, when I have reproached him with his indiscreet marriage, " that in his wife he possessed kingdoms!" Do you suppose I will give any part of my fortune to a man who enjoys such extensive domains? No:—let him preserve his territories, and I will keep my little estate for my own use.   [*Exit.*

Plac. John! John!

Enter Servant.

Has your mistress been enquiring for me?

John. Yes, sir:—My lady asked, just now, if I knew who was with you ?

Plac. Did she seem angry ?

John. No, sir ;—pretty well.

Plac. You scoundrel, what do you mean by " pretty well ?"   [*In Anger.*

John. Much as usual, sir.

Plac. And do you call that " pretty well ?" You
scoundrel, I have a great mind——

Enter MRS PLACID, *speaking very loud.*

Mrs P. What is the matter, Mr Placid ? What is
all this noise about ? You know I hate a noise. What
is the matter ?

Plac. My dear, I was only finding fault with that
blockhead.

Mrs P. Pray, Mr Placid, do not find fault with
any body in this house. But I have something which
I must take *you* very severely to task about, sir.

Plac. No, my dear, not just now, pray.

Mrs P. Why not now?

Plac. [*Looking at his Watch.*] Because dinner will
be ready in a very few minutes. I am very hungry,
and it will be cruel of you to spoil my appetite.
John, is the dinner on table ?

Mrs P. No, John, don't let it be served yet—Mr
Placid, you shall first hear what what I have to say.
                         [*Sitting down.—Exit* SERVANT.

Plac. But then I know I shall not be able to eat a
morsel.

Mrs P. Sit down. [PLACID *sits.*]—I believe, Mr
Placid, you are going to do a very silly thing. I am
afraid you are going to lend some money ?

Plac. Well, my dear, and suppose I am ?

Mrs.P. Then, I don't approve of people lending
their money.

Plac. But, my dear, I have known you approve of
borrowing money: and, once in our lives, what should
we have done, if every body had refused to lend ?

Mrs P. That is nothing to the purpose.—And,
now, I desire you will hear what I say, without
speaking a word yourself.

Plac. Well, my dear.

Mrs P. Now, mind you don't speak till I have done.—Our old acquaintance, Captain Irwin, and Lady Eleanor, his wife (with whom we lived upon very intimate terms, to be sure, while we were in America), are returned to London; and, I find, you have visited them very frequently.

Plac. Not above two or three times, upon my word; for it hurts me to see them in distress, and I forbear to go.

Mrs P. There! you own they are in distress; I expected as much. Now, own to me that they have asked you to lend them money.

Plac. I do own it—I do own it. Now, are you satisfied?

Mrs P. No; for I have no doubt but you have promised they shall have it.

Plac. No: upon my word I have not promised.

Mrs P. Then promise me they shall not.

Plac. Nay, my dear, you have no idea of their unhappy situation.

Mrs P. Yes, I have; and 'tis that which makes me suspicious.

Plac. His regiment is now broken; all her jewels, and little baubles, are disposed of; and he is in such dread of his old creditors, that, in the lodging they have taken, he passes by the name of Middleton—They have three more children, my dear, than when we left them in New York; and they have, in vain, sent repeated supplications, both to his uncle, and her father, for the smallest bounty.

Mrs P. And is not her father, my Lord Norland, a remarkable wise man, and a good man? and ought you to do for them what he has refused?

Plac. They have offended him, but they have never offended me.

Mrs P. I think, 'tis an offence, to ask a friend for money, when there is no certainty of returning it.

Plac. By no means : for, if there were a certainty, even an enemy might lend.

Mrs P. But I insist, Mr Placid, that they shall not find a friend in you upon this occasion.—What do you say, sir ?

Plac. [*After a Struggle.*] No, my dear, they shall not.

Mrs P. Positively shall not ?

Plac. Positively shall not—since they have found an enemy in you.

Enter SERVANT.

Serv. Dinner is on table.

Plac. Ah! I am not hungry now.

Mrs P. What do you mean by that, Mr Placid ? I insist on your being hungry.

Plac. Oh, yes! I have a very excellent appetite. I shall eat prodigiously.

Mrs P. You had better.   [*Exeunt.*

SCENE II.

An Apartment at MR HARMONY's.

Enter MR HARMONY, *followed by* MISS SPINSTER.

Miss S. Cousin, cousin Harmony, I will not forgive you, for thus continually speaking in the behalf of every servant whom you find me offended with. Your philanthropy becomes insupportable ; and, instead of being a virtue, degenerates into a vice.

Har. Dear madam, do not upbraid me for a constitutional fault.

Miss S. Very true; you had it from your infancy. I have heard your mother say, you were always foolishly tender-hearted, and never showed one of

those discriminating passions of envy, hatred, or revenge, to which all her other children were liable.

Har. No : since I can remember, I have felt the
most unbounded affection for all my fellow creatures.
I even protest to you, dear madam, that, as I walk
along the streets of this large metropolis, so warm is
my heart towards every person who passes me, that
I long to say, " How do you do ?" and " I am glad
to see you," to them all. Some men, I should like
even to stop, and shake hands with ;—and some women, I should like even to stop, and kiss.

Miss S. How can you be so ridiculous !

Har. Nay 'tis truth: and I sincerely lament, that
human beings should be such strangers to one another
as we are ! We live in the same street, without knowing one another's necessities; and oftentimes meet
and part from each other at church, at coffeehouses,
playhouses, and all public places,—without ever
speaking a single word, or nodding " Good b'ye !"
though 'tis a hundred chances to ten we never see one
another again.

Miss S. Let me tell you, kinsman, all this pretended philanthropy renders you ridiculous. There
is not a fraud, a theft, or hardly any vice committed,
that you do not take the criminal's part, shake your
head, and cry, " Provisions are so scarce !" And
no longer ago than last Lord Mayor's Day, when you
were told that Mr Alderman Ravenous was ill with
an indigestion, you endeavoured to soften the matter,
by exclaiming, " Provisions are so scarce !"—But,
above all, I condemn that false humanity, which
induces you to say many things in conversation,
which deserve to stigmatize you with the character of
deceit.

Hor. This is a weakness, I confess. But though
my honour sometimes reproaches me with it, my
conscience never does : for it is by this very failing,
that I have frequently made the bitterest enemies

B

friends—Just by saying a few harmless sentences,
which, though a species of falsehood and deceit, yet,
being soothing and acceptable to the person offended,
I have immediately inspired him with lenity and forgiveness; and then, by only repeating the self-same
sentences to his opponent, I have known hearts cold
and closed to each other, warmed and expanded, as
every human creature's ought to be.

Enter a SERVANT.

Serv. Mr Solus.   [*Exit* SERVANT.
Miss S. I cannot think, Mr Harmony, why you
keep company with that old bachelor; he is a man,
of all others on earth, I dislike; and so I am obliged
to quit the room, though I have a thousand things
more to say.   [*Exit angrily.*

Enter SOLUS.

Har. Mr Solus, how do you do?
Sol. I am very lonely at home; will you come and
dine with me?
Har. Now you are here, you had better stay with
me: we have no company; only my cousin Miss
Spinster and myself.
Sol. No, I must go home: do come to my house.
Har. Nay, pray, stay: what objection can you
have?
Sol. Why, to tell you the truth, your relation, Miss
Spinster, is no great favourite of mine; and I don't
like to dine with you, because I don't like her company.
Har. That is, to me, surprising!
Sol. Why, old bachelors and old maids never
agree: we are too much alike in our habits: we know
our own hearts so well, we are apt to discover every
foible we would wish to forget, in the symptoms dis-
played by the other. Miss Spinster is peevish, fretful,

and tiresome, and I am always in a fidget when I am in her company.

Har. How different are her sentiments of you! for one of her greatest joys is to be in your company. [SOLUS *starts and smiles.*] Poor woman! she has, to be sure, an uneven temper—

Sol. No, perhaps I am mistaken.

Har. But I will assure you, I never see her in half such good humour as when you are here: for I believe you are the greatest favourite she has.

Sol. I am very much obliged to her, and I certainly am mistaken about her temper—Some people, if they look ever so cross, are good-natured in the main; and I dare say she is so. Besides, she never has had a husband to sooth and soften her disposition; and there should be some allowance made for that.

Har. Will you dine with us?

Sol. I don't care if I do. Yes, I think I will. I must however step home first:—but I'll be back in a quarter of an hour.—My compliments to Miss Spinster, if you should see her before I return. [*Exit.*

Enter SERVANT,

Serv. My lady begs to know, sir, if you have invited Mr Solus to dine? because if you have, she shall go out. [*Exit* SERVANT.

Enter MISS SPINSTER.

Har. Yes, madam, I could not help inviting him; for, poor man, his own house is in such a state for want of proper management, he cannot give a comfortable dinner himself.

Miss S. And so he must spoil the comfort of mine.

Har. Poor man! poor man! after all the praises he has been lavishing upon you!

Miss S. What praises?

Har. I won't tell you: for you won't believe them.

Miss S. Yes, I shall.—Oh no—now I recollect, this is some of your invention.

Har. Nay, I told him it was *his* invention: for he declared you looked better last night, than any other lady at the Opera.

Miss S. Well, this sounds like truth:—and, depend upon it, though I never liked the manners of Mr Solus much, yet—

Har. Nay, Solus has his faults.

Miss S. So we have all.

Har. And will you leave him and me to dine by ourselves?

Miss S. Oh no, I cannot be guilty of such ill manners, though I talked of it. Besides, poor Mr Solus does not come so often, and it would be wrong not to show him all the civility we can. For my part, I have no dislike to the man; and, if taking a bit of dinner with us now and then can oblige either you or him, I should be to blame to make any objection.— Come, les us go into the drawing-room to receive him.

Har. Ay! this is right: this is as it should be.

                              [Exeunt.

SCENE III.

A Room at the Lodgings of MR IRWIN.

MR IRWIN *and* LADY ELEANOR IRWIN *discovered.*

Lady E. My dear husband, my dear Irwin, I cannot bear to see you thus melancholy. Is this the joy of returning to our native country, after a nine years' banishment?

Irw. Yes: For I could bear my misfortunes, my wretched poverty, with patience, in a land where our sorrows were shared by those about us; but here, in London, where plenty and ease smile upon every face ; where by your birth you claim distinction, and I by services ;—here to be in want,—to be obliged to take another name, through shame of our own,—to tremble at the voice of every stranger, for fear he should be a creditor,—to meet each old acquaintance with an averted eye, because we would not feel the pang of being shunned,—to have no reward for all this even in a comfortable home, but in this our habitation, to see our children looking up to me for that support I have not in my power to give —Can I,—can I love them and you, and not be miserable ?

Lady E. Yet I am not so.   And I am sure you will not doubt my love to you or them.

Irw. I met my uncle this morning, and was mean enough to repeat my request to him : he burst into a fit of laughter, and told me my distresses were the result of my ambition, in marrying the daughter of a nobleman, who himself was too ambitious ever to pardon us.

Lady E. Tell me no more of what he said.

Irw. This was a day of trials ;—I saw your father too.

Lady E. My father! Lord Norland!   Oh Heavens !

Irw. He passed me in his carriage.

Lady E. I envy you the blessing of seeing him ! For, oh !—excuse my tears—he is my father still.— How did he look ?

Irw. As well as he did at the time I used to watch him from his house, to steal to you—But I am sorry to aquaint you, that, to guard himself against all returning love for you, he has, I am informed, adopted

B 2

a young lad, on whom he bestows every mark of
that paternal affection, of which you lament the
loss.

Lady E. May the young man deserve his tenderness better than I have done—May he never disobey
him—May *he* be a comfort, and cherish his benefactor's declining years—and when his youthful passions
teach him to love, may they not, like mine, teach him
disobedience!

Enter a SERVANT, *with a Letter.*

What is that letter?

Serv. It comes from Mr Placid, the servant, who
brought it, said, and requires no answer.   [*Exit.*

Irw. It's strange how I tremble at every letter I see,
as if I dreaded the contents.   How poverty has un-
manned me! [*Aside.*] I must tell you, my dear, that,
finding myself left this morning without a guinea, I
wrote to Mr Placid, to borrow a small sum: This is
his answer: [*Reading the Superscription.*] *To Mr
Middleton.*—That's right: he remembers the caution
I gave him.   I had forgot whether I had done so, for
my memory is not so good as it was.   I did not even
now recollect his hand, though it is one I am so well
acquainted with, and ought to give me joy rather than
sorrow. [*Opens the Letter hastily, reads, and lets it
drop.*] Now I have not a friend on earth.

Lady E. Yes, you have me.   You forget me.

Irw [*In a Transport of Grief.*] I would forget you
—you—and all your children.

Lady E. I would not lose the remembrance of you
or them for all my father's fortune.

Irw. What am I to do? I must leave you! I must
go, I know not whither! I cannot stay to see you
perish.   [*Takes his hat and is going.*

Lady E. [*Holding him.*] Where would you go? 'tis
evening—'tis dark—Whither would you go at this
time?

Irw. [*Distracted.*] I must consider what's to be done—and in this room my thoughts seem too confined to reflect.

Lady E. And are London streets calculated for reflection?

Irw. No; for action. To hurry the faint thought to resolution.

Lady E. You are not well—Your health has been lately impaired.—Your temper has undergone a change too;—I tremble lest any accident—

Irw. What accident?   [*Wildly.*

Lady E. I know your provocations from an ungrateful world: But despise it, as that despises you.

Irw. But for your sake, I could.

Lady E. Then witness, Heaven, I am happy!—Though bred in all the delicacy, the luxury of wealth and splendour, yet I have never murmured at the change of fortune, while that change has made me wife to you, and mother of your children.

Irw. We will be happy, if possible. But give me this evening to consider what plan to fix upon.—There is no time to lose: we are without friends—without money—without credit. Farewell for an hour.—I will see Mr Placid, if I can; and though he have not the money to lend, he may perhaps give me some advice.

Lady E. Suppose I call on her?—Women are sometimes more considerate than men, and—

Irw. Do you for the best, and so will I.—Heavens bless you!   [*Exeunt separately.*

ACT THE SECOND.

SCENE I.

A Coffee or Club Room at a Tavern.

Enter SIR ROBERT RAMBLE—MR SOLUS *and*
MR PLACID *at the opposite Side.*

Sol. Sir Robert Ramble, how do you do?

Sir R. My dear Mr Solus, I am glad to see you.
I have been dining by myself, and now come into
this public room, to meet with some good company.

Sol. Ay, Sir Robert, you are now reduced to the
same necessity which I frequently am—I frequently
am obliged to dine at taverns and coffeehouses, for
want of company at home.

Sir R. I protest I am never happier than in a house
like this, where a man may meet his friend without
the inconvenience of form, either as a host or a visitor.

Sol. Sir Robert, give me leave to introduce to you
Mr Placid, he has been many years abroad; but I
believe he now means to remain in his own country
for the rest of his life. This, Mr Placid, is Sir Robert Ramble.

Sir R. [*To* MR PLACID.] Sir, I shall be happy
in your acquaintance, and I assure you, if you will

do me the honour to meet me now and then at this
house, you will find every thing very pleasant. I verily
believe that since I lost my wife, which is now about
five months ago, I verily believe I have dined here
three days out of the seven.

Plac. Have you lost your wife, sir? And so
lately?

Sir R. [*With great Indifference.*] Yes, sir; about
five months ago—Is it not, Mr Solus? You keep
account of such things better than I do.

Sol. Oh! ask me no questions about your wife, Sir
Robert; if she had been mine, I would have had her
to this moment.

Plac. What, wrested her from the gripe of death?

Sir R. No, sir; only from the gripe of the Scotch
lawyers.

Sol. More shame for you. Shame to wish to be
divorced from a virtuous wife.

Plac. Was that the case? Divorced from a virtuous
wife! I never heard of such a circumstance before.
Pray, Sir Robert, [*Very anxiously.*] will you indulge
me, by letting me know in what manner you were
able to bring about so great an event?

Sir R. It may appear strange to you, sir; but my
wife and I did not live happy together.

Plac. Not at all strange, sir: I can conceive—I can
conceive very well.

Sol. Yes, he can conceive that part to perfection.

Sir R. And so, I was determined on a divorce.

Plac. But then her character could not be unimpeached.

Sir R. Yes, it was, sir. You must know, we were
married in Scotland, and by the laws there, a wife
can divorce her husband for breach of fidelity; and
so, though my wife's character was unimpeached,
mine was not—and she divorced me.

Plac. Is this the law in Scotland?

Sol. It is. Blessed, blessed, country! that will bind young people together before the years of discretion, and, as soon as they have discretion to repent, will unbind them again !

Plac. I wish I had been married in Scotland.

Sol. But, Sir Robert, with all this boasting, you must own that your divorce has greatly diminished your fortune.

Sir R. [*Taking* SOLUS *aside.*] Mr Solus, you have frequently hinted at my fortune being impaired ; but I do not approve of such notions being received abroad.

Sol. I beg your pardon; but every body knows that you have played very deep lately, and have been a great loser : and every body knows——

Sir R. No, sir, every body does not know it, for I contradict the report wherever I go. A man of fashion does not like to be reckoned poor, no more than he likes to be reckoned unhappy. We none of us endeavour to be happy, sir, but merely to be thought so ; and for my part, I had rather be in a state of misery, and envied for my supposed happiness, than in a state of happiness, and pitied for my supposed misery.

Sol. But, consider, these misfortunes, which I have just hinted at, are not of any serious nature, only such as a few years economy——

Sir R. But, were my wife and her guardian to become acquainted with these little misfortunes, they would triumph in my embarrassments.

Sol. Lady Ramble triumph ! [*They join* MR PLACID.] She, who was so firmly attached to you, that I believe nothing but a compliance with your repeated request to be separated, caused her to take the step she did ?

Sir R. Yes, I believe she did it to oblige me, and I am very much obliged to her.

Sol. As good a woman, Mr Placid——

Sir R. Very good—but very ugly.

Sol. She is beautiful.

Sir R. [*To* SOLUS.] I tell you, sir, she is hideous. And then she was grown so insufferably peevish.

Sol. I never saw her out of temper.

Sir R. Mr Solus, it is very uncivil of you to praise her before my face. Lady Ramble, at the time I parted with her, had every possible fault both of mind and person, and so I made love to other women in her presence; told her bluntly, that I was tired of her; that I was very sorry to make her uneasy, but that I could not love her any longer.—And was not that frank and open?

Sol. Oh that I had but such a wife as she was!

Sir R. I must own I loved her myself when she was young.

Sol. Do you call her old?

Sir R. In years I am certainly older than she, but the difference of sex makes her a great deal older than I am. For instance, Mr Solus, you have often lamented not being married in your youth; but if you had, what would you have now done with an old wife, a woman of your own age?

Sol. Loved and cherished her.

Sir R. What, in spite of her loss of beauty?

Sol. When she had lost her beauty, most likely I should have lost my eyesight, and have been blind to the wane of her charms.

Plac. [*Anxiously*] But, Sir Robert, you were explaining to me—Mr Solus, give me leave to speak to Sir Robert—I feel myself particularly interested on this subject—And, sir, you were explaining to me—

Sir R. Very true: Where did I leave off? Oh! at my ill usage of my Lady Ramble. Yes, I did use her very ill, and yet she loved me. Many a time, when she has said to me,—"Sir Robert, I detest your principles, your manners, and even your person,"—often at that very instant I have seen a little sparkle of a wish peep out of the corner of one eye, that has called out

4

to me, " Oh! Sir Robert, how I long to make it up
with you !"

Sol. [*To* MR PLACID.] Do not you wish that
your wife had such a little sparkle at the corner
of one of her eyes ?

Sir R. [*To* MR PLACID.] Sir, do you wish to be
divorced ?

Plac. I have no such prospect. Mrs Placid is faithful, and I was married in England.

Sir R. But if you have an unconquerable desire to
part, a separate maintenance will answer nearly the
same end—for if your lady and you will only lay
down the plan of separation, and agree—

Plac. But, unfortunately, we never do agree !

Sir R. Then speak of parting, as a thing you dread
worse than death ; and make it your daily prayer to
her, that she will never think of going from you—She
will determine upon it directly.

Plac. I thank you; I am very much obliged to
you : I thank you a thousand times.

Sir R. Yes, I have studied the art of teasing a
wife; and there is nothing vexes her so much as
laughing at her. Can you laugh, Mr Placid ?

Plac. I don't know whether I can; I have not
laughed since I married. But I thank you, sir, for
your instructions—I sincerely thank you.

Sol. And now, Sir Robert, you have had the good-
nature to teach this gentleman how to get rid of his
wife, will you have the kindness to teach me how to
procure one ?

Enter MR IRWIN.

Sir R. Hah! sure I know that gentleman's face ?

Sol. My nephew! Let me escape his solicitations.
[*Aside.*]—Here, waiter!

Plac. Irwin! [*Starting.*] Having sent him a denial

I am ashamed to see him. [*Aside.*] Here, Mr Solus!——   [*Exit, following* Mr SOLUS.

Irw. [*Aside.*] More cool faces! My necessitous
visage clears even a club-room.

Sir R. My dear Captain Irwin, is it you? Yes,
'faith it is—After a nine years' absence, I most sincerely rejoice to see you.

Irw. Sir Robert, you shake hands with a cordiality
I have not experienced these many days, and I thank
you.

Sir R. But what's the matter? You seem to droop
—Where have you left your usual spirits? has absence from your country changed your manners?

Irw. No, sir; but I find some of my countrymen
changed. I fancy them less warm, less friendly, than
they were; and it is that which, perhaps, has this
effect upon me.

Sir R. Am I changed?

Irw. You appear an exception.

Sir R. And I assure you, that instead of being
more gloomy, I am even more gay than I was seven
years ago; for then, I was upon the point of matrimony—but now, I am just relieved from its cares.

Irw. I have heard so. But I hope you have not taken so great an aversion to the marriage state as never to marry again?

Sir R. Perhaps not: But then it must be to some
rich heiress.

Irw. You are right to pay respect to fortune. Money is a necessary article in the marriage contract.

Sir R. As to that—that would be no great object
at present. No, thank Heaven, my estates are pretty
large; I have no children; I have a rich uncle, excellent health, admirable spirits;—and thus happy,
it would be very strange if I did not meet my old
friends with those smiles which never for a moment
quit my countenance.

C

Irw. In the dispensation of the gifts of Providence, how few are blest like you !   [*Sighing.*

Sir R. And I assure you, my dear Mr Irwin, it gives me the most serious reflections, and the most sincere concern, that the bulk of mankind are not.

Irw. I thank you, sir, most heartily : I thank you for mankind in general, and for myself in particular. For after this generous, unaffected declaration (with less scruple than I should to any one in the world) I will own to you—that I am at this very time in the utmost want of an act of friendship.

Sir R. [*Aside.*] And so am I—Now must I confess myself a poor man ; or pass for an unfeeling one ; and I will chuse the latter. [*Bowing with great Ceremony and Coldness.*] Any thing that I can command is at your service.

Irw. [*Confounded, and hesitating.*] Why, then, Sir Robert—I am almost ashamed to say it—but circumstances have been rather unfavourable.—My wife's father [*Affecting to smile.*] is not reconciled to us yet —My regiment is broke—My uncle will not part with a farthing.—Lady Eleanor, my wife, [*Wipes his Eyes.*] has been supported as yet, with some little degree of tenderness, elegance, and—in short, I owe a small sum, which I am afraid of being troubled for ; I want a trifle also for our immediate use, and if you would lend me a hundred pounds—though, upon my honour, I am not in a situation to fix the exact time when I can pay it—

Sir R. My dear sir, never trouble yourself about the time of paying it, because it happens not to be in my power to lend it you.

Irw. Not in your power ! I beg your pardon ; but have not you this moment been saying, you are rich ?

Sir R. And is it not very common to be rich without money ? Are not half the town rich ? And yet half the town has no money. I speak for this end of

the town, the west end; the Squares, for instance,
part of Piccadilly, down St James's Street, and so
home by Pall Mall. We have all estates, bonds,
drafts, and notes of hand without number; but as for
money, we have no such thing belonging to us.

Irw. I sincerely beg your pardon. And be assured, sir, nothing should have induced me to have
taken the liberty I have done, but the misfortunes of
my unhappy family, and having understood by your
own words, that you were in affluence.

Sir R. I *am* in affluence, I am, I am ; but not in so
much, perhaps, as my hasty, inconsiderate account
may have given you reason to believe. I forgot to
mention several heavy incumbrances, which you will
perceive are great drawbacks on my income.—As my
wife sued for the divorce, I have her fortune to return ; I have also two sisters to portion off—a circumstance I totally forgot. But, my good friend, though
I am not in circumstances to do what you require,
I will do something that shall be better. I'll wait upon your father-in-law, (Lord Norland) and entreat
him to forgive his daughter : and I am sure he will if
I ask him.

Irw. Impossible.

Sir R. And so it is, now I recollect : for he is the
guardian of my late wife, and a request from me will
be received worse than from any other person.—However, Mr Irwin, depend upon it, that whenever I
have an opportunity of serving you, I will. And
whenever you shall do me the favour to call upon me,
I shall be heartily glad to see you. If I am not at
home, you can leave your card, which, you know, is
all the same; and depend upon it, I shall be extremely glad to see you, or that, at any time. [*Exit.*

Irw. Is this my native country ? Is this the hospita-
ble land which we describe to strangers ? No—We
are savages to each other ; nay, worse—The savage
makes his fellow-savage welcome ; divides with him

his homely fare; gives him the best apartment his hut
affords, and tries to hush those griefs that are confided
to his bosom—While in this civilized city, among my
own countrymen, even among my brother officers in
the army, and many of my nearest relations, so very
civilized they are, I could not take the liberty to enter
under one roof, without a ceremonious invitation,—
and that they will not give me. I may leave my card
at their door, but as for me, or any one of mine, they
would not give us a dinner; unless, indeed, it was in
such a style, that we might behold with admiration
their grandeur, and return still more depressed to our
own poverty.—Can I bear this treatment longer? No,
not even for you, my Eleanor. And this [*Takes out a
Pistol.*] shall now be the only friend to whom I will
apply—And yet I want the courage to be a villain.

Enter MR HARMONY, *speaking as he enters.*—IRWIN
conceals the Pistol instantly.

Har. Let me see half a dozen newspapers—every
paper of the day.

Enter WAITER.

Wait. That is about three dozen, sir.
Har. Get a couple of porters, and bring them all.
     [*He sits down; they bring him Papers, and he reads.
     —*IRWIN *starts, sits down, leans his head on one
     of the Tables, and shows various Signs of Unea-
     siness, then comes forward.*
Irw. Am I a man, a soldier?—And a coward? Yes,
I run away, I turn my back on life—I forsake the
post, which my commander, Providence, has allotted
me, and fly before a banditti of rude misfortunes.
Rally me, love, connubial and parental love, rally
me back to the charge! No, those very affections
sound the retreat.
     [*Sits down with the same emotions of Distraction
     as before.*

Har. That gentleman does not seem happy. I wish
I had an opportunity of speaking to him.   [*Aside.*

Irw. [*Coming forward, and speaking again.*] But
oh, my wife! what will be your sufferings, when I am
brought home to your wretched abode!—And by my
own hand!

Har. I am afraid, sir, I engross all the news here.
[*Holding up the Papers.*

Irw. [*Still apart.*] Poor soul, how her heart will
be torn!

Har. [*After looking stedfastly on him.*] Captain
Irwin, till this moment I had not the pleasure of recollecting you! It is Mr Irwin, is it not?

Irw. [*His Mind deranged by his Misfortunes.*] Yes,
sir : but what have you to say to him, more than to
a stranger?

Har. Nothing more, sir, than to apologize to you
for having addressed you just now in so familiar a
manner, before I knew who you were, and to assure
you, that although I have no other knowledge of you
than from report, and having been once, I believe, in
your company at this very house, before you left
England, yet any services of mine, as far as my abi-
lities can reach, you may freely command.

Irw. Pray, sir, do you live at the west end of the
town?

Har. I do.

Irw. Then, sir, your services can be of no use to
me.

Har. Here is the place where I live, here is my
card.   [*Gives it to him.*

Irw. And here is mine. And now I presume we
have exchanged every act of friendship, which the
strict forms of etiquette, in this town, will admit of.

Har. By no means, sir. I assure you my profes-
sions never go beyond my intentions; and if there is
any thing that I can serve you in——

Irw. Have you no sisters to portion off? no lady's
c 2

fortune to return? Or, perhaps, you will speak to my wife's father, and entreat him to forgive his child.

Har. On that subject, you may command me; for I have the honour to be intimately acquainted with Lord Norland.

Irw. But is there no reason you may recollect, why you would be the most unfit person in the world to apply to him?

Har. None. I have been honoured with marks of his friendship for many years past: and I do not know any one who could, with less hazard of his resentment, venture to name his daughter to him.

Irw. Well, sir, if you should see him two or three days hence—when I am set out on a journey I am going—if you will then say a kind word to him for my wife and children, I'll thank you.

Har. I will go to him instantly.   [*Going.*

Irw. No, do not see him yet; stay till I am gone. He will do nothing till I am gone.

Har. May I ask where you are going?

Irw. No very tedious journey; but it is a country, to those who go without a proper passport, always fatal.

Har. I'll see Lord Norland to-night: perhaps I may persuade him to prevent your journey. I'll see him to-night, or early in the morning, depend upon it.—I am a man of my word, sir, though I must own I do live at the west end of the town.   [*Exit.*

Irw 'Sdeath! am I become the ridicule of my fellow-creatures! or am I not in my senses?—I know this is London—this house a tavern—I know I have a wife—Oh! 'twere better to be mad than to remember her!—She has a father—he is rich and proud—that I will not forget. But I will pass his house, and send a malediction as I pass it. [*Furiously.*] No; breathe out my last sigh at his inhospitable door, and that sigh shall breathe—forgiveness.   [*Exit.*

SCENE II.

The Lodgings of Mr Irwin.

Enter Mrs Placid, *followed by* Lady Eleanor
Irwin.

Lady E. I am ashamed of the trouble I have given
you, Mrs Placid.　It had been sufficient to have sent
me home in your carriage; to attend me yourself
was ceremonious.

Mrs P. My dear Lady Eleanor, I was resolved to
come home with you, as soon as Mr Placid desired
I would not.

Lady E. Was that the cause of your politeness? I
am sorry it should.

Mrs P. Why sorry? It is not proper he should
have his way in every thing.

Lady E. But I am afraid you seldom let him have
it at all.

Mrs P. Yes I do.—But where, my dear, is Mr
Irwin?

Lady E. [*Weeping.*] I cannot hear the name of Mr
Irwin, without shedding tears; his health has so de-
clined of late, and his spirits been so bad—sometimes I even fear for a failure in his mind.

[*Weeps again.*

Mrs P. Is not he at home?

Lady E. I hope he is. [*Goes to the Side of the
Scenes.*] Tell your master Mrs Placid is here.

Enter a Servant.

Serv. My master is not come in yet, madam.

Lady E. Not yet? I am very sorry for it;—very sorry indeed.

Mrs P. Bless me, my dear, don't look thus pale. Come, sit down, and I'll stay with you till he returns.
[*Sits down herself.*

Lady E. My dear, you forget, that Mr Placid is in the carriage at the door all this time.

Mrs P. No, I don't.—Come, let us sit and have half an hour's conversation.

Lady E. Nay, I insist upon your going to him, or desiring him to walk in.

Mrs P. Now I think of it, they may as well drive him home, and come back for me.

Enter Mr Placid.

Why, surely, Mr Placid, you were very impatient! —I think you might have waited a few minutes longer.

Plac. I would have waited, my dear, but the evening is so damp.

Lady E. Ah! 'tis this evening—that makes me alarmed for Mr Irwin.

Plac. Lady Eleanor, you are one of the most tender, anxious, and affectionate wives, I ever knew.

Mrs P. There! Now he wishes he was your husband—he admires the conduct of every wife but his own, and envies every married man of his acquaintance. But it is very ungenerous in you.

Plac. So it is, my dear, and not at all consistent with the law of equity; for I am sure, there is not one of my acquaintance who envies me.

Mrs P. Mr Placid, your behaviour throughout this whole day has been so totally different from what it ever was before, that I am half resolved to live no longer with you.

Plac. [*Aside.*] It will do—it will do.

Lady E. Oh, my dear friends, do not talk of parting :—how can you, while every blessing smiles on

your union ? Even I, who have reason to regret mine,
yet, while that load of grief, a separation from Mr
Irwin, is but averted, I will think every other affliction supportable. [*A loud Rapping at the Door.*] That
is he !

Mrs P. Why, you seem in raptures at his return.
Lady E. I know no greater rapture.

Enter IRWIN, *pale, trembling, and disordered.*

My dear, you are not well, I see.
Irw. [*Aside to her in Anger.*] Why do you speak
of it ?
Plac. How do you do, Irwin ?
Irw. I am glad to see you. [*Bows.*
Mrs P. But I am sorry to see you look so ill.
Irw. I have only been taking a glass too much.
[LADY ELEANOR *weeps.*
Plac. Pshaw ! don't I know you never drink ?
Irw. You are mistaken—I do, when my wife is not
by. I am afraid of her.
Plac. Impossible.
Irw. What ! to be afraid of one's wife ?
Plac. No, I think that very possible.
Mrs P. But it does not look well when it is so ; it
makes a man appear contemptible, and a woman a
termagant. Come, Mr Placid, I cannot stay another
moment. Good night. Heaven bless you ! [*To*
LADY ELEANOR.]—Good night, my dear Mr Irwin;
—and now, pray take my advice, and keep up your
spirits.
Irw. I will, madam,—[*Shaking Hands with* PLA-
CID.] And do you keep up your spirits. [*Exeunt* MR
and MRS PLACID.—IRWIN *shuts the Door with Care
after them, and looks around the Room, as if he feared
to be seen or overheard.*] I am glad they are gone—
I spoke unkindly to you just now, did I not? My
temper is altered lately ; and yet I love you.
Lady E. I never doubted it, nor ever will.

Irw. If you did, you would wrong me ; for there is no danger I would not risk for your sake : there is not an infamy I would not be branded with, to make you happy, nor a punishment I would not undergo, with joy, for your welfare.—But there's a bar to this; we are unfortunately so entwined together, so linked, so riveted, so cruelly, painfully fettered, to each other, you could not be happy unless I shared the self-same happiness with you.—But you will learn better.—now you are in London, and amongst fashionable wives; you must learn better.

[*Walks about, and smiles with a ghastly Countenance.*

Lady E Do not talk, do not look, thus wildly—Indeed, indeed, you make me very uneasy.

Irw. What! uneasy when I come to bring you comfort; and such comfort as you have not experienced for many a day? [*He pulls out a Pocketbook.*] Here is a friend in our necessity,—a friend, that brings a thousand friends; plenty and—no, not always—peace.

[*He takes several Papers from the Book, and puts them into her Hands—She looks at them, then screams.*

Lady E. Ah! 'tis money! [*Trembling.*] These are bank-notes!

Irw. Hush! for Heaven's sake, hush! We shall be discovered. [*Trembling, and in great Perturbation.*] What alarms you thus?

Lady E. What alarms you?

Irw. Do you say, I am frightened?

Lady E. A sight so new has frightened me.

Irw. Nay, they are your own: by Heaven, they are! No one on earth has a better, or a fairer right to them than yourself. It was a laudable act, by which I obtained them.—The parent bird had forsook its young, and I but forced it back, to perform the rites of nature.

Lady E. You are insane, I fear. No, no, I do not fear—I hope you are.

[*A loud Rapping at the Street Door—He starts, takes the Notes from her, and puts them hastily into his Pocket.*

Irw. Go to the door yourself; and if 'tis any one who asks for me, say, I am not come home yet.

[*She goes out, then returns.*

Lady E. It is the person belonging to the house; no one to us.

Irw. My dear Eleanor, are you willing to quit London with me in about two hours time?

Lady E. Instantly.

Irw. Nay, not only London, but England?

Lady E. This world, if you desire it. To go in company with you, will make the journey pleasant; and all I loved on earth would still be with me.

Irw. You can, then, leave your father without regret, never, never, to see him more?

Lady E. Why should I think on him, who will not think on me? [*Weeps.*

Irw. But our children——

Lady E. We are not to leave them?

Irw. One of them we must; but do not let that give you uneasiness. You know he has never lived with us since his infancy, and cannot pine for the loss of parents, whom he has never known.

Lady E. But I have known him. He was my first; and, sometimes, I think, more closely wound around my heart, than all the rest. The grief I felt on being forced to leave him, when we went abroad, and the constant anxiety I have since experienced, lest he should not be kindly treated, have augmented, I think, my tenderness.

Irw. All my endeavours to-day, as well as every other day, have been in vain, to find into what part of the country his nurse has taken him.—Nay, be not thus overcome with tears; we will (in spite of all my haste to be gone) stay one more miserable day here, in hopes to procure intelligence, so as to take him with us; and then—smile with contempt on all we leave behind.   [*Exeunt.*

ACT THE THIRD.

SCENE I.

A Library at LORD NORLAND'S.

Enter LORD NORLAND, *followed by* MR HAR-
MONY.

Lord N. [*In Anger.*] I tell you, Mr Harmony, that if an indifferent person, one on whom I had never bestowed a favour in my life, were to offend me, it is in my nature never to forgive. Can I then forgive my own daughter, my only child, on whom 1 heaped continual marks of the most affectionate fondness ? Shall she dare to offend me in the tenderest point, and you dare to suppose I will pardon her ?

Har. Your child, consider.

Lord N. The weakest argument you can use. As my child, was she not most bound to obey me ? As my child, ought she not to have sacrificed her own happiness to mine ? Instead of which, mine has been yielded up for a whim, a fancy. a fancy to marry a beggar; and, as such is her choice, let her beg with him.

Har. She does, by me;—pleads hard for your forgiveness.

Lord N. If I thought she dared to send a message to me, though dictated on her knees, she should find, that she had not yet felt the full force of my resentment.

Har. What could you do more?

Lord N. I have done nothing yet.   At present, I have only abandoned her;—but I can persecute.

Har. I have no doubt of it: and, that I may not be the means of aggravating your displeasure, I assure you, that what I have now said has been entirely from myself, without any desire of hers; and, at the same time, I give you my promise, I will never presume to introduce the subject again.

Lord N. On this condition (but on no other) I forgive you now.

Har. And now, then, my lord, let us pass from those who have forfeited your love, to those who possess it.—I heard, some time ago, but I never felt myself disposed to mention it to you, that you had adopted a young man as your son.

Lord N. A young man! Pshaw! No; a boy—a mere child, who fell in my way by accident.

Har. A chance child!—Ho! ho! I understand you.

Lord N. Do not jest with me, sir. Do I look——

Har. Yes, you look as if you would be ashamed to own it, if you had one.

Lord N. But this boy I am not ashamed of: he is a favourite—rather a favourite. I did not like him so well at first;—but custom,—and having a poor creature entirely at one's mercy, one begins to love it merely from the idea of——what would be its fate if one did not.

D

Har. Is he an orphan, then?

Lord N. No

Har. You have a friendship for his parents?

Lord N. I never saw the father: his mother I had a friendship for once.   [*Sighing.*

Har. Ay, while the husband was away?

Lord N. I tell you, no. [*Violently.*]—But ask no more questions. Who his parents are is a secret, which neither he, nor any one (that is now living) knows, except myself: nor ever shall.

Har. Well, my lord, since 'tis your pleasure to consider him as your child, I sincerely wish you may experience more duty from him, than you have done from your daughter.

Lord N. Thank Heaven, his disposition is not in the least like hers—No : [*Very much impassioned.*] I have the joy to say, that never child was so unlike its mother.

Har. [*Starting.*] How! his mother !

Lord N. Confusion!—what have I said?—I am ashamed——

Har. No,—be proud.

Lord N. Of what?

Har. That you have a lawful heir to all your riches; proud, that you have a grandson.

Lord N. I would have concealed it from all the world ; I wished it even unknown to myself. And, let me tell you, sir, (as not by my design, but through my inadvertency, you are become acquainted with this secret) that, if ever you breathe it to a single creature, the boy shall answer for it ; for, were he known to be hers, though he were dearer to me than ever she was, I would turn him from my house, and cast him from my heart, as I have done her.

Har. I believe you ;—and, in compassion to the child, give you my solemn promise, never to reveal who he is. I have heard that those unfortunate parents left an infant behind when they went abroad,

and that they now lament him as lost.   Will you satisfy my curiosity, in what manner you sought and
found him out?

Lord N. Do you suppose I searched for him ?
No —he was forced upon me.   A woman followed
me, about eight years ago, in the fields adjoining to
my country seat, with a half starved boy in her
hand, and asked my charity for my grandchild : the
impression of the word made me turn round involun-
tarily ; and, casting my eyes upon him, I was rejoiced not to find a feature of his mother's in all his
face ; and I began to feel something like pity for him.
In short, he caught such fast hold by one of my
fingers, that I asked him carelessly, " If he would
go home and live with me ?"   On which, he answered me so willingly, " Yes," I took him at his
word.

Har. And did never your regard for him plead in
his mother's behalf?

Lord N. Never :—for, by Heaven, I would as soon
forgive the robber, who met me last night at my own
door, and, holding a pistol to my breast, took from
me a sum to a considerable amount, as I would pardon her.

Har. Did such an accident happen to you ?

Lord N. Have you not heard of it ?

Har. No.

Lord N. It is amazing we cannot put a stop to
such depredations.

Har. Provisions are so scarce !

Enter a SERVANT.

Serv. Miss Wooburn, my lord, if you are not engaged, will come and sit an hour with you.

Lord N. I have no company but such as she is
perfectly acquainted with, and I shall be glad of her
visit.   [*Exit* SERVANT.

Har. You forget I am a stranger, and my presence may not be welcome.

Lord N. A stranger! What, to my ward? to Lady Ramble? for that is the name which custom would authorize her to keep; but such courtesy she disdains, in contempt of the unworthy giver of the title.

Har. I am intimate with Sir Robert, my lord: and, though I acknowledge that both you and his late wife have cause for complaint, yet Sir Robert has still many virtues.

Lord N. Not one. He is the most vile, the most detestable of characters. He not only contradicted my will in the whole of his conduct, but he seldom met me that he did not give me some personal affront.

Har. It is, however, generally held better to be uncivil in a person's presence, than in his absence.

Lord N. He was uncivil to me in every respect.

Har. That I will deny; for I have heard Sir Robert, in your absence, say such things in your favour!——

Lord N. Indeed!

Har. Most assuredly.

Lord N. I wish he had sometimes done me the honour to have spoken politely to my face.

Har. That is not Sir Robert's way;—he is no flatterer. But then, no sooner has your back been turned, than I have heard him lavish in your praise.

Lord N. I must own, Mr Harmony, that I never looked upon Sir Robert as incorrigible. I could always discern a ray of understanding, and a beam of virtue, through all his foibles; nor would I have urged the divorce, but that I found his wife's sensibility could not bear his neglect; and, even now, notwithstanding her endeavour to conceal it, she pines in secret, and laments her hard fortune. All my

hopes of restoring her health rest on one prospect—
that of finding a man worthy my recommendation
for her second husband, and, by thus creating a second passion, expel the first.—Mr Harmony, you and
I have been long acquainted—I have known your
disposition from your infancy—Now, if such a man
as you were to offer—

Har. You flatter me.

Lord N. I do not—would you venture to become
her husband?

Har. I cannot say I have any particular desire;—
but if it will oblige either you or her,—for my part,
I think the short time we live in this world, we should
do all we can to oblige each other.

Lord N. I should rejoice at such an union myself,
and, I think, I can answer for her.—You permit me,
then, to make overtures to her in your name?

Har. [*Considering.*] This is rather a serious business
—However, I never did make a difficulty when I
wished to oblige a friend.—But there is one proviso,
my lord; I must first mention it to Sir Robert.

Lord N. Why so?

Har. Because he and I have always been very intimate friends: and to marry his wife without even
telling him of it, will appear very uncivil!

Lord N. Do you mean, then, to ask his consent?

Har. Not absolutely his consent; but I will insinuate the subject to him, and obtain his approbation
in a manner suitable to my own satisfaction.

Lord N. You will oblige me, then, if you will see
him as early as possible; for it is reported he is going
abroad.

Har. I will go to him immediately;—and, my
lord, I will do all in my power to oblige you, Sir Robert, and the lady—[*Aside.*] but as to obliging
myself, that was never one of my considerations.

[*Exit.*

D 2

Enter MISS WOOBURN.

Lord N. I am sorry to see you thus; you have been weeping! Will you still lament your separation from a cruel husband, as if you had followed a kind one to the grave?

Miss W. By no means, my lord. Tears from our sex are not always the result of grief; they are frequently no more than little sympathetic tributes, which we pay to our fellow beings, while the mind and the heart are steeled against the weakness, which our eyes indicate.

Lord N. Can you say, your mind and heart are so steeled?

Miss W. I can: My mind is as firmly fixed against Sir Robert Ramble, as, at our first acquaintance, it was fixed upon him. And I solemnly protest——

Lord N. To a man of my age and observation, protestations are vain.—Give me a proof, that you have rooted him from your heart.

Miss W. Any proof you require I will give you without a moment's hesitation.

Lord N. I take you at your word; and desire you to accept a gentleman, whom I shall recommend for your second husband. [MISS WOOBURN *starts.*]— You said, you would not hesitate a moment.

Miss W. I thought I should not;—but this is something so unexpected——

Lord N. You break your word, then; and still give cause for this ungrateful man to ridicule your fondness for him?

Miss W. No, I will put an end to that humiliation; and whoever the gentleman is whom you mean to propose—Yet, do not name him at present—but give me the satisfaction of keeping the promise I have made to you (at least for a little time) without exactly knowing how far it extends; for, in return, I

have a promise to ask from you, before I acquaint
you with the nature of your engagement.

Lord N. I give my promise.   Now name your request.

Miss W. Then, my lord—[*Hesitating, and confused.*]—the law gave me back, upon my divorce from
Sir Robert, the very large fortune which I brought to
him.—I am afraid, that in his present circumstances,
to enforce the strict payment of this debt would very
much embarrass him.

Lord N. What if it did?

Miss W. It is my entreaty to you (in whose hands
is invested the power to demand this right of law) to
lay my claim aside for the present. [LORD NORLAND
offers to speak.] I know, my lord, what you are going to say; I know Sir Robert is not now, but I can
never forget that he has been, my husband.

Lord N. To show my gratitude for your compliance with the request I have just made you, [*Goes to
a Table in the Library.*] here is the bond by which
I am empowered to seize on the greatest part of his
estates in right of you: take the bond into your own
possession, till your next husband demands it of you;
and, by the time you have called him husband for a
few weeks, this tenderness, or delicacy, to Sir Robert, will be worn away.

Enter HARMONY, *hastily.*

Har. My lord, I beg pardon; but I forgot to mention——

Miss W. Oh, Mr Harmony, I have not seen you
before I know not when: I am particularly happy
at your calling just now, for I have—[*Hesitating.*]—
a little favour to ask of you.

Har. If it were a great favour, madam, you might
command me.

Miss W. But—my lord, I beg your pardon—the

favour I have to ask of Mr Harmony must be told to him in private.

Lord N. Oh! I am sure I have not the least objection to you and Mr Harmony having a private conference. I'll leave you together. [HARMONY *appears embarrassed.*] You do not derange my business —I'll be back in a short time.   [*Exit.*

Miss W. Mr Harmony, you are the very man on earth whom I most wanted to see. [HARMONY *bows.*] I know the kindness of your heart, the liberality of your sentiments, and I wish to repose a charge to your trust, very near to me indeed—but you must be secret.

Har. When a lady reposes a trust in me, I shouldn't be a man if I were not.

Miss W. I must first inform you, that Lord Norland has just drawn from me a promise, that I will once more enter into the marriage state : and without knowing to whom he intends to give me, I will keep my promise.   But it is in vain to say, that though I mean all duty and fidelity to my second husband, I shall not experience moments when my thoughts— will wander on my first.

Har. [*Starting.*] Hem!—Hem!—[*To her.*]—Indeed!

Miss W. I must always rejoice in Sir Robert's successes, and lament over his misfortunes.

Har. If that is all—

Miss W. No, I would go one step further : [HARMONY *starts again.*] I would secure him from those distresses, which to hear of, will disturb my peace of mind.   I know his fortune has suffered very much, and I cannot, will not, place it in the power of the man, whom my Lord Norland may point out for my next marriage, to harass him farther—This is the writing, by which that gentleman may claim the part of my fortune from Sir Robert Ramble, which

is in landed property ; carry it, my dear Mr Harmony,
to Sir Robert instantly ; and tell him—that, in separating from him, I meant only to give him liberty, not
make him the debtor, perhaps the prisoner, of my
future husband.

Har. Madam, I will most undoubtedly take this
bond to my friend ; but will you give me leave to
suggest to you,—that the person on whom you bestow
your hand may be a little surprised to find, that while
he is in possession of you, Sir Robert is in the possession of your fortune ?

Miss W. Do not imagine, sir, that I shall marry any
man, without first declaring what I have done—I
only wish at present it should be concealed from Lord
Norland—When this paper is given, as I have required, it cannot be recalled : and when that is past,
I shall divulge my conduct to whom I please : and
first of all, to him, who shall offer me his addresses.

Har. And if he is a man of my feelings, his addresses will be doubly importunate for this proof
of liberality to your former husband.—But are you
sure, that in the return of this bond, there is no secret affection, no latent spark of love ?

Miss W. None, I know my heart ; and if there was,
I could not ask you, Mr Harmony (nor any one like
you,) to be the messenger of an imprudent passion.
Sir Robert's vanity, I know, may cause him to judge
otherwise ; but undeceive him ; let him know, this
is a sacrifice to the golden principles of duty, and not
an offering to the tinselled shrine of love.

Enter LORD NORLAND.

Miss W. Put up the bond.——

[HARMONY *conceals it.*

Lord N. Well, my dear, have you made your request ?

Miss W. Yes, my lord,

Lord N. And has he granted it?

Har Yes, my lord. I am going to grant it.

Lord N. I sincerely wish you both joy of this good understanding between you. But, Mr Harmony, [*In a Whisper.*] are not you going to Sir Robert?

Har Yes, my lord, I am going this moment.

Lord N. Make haste, then, and do not forget your errand.

Har. No, my lord, I sha'n't forget my errand: it won't slip my memory—Good morning, my lord:— good morning, madam.   [*Exit.*

Lord N. Now, my dear, as you and Mr Harmony seem to be on such excellent terms, I think I may venture to tell you (if he has not yet told you himself,) that he is the man who is to be your husband.

Miss W. He! Mr Harmony!—No, my lord, he has not told me; and I am confident he never will.

Lord N. What makes you think so?

Miss W. Because—because—he must be sensible he would not be the man I should chuse.

Lord N. And where is the woman who marries the man she would chuse? You are reversing the order of society; men only have the right of choice in marriage. Were women permitted theirs, we should have handsome beggars allied to our noblest families, and no such object in our whole island as an old maid.

Miss W. But being denied that choice, why am I forbid to remain as I am?

Lord N. What are you now? Neither a widow, a maid, nor a wife. If I could fix a term to your present state, I should not be thus anxious to place you in another.

Miss W. I am perfectly acquainted with your friendly motives, and feel the full force of your advice. —I therefore renew my promise—and although Mr Harmony (in respect to the marriage state) is as little to my wishes as any man on earth, I will nevertheless endeavour—whatever struggles it may cost me—to be to him, if he prefers his suit, a dutiful, an obedient—but, for a loving wife, that I can never be again. [*Exeunt severally.*

SCENE II.

An Apartment at SIR ROBERT RAMBLE'S.

Enter SIR ROBERT *and* MR HARMONY.

Sir R. I thank you for this visit. I was undetermined what to do with myself. Your company has determined me to stay at home.

Har. I was with a gentleman just now, Sir Robert, and you were the subject of our conversation.

Sir R. Had it been a lady, I should be anxious to know what she said.

Har. I have been with a lady, likewise; and she made you the subject of her discourse.

Sir R. But was she handsome?

Har. Very handsome.

Sir R. My dear fellow, what is her name? What did she say, and where may I meet with her?

Har. Her name is Wooburn.

Sir R. That is the name of my late wife!

Har. It is her I mean.

Sir R. Zounds, you had just put my spirits into a flame, and now you throw cold water all over me.

Har. I am sorry to hear you say so, for I came from her this moment;—and what do you think is the present she has given me to deliver to you?

8

Sir R. Pshaw! I want no presents. Some of my old love-letters returned, I suppose, to remind me of my inconstancy.

Har. Do not undervalue her generosity; this is her present :—this bond, which has power to take from you three thousand a year, her right.

Sir R. Ah! this is a present, indeed! Are you certain you speak truth? Let me look at it :—Sure my eyes deceive me!—No, by Heaven it is true! [*Reads.*] The very thing I wanted, and will make me perfectly happy. Now I'll be generous again ; my bills shall be paid, my gaming debts cancelled, poor Irwin shall find a friend; and I'll send Miss Wooburn as pretty a copy of verses as ever I wrote in my life.

Har. Take care how you treat with levity a woman of her elevated mind. She charged me to assure you, that love had no share whatever in this act, which is mere compassion to the embarrassed state of your affairs.

Sir R. Sir, I would have you to know, I am no object of compassion. However, a lady's favour one cannot return; and so I'll keep this thing.

[*Puts the Bond in his Pocket.*

Har. Nay, if your circumstances are different from what she imagines, give it me back, and I will restore it to her.

Sir R. No, poor thing! it would break her heart to send it back —No, I'll keep it—She would never forgive me, were I to send it back. I'll keep it. And she is welcome to attribute her concern for me to what she pleases. But surely you can see—you can understand—But Heaven bless her for her love! and I would love her in return—if I could.

Har. You would not talk thus, if you had seen the firm dignity with which she gave me that paper— "Assure him," said she, "no remaining affection comes along with it, but merely a duty which I owe him,

to protect him from the humiliation of being a debtor
to the man, whom I am going to marry."

Sir R. [*With the utmost Emotion.*] Why, she is not
going to be married again?

Har. I believe so.

Sir R. But are you sure of it, sir? Are you sure
of it?

Har. Both she and her guardian told me so.

Sir R. That guardian, my Lord Norland, is one
of the basest, vilest of men.—I tell you what, sir,
I'll resent this usage.

Har. Wherefore?—As to his being the means of
bringing about your separation, in that he obliged
you.

Sir R. Yes, sir, he did, he certainly did ;—but
though I am not in the least offended with him on
that account (for at that I rejoice), yet I will resent
his disposing of her a second time.

Har. And wherefore?

Sir R. Because, little regard as I have for her myself, yet no other man shall dare to treat her so ill as
I have done.

Har. Do not fear it—Her next husband will be a
man, who, I can safely say, will never insult, or
even offend her; but sooth, indulge, and make her
happy.

Sir R. And do you dare to tell me, that her next
husband shall make her happy? Now that is worse
than the other—No, sir, no man shall ever have it to
say, he has made her either happy or miserable, but
myself.

Har. I know of but one way to prevent it.

Sir R. And what is that?

Har. Pay your addresses to her, and marry her
again yourself.

Sir R. And I would, rather than she should be
happy with any body else.

E

Har. To show that I am wholly disinterested in this affair, I will carry her a letter from you, if you like. and say all I can in your behalf.

Sir R. Ha! ha! ha! Now, my dear Harmony, you carry your good natured simplicity too far. However, I thank you—I sincerely thank you—But do you imagine I would be such a blockhead, as to make love to the same woman I made love to seven years ago, and who for the last six years I totally neglected?

Har. Yes; for if you have neglected her six years, she will now be a novelty.

Sir R. Egad, and so she will.   You are right.

Har. But being in possession of her fortune, you can be very happy without her.

Sir R. Take her fortune back, sir. [*Taking the Bond from his Pocket, and offering it to* HARMONY.] I would starve, I would perish, die in poverty, and infamy, rather than owe an obligation to a vile, perfidious, inconstant woman.

Har. Consider, Sir Robert, if you insist on my taking this bond back, it may fall into the husband's hands.

Sir R. Take it back—I insist upon it. [*Gives it him, and* HARMONY *puts it up.*] But, Mr Harmony, depend on it, Lord Norland shall hear from me, in the most serious manner, for his interference—I repeat, he is the vilest, the most villainous of men.

Har. How can you speak with such rancour of a nobleman, who speaks of you in the highest terms?

Sir R. Does he, 'faith?

Har. He owns you have some faults.

Sir R. I know I have.

Har. But he thinks your good qualities are numberless.

Sir R. Now, dam'me if ever I thought so ill of him as I have appeared to do—But who is the intended husband, my dear friend?   Tell me, that I may laugh at him, and make you laugh at him.

Har. No, I am not inclined to laugh at him.

Sir R. Is it old Solus?

Har. No.

Sir R. But I will bet you a wager it is somebody equally ridiculous.

Har. I never bet.

Sir R. Solus is mad for a wife, and has been praising mine up to the heavens,—you need say no more —I know it is he.

Har. Upon my honour, it is not However, I cannot disclose to you at present the person's name; I must first obtain Lord Norland's permission.

Sir R. I shall ask you no more. I'll write to her, she will tell me ;—or I'll pay her a visit, and ask her boldly myself.——Do you think [*Anxiously.*]—do you think she would see me?

Har. You can try.

Enter a SERVANT.

Serv. Mr Solus.

Sir R. Now I will find out the secret immediately. —I'll charge him with being the intended husband.

Har. I won't stay to hear you.

Enter SOLUS.

Mr Solus, how do you do? I am extremely sorry that my engagements take me away as soon as you enter.

[*Exit* HARMONY, *running, to avoid an Explanation.*

Sol. Sir Robert, what is the matter? Has any thing ruffled you? Why, I never saw you look more out of temper, even while you were married.

Sir R. Ah! that I had never married! never known what marriage was! for, even at this moment, I feel its torments in my heart.

Sol. I have often heard of the torments of matri-

mony; but I conceive, that at the worst, they are
nothing more than a kind of violent tickling, which
will force the tears into your eyes, though at the same
time you are bursting your sides with laughter.

Sir R. You have defined marriage too favourably;
there is no laughter in the state; all is melancholy,
all gloom.

Sol. Now I think marriage is an excellent remedy
for the spleen. I have known a gentleman at a feast
receive an affront, disguise his rage, step home, vent
it all upon his wife, return to his companions, and be
as good company as if nothing had happened.

Sir R. But even the necessary expenses of a wife
should alarm you.

Sol. I can then retrench some of my own. Oh!
my dear sir, a married man has so many delightful
privileges to what a bachelor has:—An old lady will
introduce her daughters to you in a dishabille—"It
does not signify, my dears, it's a married man"—One
lady will suffer you to draw on her glove—"Never
mind, it's a married man"—Another will permit you
to pull on her slipper; a third will even take you into
her bedchamber—"Pshaw, it's *nothing* but a married
man."

Sir R. But the weight of your fetters will overba-
lance all these joys.

Sol. And yet I cannot say, notwithstanding you are
relieved from those fetters, that I see much joy or
content here.

Sir R. I am not very well at present; I have the
head-ache; and, if ever a wife can be of comfort to
her husband, it must be when he is indisposed. A
wife, then, binds up your head, mixes your powders,
bathes your temples, and hovers about you, in a way
that is most endearing.

Sol. Don't speak of it; I long to have one hover
about me. But I will—I am determined I will, before I am a week older. Don't speak, don't attempt

to persuade me not. Your description has renewed my eagerness—I will be married.

Sir R. And without pretending not to know whom you mean to make your choice, I tell you plainly, it is Miss Wooburn, it is my late wife.—I know you have made overtures to my Lord Norland, and that he has given his consent.

Sol. You tell me a great piece of news—I'll go ask my lord if it be true ; and if he says it is, I shall be very glad to find it so.

Sir R. That is right, sir ; marry her, marry her ;— I give you joy,—that's all.—Ha ! ha ! ha ! I think I should know her temper.—But if you will venture to marry her, I sincerely wish you happy.

Sol. And if we are not, you know we can be divorced.

Sir R. Not always. Take my advice, and live as you are.

Sol. You almost stagger my resolution.—I had painted such bright prospects in marriage:—Good day to you. [*Going, returns.*] —You think I had better not marry ?

Sir R. You are undone if you do.

Sol. [*Sighing.*] You ought to know from experience.

Sir R. From that I speak.

Sol. [*Going to the Door, and returning once or twice, as undetermined in his Resolution.*] But then, what a poor disconsolate object shall I live, without a wife to hover about me ; to bind up my head and bathe my temples ! Oh ! I am impatient for all the chartered rights, privileges, and immunities of a married man. [*Exit.*

Sir R. Furies ! racks ! torments !—I cannot bear what I feel, and yet I am ashamed to own I feel any thing !

Enter Mr Placid.

Plac. My dear Sir Robert, give me joy! Mrs Placid and I are come to the very point you advised: matters are in the fairest way for a separation.

Sir R. I do give you joy, and most sincerely.—You are right: you will soon be as happy as I am. [*Sighing.*] But, would you suppose it? that deluded woman, my wife, is going to be married again! I thought she had experienced enough from me.

Plac. You are hurt, I see, lest the world should say, she has forgot you.

Sir R. She cannot forget me; I defy her to forget me.

Plac. Who is her intended husband?

Sir R. Solus, Solus. An old man—an ugly man. He left me this moment, and owned it—owned it! Go after him, will you, and persuade him not to have her.

Plac. My advice will have no effect, for you know he is determined upon matrimony.

Sir R. Then could not you, my dear sir (as you are going to be separated,) could not you recommend him to marry your wife?—It will be all the same to him, and I shall like it much better.

Plac. Ours will not be a divorce, consider, but merely a separate maintenance. But were it otherwise, I wish no man so ill, as to wish him married to Mrs Placid.

Sir R. That is my case exactly—I wish no man so ill, as to wish him married to my Lady Ramble; and poor old Solus in particular, poor old man! a very good sort of man—I have a great friendship for Solus, —I can't stay a moment in the house—I must go somewhere—I'll go to Solus—No, I'll go to Lord Norland—No, I'll go to Harmony; and then I'll

call on you, and we'll take a bottle together; and
when you are become free [*Takes his Hand.*] we'll
both join, from that moment we'll join, to laugh at,
to contemn, to despise, all those who boast of the joys
of conjugal love.   [*Exeunt.*

ACT THE FOURTH.

SCENE I.

An Apartment at MR HARMONY's.

Enter MR HARMONY.

Har. And now for one of the most painful tasks
that brotherly love ever draws upon me; to tell another the suit, of which I gave him hope, has failed.
—Yet, if I can but overcome Captain Irwin's delicacy
so far as to prevail on him to accept one proof more
of my good wishes towards him:—but to a man of
his nice sense of obligations, the offer must be made
with caution.

Enter LORD NORLAND.

Lord N. Mr Harmony, I beg your pardon: I
come in thus abruptly, from the anxiety I feel concerning what passed between us this morning in respect to Miss Wooburn. You have not changed your
mind, I hope?

Har. Indeed, my lord, I am very sorry that it will not be in my power to oblige you.

Lord N. [*In Anger.*] How, sir ? Did not you give me your word?

Har. Only conditionally, my lord.

Lord N. And what were the conditions ?

Har. Have you forgot them ? Her former husband—

Enter a SERVANT.

Serv. Sir Robert Ramble is in his carriage at the door, and, if you are at leisure, will come in.

Har. Desire him to walk up. I have your leave, I suppose, my lord ?   [*Exit* SERVANT.

Lord N. Yes; but let me get out of the house without meeting him. [*Going to the opposite Door.*] Can I go this way ?

Har. Why should you shun him ?

Lord N. Because he used his wife ill.

Har. He did. But I believe he is very sorry for it.—And as for you,—he said to me only a few hours ago— but no matter.

Lord N. What did he say ? I insist upon knowing.

Har. Why, then, he said, that if he had a sacred trust to repose in any one, you should be the man on earth to whom he would confide it.

Lord N. Well, I am in no hurry; I can stay a few minutes.

Enter SIR ROBERT RAMBLE.

Sir R. Oh ! Harmony ! I am in such a distracted state of mind—

    [*Seeing* LORD NORLAND, *he starts, and bows with the most humble Respect.*

Lord N. Sir Robert, how do you do ?

Sir R. My lord, I am pretty well.—I hope I have the happiness of seeing your lordship in perfect health.

Lord N. Very well, sir, I thank you.

Sir R. Indeed, my lord, I think I never saw you
look better.

Lord N. Mr Harmony, you and Sir Robert may
have some business—I wish you a good morning.

Har. No, my lord, I fancy Sir Robert has nothing
particular.

Sir R. Nothing, nothing, I assure you, my lord.

Lord N. However, I have business myself in another place, and so you will excuse me.   [*Going.*

Sir R. [*Following him.*] My lord—Lord Norland,
—I trust you will excuse my enquiries.—I hope, my
lord, all your family are well?

Lord N. All very well.

Sir R. Your little éléve,—Master Edward,—the
young gentleman you have adopted—I hope he is
well—[*Hesitating and confused.*] And—your ward,—
Miss Wooburn—I hope, my lord, she is well?

Lord N. Yes, Sir Robert, Miss Wooburn is tolerably well.

Sir R. Only tolerably, my lord? I am sorry for
that.

Har. I hope, my lord, you will excuse my mentioning the subject; but I was telling Sir Robert just
now of your intentions respecting a second marriage
for that lady; but Sir Robert does not appear to approve of the design.

Lord N. What objections can he have?

Sir R. My lord, there are such a number of bad
husbands;—there are such a number of dissipated,
unthinking, unprincipled men!—And—I should be
extremely sorry to see any lady with whom I have
had the honour of being so closely allied, united to
a man who would undervalue her worth.

Lord N. Pray, Sir Robert, were you not then extremely sorry for her while she was united to you?

Sir R. Very sorry for her, indeed, my lord. But,
at that time, my mind was so much taken up with
other cares, I own I did not feel the compassion which

was her due; but, now that I am single, I shall have leisure to pay her more attention; and should I find her unhappy, it must, inevitably, make me so.

Lord N. Depend upon it, that, on the present occasion, I shall take infinite care in the choice of her husband.

Sir R. If your lordship would permit me to have an interview with Miss Wooburn, I think I should be able at least—

Lord N. You would not sure insult her by your presence?

Sir R. I think I should be able at least to point out an object worthy of her taste—I know that which she will like better than any one in the world.

Lord N. Her request has been, that I may point her out a husband the reverse of you.

Sir R. Then, upon my honour, my lord, she won't like him.

Lord N. Have not you liked women the reverse of her?

Sir R. Yes, my lord, perhaps I have, and perhaps I still do. I do not pretend to love her; I did not say I did; nay, I positively protest I do not; but this indifference I acknowledge as one of my faults; and, notwithstanding all my faults, give me leave to acknowledge my gratitude that your lordship has nevertheless been pleased to declare—you think my virtues are numberless. [LORD NORLAND *shews Surprise.*]

Har. [*Aside to* SIR ROBERT.] Hush, hush!—Don't talk of your virtues now.

Lord N. Sir Robert, to all your incoherent language this is my answer, this is my will: the lady, to whom I have had the honour to be guardian, shall never (while she calls me friend) see you more.

[SIR ROBERT, *at this Sentence, stands silent for some Time, then, suddenly recollecting himself:*

Sir R. Lord Norland, I am too well acquainted with the truth of your word, and the firmness of your temper, to press my suit one sentence farther.

Lord N. I commend your discernment.

Sir R. My lord, I feel myself a little embarrassed. —I am afraid I have made myself a little ridiculous upon this occasion—Will your lordship do me the favour to forget it ?

Lord N. I will forget whatever you please.

Har. [*Following him, whispers.*] I am sorry to see you going away in despair.

Sir R. I never did despair in my life, sir ; and while a woman is the object of my wishes, I never will.   [*Exit.*

Lord N. What did he say ?

Har. That he thought your conduct, that of a just and an upright man.

Lord N. To say the truth, he has gone away with better manners than I could have imagined, considering his jealousy is provoked.

Har. Ah! I always knew he loved his wife, notwithstanding his behaviour to her; for, if you remember, he always spoke well of her behind her back.

Lord N. No, I do not remember it.

Har. Yes, he did ; and that is the only criterion of a man's love, or of his friendship.

Enter a SERVANT.

Serv. A young gentleman is at the door, sir, enquiring for Lord Norland.

Lord N. Who can it be ?

Har. Your young gentleman from home, I dare say. Desire him to walk in. Bring him here.

[*Exit* SERVANT.

Lord N. What business can he have to follow me ?

Enter EDWARD.

Edw. Oh, my lord, I beg your pardon for coming hither, but I come to tell you something you will be glad to hear.

Har. Good Heaven, how like his mother!

Lord N. [*Taking him by the Hand.*] I begin to think he is—But he was not so when I first took him. No, no, if he had, he would not have been thus near me now;—but to turn him away because his countenance is a little changed, I think would not be right.

Edw. [*To* HARMONY.] Pray, sir, did you know my mother?

Har. I have seen her.

Edw. Did you ever see her, my lord?

Lord N. I thought, you had orders never to enquire about your parents?—Have you forgot those orders?

Edw. No, my lord;—but when this gentleman said, I was like my mother, it put me in mind of her.

Har. You do not remember your mother, do you?

Edw. Sometimes I think I do. I think sometimes I remember her kissing me, when she and my father went on board of a ship; and so hard she pressed me—I think I feel it now.

Har. Perhaps she was the only lady that ever saluted you?

Edw. No, sir, not by many.

Lord N. But, pray, young man, (to have done with this subject,) what brought you here? You seem to have forgot your errand?

Edw. And so I had, upon my word. Speaking of my mother, put it quite out of my mind.—But, my lord, I came to let you know, the robber, who stopped you last night, is taken.

Lord N. I am glad to hear it.

Edw. I knew you would, and therefore I begged to be the first to tell you.

Har. [*To* LORD NORLAND.] Should you know the person again?

Lord N. I cannot say, I should; his face seemed so much distorted.

Har. Ah, wretched man! I suppose with terror.

Lord N. No; it appeared a different passion from fear.

Har. Perhaps, my lord, it was your fear that made you think so.

Lord N. No, sir, I was not frightened.

Edw. Then, why did you give him your money?

Lord N. It was surprise, caused me to do that.

Edw. I wondered what it was! You said it was not fear, and I was sure it could not be love.

Har. How has he been taken?

Edw. A person came to our steward, and informed against him——And, Oh! my lord, his poor wife told the officers, who took him, they had met with misfortunes, which she feared had caused a fever in her husband's head: and, indeed, they found him too ill to be removed; and so, she hoped, she said, that, as a man not in his perfect mind, you would be merciful to him.

Lord N. I will be just.]

Edw. And that is being merciful, is it not, my lord?

Lord N. Not always.

Edw. I thought it had been.—It is not just to be unmerciful, is it?

Lord N. Certainly not.

Edw. Then it must be just to have mercy.

Lord N. You draw a false conclusion——Great

F

as the virtue of mercy is, justice is greater still.—
Justice holds its place among those cardinal virtues,
which include all the lesser.—Come, Mr Harmony,
will you go home with me? And, before I attend to
this business, let me persuade you to forget there is
such a person in the world as Sir Robert Ramble, and
suffer me to introduce you to Miss Wooburn, as the
man who——

Har. I beg to be excused—Besides the consideration of Sir Robert, I have another reason why I cannot go with you.—The melancholy tale, which this
young gentleman has been telling, has cast a gloom
on my spirits, which renders me unfit for the society
of a lady.

Lord N. Now I should not be surprised, were you
to go in search of this culprit and his family, and
come to me to entreat me to forego the prosecution;
but, before you ask me, I tell you it is in vain—I will
not.

Har. Lord Norland, I have lately been so unsuc-
cessful in my petitions to you, I shall never presume
to interpose between your rigour and a weak sufferer
more.

Lord N. Plead the cause of the good, and I will
listen; but you find none but the wicked for your
compassion.

Har The good, in all states, even in the very grasp
of death, are objects of envy; it is the bad who are
the only sufferers. There, where no internal consolation cheers, who can refuse a little external comfort?
—And, let me tell you, my lord, that, amidst all
your authority, your state, your grandeur, I often
pity you.   [*Speaking with unaffected Compassion.*

Lord N. Good day, Mr Harmony; and when you
have apologized for what you have said, we may be
friends again.

[*Exit, leading off* EDWARD.

Har. Nay, hear my apology now. I cannot—no, it is not in my nature, to live in resentment, nor under the resentment of any creature in the world.

[*Exit, following* LORD NORLAND.

SCENE II.

An Apartment at LORD NORLAND'S.

Enter SIR ROBERT RAMBLE, *followed by a* SERVANT.

Sir R. Do not say who it is—but say, a gentleman, who has some particular business with her.

Serv. Yes, sir.   [*Going.*

Sir R. Pray,—[SERVANT *returns.*] You have but lately come into this service, I believe ?

Serv. Only a few days, sir.

Sir R. You don't know me, then ?

Serv. No, sir.

Sir R. I am very glad of it. So much the better. ——Go to Miss Wooburn, with a stranger's compliments, who is waiting, and who begs to speak with her upon an affair of importance.

Serv. Yes, sir.   [*Exit.*

Sir R. I wish I may die, if I don't feel very unaccountably ! How different are our sensations towards our wives, and all other women ! This is the very first time she has given me a palpitation since the honeymoon.

Enter MISS WOOBURN, *who starts on seeing* SIR ROBERT ;—*he bows in great Confusion.*

Miss W. Support me, Heaven !   [*Aside.*

Sir R. [*Bows repeatedly, and does not speak till after many Efforts.*] Was ever man in such confusion before his wife !   [*Aside.*

Miss W. Sir Robert, having recovered, in some measure, from the surprise into which this intrusion first threw me, I have only to say,—that, whatever pretence may have induced you to offer me this insult, there is not any that can oblige me to bear with it.   [*Going.*

Sir R. Lady Ramb—[*Recalling himself.*] Miss Woo —[*She turns.*]—Lady Ramble—[*Recalling himself again.*] Miss Wooburn—Madam—You wrong me ——There was a time when I insulted you, I confess; but it is impossible that time should ever return.

Miss W. While I stay with you, I incur the danger.   [*Going.*

Sir R. [*Holding her.*] Nay, listen to me, as a friend, whom you have so often heard as an enemy.—You offered me a favour by the hands of Mr Harmony——

Miss W. And is this the motive of your visit—this the return—

Sir R. No, madam, that obligation was not the motive which drew me hither—The real cause of this seeming intrusion is—you are going to be married once more, and I come to warn you of your danger.

Miss W. That you did sufficiently in the marriage state.

Sir R. But now I come to offer you advice, that may be of the most material consequence, should you really be determined to yield yourself again into the power of a husband.

Miss W. Which I most assuredly am.

Sir R. Happy, happy man ! How much is he the object of my envy ! None so well as I know how to envy him, because none so well as I know how to value you. [*She offers to go.*] Nay, by Heaven, you shall not go, till you have heard all that I came to say.

Miss W. Speak it then instantly.

Sir R. No, it would take whole ages to speak; and should we live together, as long as we have lived together, still I should not find time to tell you—how much I love you!

[*A loud Rapping at the Street Door.*

Miss W. That, I hope, is Lord Norland.

Sir R. And what has Lord Norland to do with souls free as ours? Let us go to Scotland again; and again bid defiance to his stern commands.

Miss W. Be assured, that through him only will I ever listen to a syllable you have to utter.

Sir R. One syllable only, and I am gone that instant.

Miss W. Well, sir!

[*He hesitates, trembles, seems to struggle with himself; then approaching her slowly, timidly, and, as if ashamed of his Humiliation, kneels to her—She turns away.*

Sir R. [*Kneeling.*] Maria, Maria, look at me!—Look at me in this humble state—Could you have suspected this, Maria?

Miss W. No: nor can I conceive what this mockery means.

Sir R. It means, that, now you are no longer my wife, you are my goddess; and thus I offer you my supplication, that, (if you are resolved not to live single,) amongst the numerous train who present their suit,—you will once more select me.

Miss W. You!—You, who have treated me with cruelty; who made no secret of your love for others; but gloried, boasted of your gallantries.

Sir R. I did, I did—But here I swear, only trust me again—do but once more trust me, and I swear by all I hold most sacred, that I will, for the future, carefully conceal all my gallantries from your know-

F 2

ledge—though they were ten times more frequent
than before.

Enter EDWARD.

Edw. Oh, my dear Miss Wooburn—What! Sir
Robert here too ! [*Goes to* SIR ROBERT, *and shakes
Hands.*] How do you do, Sir Robert? Who would
have thought of seeing you here ? I am glad to see
you, though, with all my heart ; and so, I dare say,
is Miss Wooburn, though she may not like to say so.

Miss W. You are impertinent, sir.

Edw. What, for coming in ? I will go away then.

Sir R. Do, do—there's a good boy—do.

Edw. [*Going, returns.*] I cannot help laughing,
though, to see you two together !—for you know
you never were together when you lived in the same
house.

Sir R. Leave the room instantly, sir, or I shall call
Lord Norland.

Edw. Oh, don't take that trouble ; I will call him
myself. [*Runs to the Door.*] My lord ! my lord ! pray
come hither this moment—As I am alive, here is Sir
Robert Ramble along with Lady Ramble !

Enter LORD NORLAND.

[SIR ROBERT, *looks confounded*—LORD NOR-
LAND *points to* EDWARD *to leave the Room.*
[*Exit* EDWARD.

Lord N. Sir Robert, on what pretence do you
come hither ?

Sir R. On the same pretence as when I was, for
the first time, admitted into your house ; to solicit
this lady's hand : and, after having had it once, no
force shall compel me to take a refusal.

Lord N. I will try, however—Madam, quit the
room instantly.

Sir R. My lord, she shall not quit it.

Lord N. I command her to go.

Sir R. And I command her to stay.

Lord N. Which of us will you obey?

Miss W. My inclination, my lord, disposes me to obey you —but I have so lately been accustomed to obey him, that custom inclines me to obey him still.

Sir R. There! there! there, my lord! Now I hope you will understand better for the future, and not attempt to interfere between a man and his wife?

Lord N. [*To* MISS WOOBURN.] Be explicit in your answer to this question——Will you consent to be his wife?

Miss W. No, never.

Sir R. Zounds, my lord! now you are hurrying matters. You should do it by gentle means ;—let me ask her gently.—[*With a most soft Voice.*] Maria, Maria, will you be my wife once again?

Miss W. Never.

Sir R. So you said seven years ago, when I asked you, and yet you consented.

Lord N. And now, Sir Robert, you have had your answer ; leave my house.   [*Going up to him.*

Sir R. Yes, sir ; but not without my other half.

Lord N. Your other half?

Sir R. Yes ; the wife of my bosom—the wife, whom I swore at the altar " to love and to cherish, and, forsaking all others, cleave only to her, as long as we both should live."

Lord N. You broke your oath, and made the contract void.

Sir R. But I am ready to take another oath, and another after that, and another after that—And, oh! my dear Maria, be propitious to my vows, and give me hopes you will again be mine.

[*He goes to her, and kneels in the most suppli-cating Attitude.*

Enter EDWARD, *showing in* MR SOLUS *and* MR
PLACID : EDWARD *points to* SIR ROBERT (*who
has hi Back to them*) *and goes off.*

Sir R. [*Still on his Knees, and not perceiving their
Entrance.*] I cannot live without you — Receive your
penitent husband, thus humbly acknowledging his
faults, and imploring you to accept him once again.

Sol. [*Going up to* SIR ROBERT.] Now, is it wonderful that I should want a wife ?

Plac. And is it to be wondered at, if I should hesitate about parting with mine ?

Sir R. [*Starts up with great Confusion.*] Mr Solus,
Mr Placid, I am highly displeased that my private
actions should be thus inspected.

Sol. No one shall persuade me now, to live a day
without a wife.

Plac. And no one shall persuade me now, not to
be content with my own.

Sol. I will procure a special licence, and marry the
first woman I meet.

Sir R. Mr Solus, you are, I believe, interested
in a peculiar manner, about the marriage of this
lady.

Sol. And, poor man, you are sick, and want somebody to bathe your temples, and to hover about
you.

Miss W. You come in most opportunely, my dear
Mr Solus, to be a witness——

Sir R. My dear Mr Solus!

Sol. To be a witness, madam, that a man is miserable without a wife. I have been a fatal instance of
that for some time.

Miss W. Come to me, then, and receive a lesson.

Sir R. No, madam, he shall not come to you ; nor
shall he receive a lesson. No one shall receive a
lesson from you but myself.

Lord N. Sir Robert, one would suppose, by this extraordinary behaviour, you were jealous.

Sir R. And so I am, my lord: I have cause to be so.

Lord N. No cause to be jealous of Mr Solus—he is not Miss Wooburn's lover, I assure you.

Sir R. Then, my lord, I verily believe it is your-self. Yes, I can see it is : I can see it in her eyes, and by every feature in your face.

Miss W. Oh! my good friend, Mr Placid, only lis-ten to him.

Sir R. And why my good friend Mr Placid ?— [*To* PLACID.] By Heavens, sir, I believe that you only wished to get rid of your own wife, in order to marry mine.

Plac. I do not wish to part with my own wife, Sir Robert, since what I have just seen.

Sir R. [*Going up to* SOLUS *and* LORD NORLAND.] Then, pray, gentlemen, be so good as to tell me, which of you two is the happy man, that I may know how to conduct myself towards him ?

Miss W. Ha! ha! ha!

Sir R. Do you insult me, Maria ?—Oh! have pity on my sufferings.

Sol. If you have a mind to kneel down again, we will go out of the room.

Plac. Just as I was comforting myself with the pro-spect of a divorce, I find my instructor and director pleading on his knees to be remarried !

Enter MRS PLACID, *who steals upon* MR PLACID *unperceived.*

Mrs P. What were you saying about a divorce ?

Sir R. Now, down on your knees, and beg par-don.

Miss W. My dear Mrs Placid, if this visit is to me, I take it very kind.

Mrs P. Not absolutely to you, my dear. I saw

Mr. Placid's carriage at the door, and so I stepped in to desire him to go home directly.

Plac. Presently, my dear; I will go presently.

Mrs P Presently won't do : I say, directly. There is a lady at my house in the greatest possible distress —[*Whispers him.*]—Lady Eleanor—I never saw a creature in such distraction ; [*Raising her Voice.*] therefore go home this moment ; you sha'n't stay an instant longer.

Sol. Egad, I don't know whether I will marry or no.

Mrs P. Why don't you go, Mr Placid, when I bid you ?

Sol No ;—I think I won't marry.

Plac. But, my dear, will not you go home with me ?

Mrs P. Did not I tell you to go by yourself?

                [PLACID *bows, and goes off.*

Sol. No ;—I am sure I won't marry.

Lord N. And now, Mr Solus and Sir Robert, these ladies may have some private conversation. Do me the favour to leave them alone.

Miss W. My lord, with your leave, we will re-tire. [*Turns when she gets to the Door.*] Sir Robert, I have remained in your company, and compelled myself to the painful task of hearing all you have had to say, merely for the satisfaction of exposing your love ; and then enjoying the triumph, of bidding you farewell for ever.   [*Exit with* MRS PLACID.

Sol. [*Looking stedfastly at* SIR ROBERT.] He turns pale at the thoughts of losing her. Yes, I think I'll marry.

Lord N. Come, Sir Robert, it is in vain to loiter ; your doom is fixed.

Sir R. [*In a melancholy musing Tone.*] Shall I then never again know what it is to have a heart like hers to repose my troubles on ?

Sol. Yes, I am pretty sure I'll marry.

Sir R.—A friend in all my anxieties, a companion in all my pleasures, a physician in all my sicknesses——

Sol. Yes, I will marry.

Lord N. Come, come, Sir Robert, do not let you and I have any dispute.

[*Leading him towards the Door.*

Sir R. Senseless man, not to value those blessings —Not to know how to estimate them, till they were lost!   [LORD NORLAND *leads him off.*

Sol. [*Following.*] Yes,—I am determined;—nothing shall prevent me—I will be married.   [*Exit.*

ACT THE FIFTH.

SCENE I.

An Apartment at LORD NORLAND'S.

Enter HAMMOND, *followed by* LADY ELEANOR.

Ham. My lord is busily engaged, madam; I do not suppose he would see any one, much less a stranger.

Lady E. I am no stranger.

Ham. Your name, then, madam?

Lady E. That I cannot send in. But tell him, sir, I am the afflicted wife of a man, who, for some weeks past, has given many fatal proofs of a disordered mind. In one of those fits of phrensy, he held an

instrument of death, meant for his own destruction,
to the breast of your lord (who by accident that moment passed,) and took from him, what he vainly
hoped might preserve his own life, and relieve the
wants of his family. But, his paroxysm over, he
shrunk from what he had done, and gave the whole
he had thus unwarrantably taken into a servant's
hands, to be returned to its lawful owner. The man,
admitted to this confidence, betrayed his trust, and
instead of giving up what was thus sacredly delivered
to him, secreted it; and, to obtain the promised reward, came to this house, but to inform against the
wretched offender; who now, only resting on your
lord's clemency, can escape the direful fate he has in-
curred.

Ham. Madam, the account you give makes me interested in your behalf, and you may depend I will
repeat it all with the greatest exactness.

[*Exit* HAMMOND.

Lady E. [*Looking round.*] This is my father's house!
It is only through two rooms and one short passage,
and there he is sitting in his study. Oh! in that
study, where I (even in the midst of all his business)
have been so often welcome; where I have urged the
suit of many an unhappy person, nor ever urged in
vain. Now I am not permitted to speak for myself,
nor have one friendly voice to do that office for me,
which I have so often undertaken for others.

Enter HAMMOND, EDWARD *following.*

Ham. My lord says, that any petition concerning
the person you come about is of no use. His respect
for the laws of his country demands an example such
as he means to make.

Lady E. Am I, am I to despair then! [*To* HAM-
MOND.] Dear sir, would you go once more to him,
and humbly represent——

3

Ham. I should be happy to oblige you, but I dare not take any more messages to my lord; he has given me my answer.—If you will give me leave, madam, I'll see you to the door.

[*Crosses to the other Side, and goes off.*

Lady E. Misery—Distraction!—Oh, Mr Placid! Oh, Mr Harmony! Are these the hopes you gave me, could I have the boldness to enter this house? But you would neither of you undertake to bring me here!—neither of you undertake to speak for me!

[*She is following the* SERVANT ; EDWARD *walks softly after her, till she gets near the Door; he then takes hold of her Gown, and gently pulls it; she turns and looks at him.*

Edw. Shall I speak for you, madam?

Lady E. Who are you, pray, young gentleman?—Is it you, whom Lord Norland has adopted for his son?

Edw. I believe he has, madam; but he has never told me so yet.

Lady E. I am obliged to you for your offer; but my suit is of too much consequence for you to under-take.

Edw. I know what your suit is, madam, because I was with my lord when Hammond brought in your message ; and I was so sorry for you, I came out on purpose to see you—and, without speaking to my lord, I could do you a great kindness—if I durst.

Lady E. What kindness?

Edw. But I durst not—No, do not ask me.

Lady E. I do not. But you have increased my anxiety, and in a mind so distracted as mine, it is cruel to excite one additional pain.

Edw. I am sure I would not add to your grief for the world.—But then, pray do not speak of what I am going to say.—I heard my lord's lawyer tell him just now, that, as he said he should not know the person again, who committed the offence about which you came, and as the man who informed against him

G

is gone off, there could be no evidence that he did the action, but from a book, a particular pocketbook, of my lord's, which he forgot to deliver to his servant with the notes and money he returned, and which was found upon him at your house: and this Lord Norland will affirm to be his.—Now, if I did not think I was doing wrong, this is the very book— [*Takes a Pocketbook from his Pocket.*] I took it from my lord's table ;—but it would be doing wrong, or I am sure I wish you had it. [*Looking wishfully at her.*

Lady E. It will save my life, my husband's, and my children's.

Edw. [*Trembling.*] But what is to become of me?

Lady E. That Providence who never punishes the deed, unless the will be an accomplice, shall protect you, for saving one, who has only erred in a moment of distraction.

Edw. I never did any thing to offend my lord in my life ;—and I am in such fear of him, I did not think I ever should.—Yet I cannot refuse you ;— take it.—[*Gives her the Book.*] But pity me, when my lord shall know of it.

Lady E. Oh! should he discard you for what you have done, it will embitter every moment of my remaining life.

Edw. Do not frighten yourself about that.—I think he loves me too well to discard me quite.

Lady E. Does he indeed?

Edw. I think he does!—for often, when we are alone, he presses me to his bosom so fondly, you would not suppose.—And, when my poor nurse died, she called me to her bedside, and told me (but pray keep it a secret)—she told me I was his grandchild.

Lady E. You are !—you are his grandchild—I see —I feel you are ;—for I feel that I am your mother, [*Embraces him.*] Oh! take this evidence back. [*Returning the Book.*]—I cannot receive it from thee, my child ;—no, let us all perish, rather than my boy, my

only boy, should do an act to stain his conscience, or
to lose his grandfather's love.

Edw. What do you mean?

Lady E. The name of the person with whom you
lived in your infancy was Heyland?

Edw. It was.

Lady E. I am your mother; Lord Norland's only
child, [EDWARD *kneels.*] who, for one act of disobedience, have been driven to another part of the globe
in poverty, and forced to leave you, my life, behind.
[*She embraces and raises him.*] Your father, in his
struggles to support us all, has fallen a victim;—
but Heaven, which has preserved my son, will save
my husband, restore his senses, and once more——

Edw [*Starting.*] I hear my lord's step,—he is coming this way:—Begone, mother, or we are all undone.

Lady E. No, let him come—for though his frown
should kill me, yet must I thank him for his care of
thee.   [*She advances towards the Door to meet him.*

Enter LORD NORLAND.

[LADY E. *falls on her Knees.*] You love me,—'tis in
vain to say you do not. You love my child: and
with whatever hardship you have dealt, or still mean
to deal by me, I will never cease to think you love
me, nor ever cease my gratitude for your goodness.

Lord N. Where are my servants? Who let this
woman in?

[*She rises, and retreats from him, alarmed and
confused.*

Edw. Oh, my lord, pity her.—Do not let me see
her hardly treated—Indeed I cannot bear it.

Enter HAMMOND.

Lord N. [*To* LADY ELEANOR.] What was your

errand here? If to see your child, take him away with
you.

Lady E. I came to see my father;—I have a house
too full of such as he already.

Lord N. How did she gain admittance?

Ham. With a petition, which I repeated to your
lordship.   [*Exit* HAMMOND.

Lord N. Her husband, then, it was, who—[*To*
LADY ELEANOR.] But let him know, for this boy's
sake, I will no longer pursue him.

Lady E. For that boy's sake you will not pursue
his father; but for whose sake are you so tender of
that boy? 'Tis for mine, for my sake; and by that I
conjure you—   [*Offers to kneel.*

Lord N. Your prayers are vain——[*To* EDWARD.]
Go, take leave of your mother for ever, and instantly
follow me;—or shake hands with me for the last
time, and instantly begone with her.

Edw. [*Stands between them in doubt for some little
Time; looks alternately at each with Emotions of Affection; at last goes to his Grandfather, and takes hold
of his Hand*] Farewell, my lord,—it almost breaks
my heart to part from you;—but if I have my choice,
I must go with my mother.

[*Exit* LORD NORLAND *instantly*—LADY ELEANOR
and her Son go off on the opposite Side.

SCENE II.

Another Apartment at LORD NORLAND'S.

Enter MISS WOOBURN *and* MRS PLACID.

Mrs P. Well, my dear, farewell—I have stayed a
great while longer than I intended—I certainly forgot to tell Mr Placid to come back after he had

spoken with Lady Eleanor, or he would not have taken the liberty not to have come.

Miss W. How often have I lamented the fate of Lord Norland's daughter! But, luckily, I have no personal acquaintance with her, or I should probably feel a great deal more on her account than I do at present.—She had quitted her father's house before I came to it.

Enter Mr Harmony.

Har. My whole life is passed in endeavouring to make people happy, and yet they won't let me do it. —I flattered myself, that after I had resigned all pretensions to you, Miss Wooburn, in order to accommodate Sir Robert—that, after I had told both my lord and him, in what high estimation they stood in each other's opinion, they would of course have been friends; or, at least, not have come to any desperate quarrel!—instead of which, what have they done, but, within this hour, had a duel!—and poor Sir Robert—

Miss W. For Heaven's sake, tell me of Sir Robert——

Har. You were the only person he mentioned after he received his wound; and such encomiums as he uttered——

Miss W. Good Heaven! If he is in danger, it will be vain to endeavour to conceal what I shall suffer.
[*Retires a few Paces, to hide her Emotions.*

Mrs P. Was my husband there?

Har. He was one of the seconds.

Mrs P. Then he shall not stir out of his house this month for it.

Har He is not likely; for he is hurt too.

Mrs P. A great deal hurt?

Har. Don't alarm yourself.

Mrs P. I don't.

Har. Nay, if you had heard what he said!
G 2

Mrs P. What did he say?

Har. How tenderly he spoke of you to all his fiends——

Mrs P. But what did he say?

Har. He said, you had imperfections.

Mrs P. Then he told a falsehood.

Har. But he acknowledged they were such as only evinced a superior understanding to the rest of your sex ;—and that your heart——

Mrs P. [*Bursting into Tears.*] I am sure I am very sorry that any misfortune has happened to him, poor, silly man! But I don't suppose [*Drying up her Tears at once.*] he'll die?

Har. If you will behave kindly to him, I should suppose not.

Mrs P. Mr Harmony, if Mr Placid is either dying or dead, I shall behave with very great tenderness; but if I find him alive, and likely to live, I will lead him such a life as he has not led a long time.

Har. Then you mean to be kind?—But, my dear Miss Wooburn, [*Going to her.*] why this seeming grief? Sir Robert is still living; and should he die of his wounds, you may at least console yourself, that it was not your cruelty which killed him.

Miss W. Rather than have such a weight on my conscience, I would comply with the most extravagant of his desires, and suffer his cruelty to be the death of me.

Har. If those are your sentiments, it is my advice that you pay him a visit in his affliction.

Miss W. Oh no, Mr Harmony, I would not for the universe. Mrs Placid, do you think it would be proper?

Mrs P. No, I think it would not—Consider, my dear, you are no longer a wife, but a single woman, and would you run into the clutches of a man?

Har. He has no clutches, madam; he is ill in bed, and totally helpless.—But, upon recollection, it

would, perhaps, be needless to go; for he may be too
ill to admit you.

Miss W. If that is the case, all respect to my situation, my character, sinks before the strong desire of
seeing him once more. Oh! were I married to another, I feel, that, in spite of all my private declara-
tions, or public vows, I should fly from him to pay my
duty where it was first plighted.

Har. My coach is at the door; shall I take you to
his house? Come, Mrs Placid, waive all ceremonious
motives on the present melancholy occasion, and go
along with Miss Wooburn and me.

Miss W. But, Mrs Placid, perhaps poor Mr Placid is in want of your attendance at home.

Har. No, they were both carried in the same carriage to Sir Robert's.

Miss W. [*As* HARMONY *leads her to the Door.*]
Oh! how I long to see my dear husband, that I may
console him!

Mrs P. Oh! how I long to see my dear husband,
that I may quarrel with him! [*Exeunt.*

SCENE III.

The Hall at SIR ROBERT RAMBLE'S.

The PORTER *discovered asleep.*

Enter a FOOTMAN.

Foot. Porter, porter, how can you sleep at this
time of the day? It is only eight o'clock.

Porter. What did you want, Mr William?

5

Foot. To tell you, my master must not be disturbed, and so you must not let in a single creature.

Porter. Mr William, this is no less than the third time I have received those orders within this half hour ;—First from the butler, then from the valet, and now from the footman—Do you all suppose I am stupid ?

Foot. I was bid to tell you. I have only done what I was desired ; and mind you do the same.   [*Exit.*

Porter. I'll do my duty, I warrant you. I'll do my duty [*A loud Rapping at the Door.*] And there's a summons to put my duty to the trial. [*Opens the Door.*

Enter HARMONY, MISS WOOBURN, *and* MRS PLACID.

Har. These ladies come on a visit to Sir Robert. Desire one of the servants to conduct them to him instantly.

Porter. Indeed, sir, that is impossible—My master is not——

Har. We know he is at home, and therefore we can take no denial.

Porter. I own he is at home, sir ; but, indeed, he is not in a situation——

Miss W. We know his situation.

Porter. Then, madam, you must suppose he is not to be disturbed.   I have strict orders not to let in a single soul.

Har. This lady, you must be certain, is an exception.

Porter. No lady can be an exception in my master's present state ; for I believe, sir, but—perhaps, I should not speak of it—I believe my master is nearly gone.

Miss W. Oh ! support me, Heaven !

M s P. But ha he his senses ?

Porter. Not very clearly, I believe.

Miss W. Oh, Mr Harmony, let me see him, before they are quite lost.

Porter. It is as much as my place is worth, to let a creature farther than this hall ; for my master is but in the next room.

Mrs P. That is a dining room. Is not he in bed ?

Har. [*Aside to the Ladies.*] In cases of wounds, the patient is oftentimes propped up in his chair.

Miss W. Does he talk at all ?

Porter. Yes, madam, I heard him just now very loud.

Miss W. [*Listening.*] I think I hear him rave.

Har. No, that murmuring is the voice of other persons.

Mrs P. The physicians in consulation, I apprehend—Has he taken any thing ?

Porter. A great deal, I believe, madam.

Mrs P. No amputation, I hope ?

Porter. What, madam ?

Har. He does not understand you. [*To* Miss Woo-burn.]—Come, will you go back ?

Porter. Do, my lady, and call in the morning.

Miss W. By that time he may be totally insensible, and die without knowing how much I am attached to him.

Mrs P. And my husband may die without knowing how angry I am with him !—Mr Harmony, never mind this foolish man, but force your way into the next room.

Porter. Indeed, sir, you must not. Pray, Mr Harmony, pray, ladies, go away.

Miss W. Yes, I must go from my husband's house for ever, never to see that, or him again!

[*Faints on* Mr Harmony.

Mrs P. She is fainting—open the windows—give her air.

Porter. Pray go away :—There is plenty of air in the streets, ma'am.

Har. Scoundrel! Your impertinence is insupportable. Open these doors ; I insist on their being opened.

[*He thrusts a Door in the Centre of the Stage ; it opens, and discovers* SIR ROBERT *and* MR PLACID *at a Table, surrounded by a Company of Gentlemen.*

Sir R. A song—a song—another song——[MISS WOOBURN, *all astonishment, is supported by* MR HARMONY *and* MRS PLACID.—*The* PORTER *runs off.*] Ah ! what do I see !—Women !—Ladies !—Celestial beings we were talking of.—Can this be real?— [SIR ROBERT *and* MR PLACID *come forward—*SIR ROBERT, *perceiving it is* MISS WOOBURN, *turns himself to the Company.*] Gentlemen, gentlemen, married men and single men, hear me thus publicly renounce every woman on earth but this ; and swear henceforward to be devoted to none but my own wife.

[*Goes to her in Raptures.*

Plac. [*Looking at* MRS PLACID, *then turning to the Company.*] Gentlemen, gentlemen, married men and single men, hear me thus publicly declare, I will henceforth be master ; and from this time forward will be obeyed by my wife.

[SIR ROBERT *waves his Hand, and the Door is closed on the Company of Gentlemen.*

Mrs P. Mr Placid—Mr Placid, are you not afraid ?

Plac. No, madam, I have consulted my friends, I have drank two bottles of wine, and I never intend to be afraid again.

Miss W. [*To* SIR ROBERT.] Can it be that I see you without a wound ?

Sir R. No, my life, that you do not; for I have a wound through my heart, which none but you can cure. But, in despair of your aid, I have flown to

wine, to give me a temporary relief by the loss of reflection.

Mrs P. Mr Placid, you will be sober in the
morning.

Plac. Yes, my dear; and I will take care that you
shall be dutiful in the morning.

Har. For shame! how can you treat Mrs Placid
thus? you would not, if you knew what kind things
she has been saying of you; and how anxious she
was, when I told her you were wounded in a
duel.

Mrs P. Was not I, Mr Harmony?
                              [*Bursting into Tears.*

Plac. [*Aside to* HARMONY *and* SIR ROBERT.] I
did not know she could cry:—I never saw it before,
and it has made me sober in an instant.

Miss W. Mr Placid, I rely on you to conduct me
immediately from this house.

Sir R. That I protest against; and will use even
violent measures to prevent him.

Enter a SERVANT.

Serv. Lord Norland.

Enter LORD NORLAND.

Miss W. He will protect me.

Sir R. Who shall protect you in my house but I?
My lord, she is under my protection; and if you offer
to take her from me, I'll exert the authority of a husband, and lock her up.

Lord N. [*To* MISS WOOBURN.] Have you been
deluded hither, and wish to leave the place with me?
Tell me instantly, that I may know how to act.

Miss W. My lord, I am ready to go with you,
but——

Har. But you find she is inclined to stay;—and

do have some compassion upon two people, that are
so fond of you.

Enter Mr Solus, *dressed in a Suit of white Clothes.*

Sol. I am married!—I am married!—Wish me
joy! I am married!

Sir R. I cannot give you joy, for envy.

Sol. Nay, I do not know whether you will envy
me much when you see my spouse—I cannot say she
was exactly my choice. However, she is my wife
now; and that is a name so endearing, that I think I
love her better since the ceremony has been performed.

Mrs. P. And pray when did it take place?

Sol. This moment. We are now returning from a
friend's house, where we have been joined by a special
licence; and I felt myself so happy, I could not pass
Sir Robert's door without calling to tell him of my
good fortune. And, as I see your lady here, Sir Robert, I guess you are just married too; and so I'll
hand my wife out of the carriage, and introduce the
two brides to each other.   [*Exit* Solus.

Sir R. You see, my lord, what construction Mr
Solus has put on Miss Wooburn's visit to me: and, by
Heaven, if you take her away, it will be said, that she
came and offered herself to me, and that I rejected her!

Miss W. Such a report would kill me.

     [*Enter* Solus, *leading on* Miss Spinster.

Sol. Mistress Solus.   [*Introducing her.*

Har. [*Starting.*] My relation! Dear madam, by what
strange turn of fortune do I see you become a wife?

Mrs S. Mr Harmony, it is a weakness, I acknowledge; but you can never want an excuse for me,
when you call to mind the scarcity of provisions.

Sol. Mr Harmony, I have loved her ever since you
told me she spoke so well of me behind my back.

Enter SERVANT, *and whispers* MR HARMONY, *who follows him off.*

Lord N. I agree with you, Mr Solus, that this is a most excellent proof of a person's disposition; and in consideration, Sir Robert, that throughout all our many disagreements you have still preserved a respect for my character in my absence, I do at last say to that lady, she has my consent to trust you again.

Sir R. And she will trust me: I see it in her smiles. Oh! unexpected ecstacy!

Enter MR HARMONY.

Har. [*Holding a Letter in his Hand.*] Amidst the bright prospects of joy, which this company are contemplating, I come to announce an event that ought to cloud the splendour of the horizon—A worthy, but an ill-fated, man, whom you are all acquainted with, has just breathed his last.

Lord N. Do you mean the husband of my daughter?

Sol. Do you mean my nephew?

Plac. Is it my friend?

Sir R. And my old acquaintance?

Har. Did Mr Irwin possess all those titles you have given him, gentlemen? Was he your son? [*To* LORD NORLAND.] Your nephew? [*To* SOLUS.] Your friend? [*To* MR PLACID.] And your old acquaintance? [*To* SIR ROBERT.] How strange, he did not know it!

Plac. He did know it.

Har. Still more strange, that he should die for want, and not apply to any of you?

Sol. What! Die for want in London! Starve in the midst of plenty!

Har. No; but he seized that plenty where law, where honour, where every social and religious tie forbade the trespass; and, in punishment of the guilt, has become his own executioner.

Lord N. Then my daughter is wretched, and her boy involved in his father's infamy!

Sol. The fear of his ghost haunting me, will disturb the joys of my married life.

Plac. Mrs Placid, Mrs Placid, my complying with your injunctions, in respect to Mr Irwin, will make me miserable for ever.

Miss W. I wish he had applied to me.

Sir R. And, as I refused him his request, I would give half my estate, that he had not applied to me.

Har. And a man who always spoke so well of you all behind your backs!—I dare say that, in his dying moments, there was not one of you whom he did not praise for some virtue.

Sol. No, no—when he was dying, he would be more careful of what he said.

Lord N. Sir Robert, good day. Settle your marriage as you and your lady shall approve ; you have my good wishes. But my spirits have received too great a shock, to be capable of any other impression at present.

Miss W. [*Holding him.*] Nay, stay, my lord.

Sol. And, Mrs Solus, let me hand you into your carriage, to your company; but excuse my going home with you. My spirits have received too great a shock, to be capable of any other impression at present.

Har. [*Stopping* SOLUS.] Now, so loth am I to see any of you, only for a moment, in grief, while I have the power to relieve you, that I cannot help—Yes, my philanthropy will get the better of my justice.

[*Goes to the Door, and leads in* LADY ELEANOR IRW N *and* EDWARD.

Lord N. [*Runs to* IRWIN, *and embraces him.*] My son ! [IRWIN *falls on his Knees.*] I take a share in all your offences—The worst of accomplices, while I impelled you to them.

Irw. [*On his Knees.*] I come to offer my returning reason; to offer my vows, that, while that reason continues, so long will I be penitent for the phrensy which put your life in danger.

Lady E. [*Moving timidly to her Father, leading* EDWARD *by the Hand.*] I come to offer you this child, this affectionate child ; who, in the midst of our caresses, droops his head, and pines for your forgiveness.

Lord N. Ah ! there is a corner of my heart left to receive him.   [*Embraces him.*

Edw. Then, pray, my lord, suffer the corner to be large enough to hold my mother too.

Lord N. My heart is softened, and receives you all. [*Embraces* LADY ELEANOR, *who falls on her Knees*; *he then turns to* HARMONY.] Mr Harmony, I thank you, I most sincerely thank you, for this, the most joyful moment of my life. I not only experience release from misery, but a return to happiness.

Har. [*Goes hastily to* SOLUS, *and leads him to* IRWIN; *then turns to* MR *and* MRS PLACID.] And now, that I see you all reconciled, I can say—there are not two enemies, in the whole circle of my acquaintance, that I have not, within these three days, made friends.

Sir R. Very true, Harmony : for we should never have known half how well we all love one another, if you had not told us.

Har. And yet, my good friends, notwithstanding the merit you may attribute to me, I have one most tremendous fault; and it weighs so heavy on my conscience, I would confess what it is, but that you might hereafter call my veracity in question.

Sir R. My dear Harmony, without a fault, you would not be a proper companion for any of us.

Lord N. And whilst a man like you may have (among so many virtues) some faults, let us hope there may be found in each of us (among all our faults) some virtues.

Har. Yes, my lord—and, notwithstanding our numerous faults, it is my sincere wish, that the world may speak well of us all—behind our backs.

[*Exeunt.*

THE END.

THE

WEDDING DAY.

A DRAMA,

IN TWO ACTS,

AS PERFORMED AT

THE THEATRE ROYAL, DRURY-LANE.

BY MRS INCHBALD.

DRAMATIS PERSONÆ.

Lord RAKELAND,	*Mr Brunton.*
Sir ADAM CONTEST,	*Mr Munden.*
Mr MILLDEN,	*Mr Cresswell.*
Mr CONTEST,	*Mr Claremont.*
JOHN,	*Mr W. Murray.*
WILLIAM,	*Mr T. Blanchard.*
Lady AUTUMN,	*Mrs Humphries.*
Lady CONTEST,	*Mrs C. Kemble.*
Mrs HAMFORD,	*Mrs Emery.*
HANNAH,	*Miss Bristowe.*

Several Servants.

SCENE—*London.* TIME—*One Day.*

THE

WEDDING DAY.

ACT I.

SCENE I.—*An Apartment at Lord* RAKELAND's.

Enter WILLIAM, *followed by Lord* RAKELAND.

Lord Rake. AT home? to be sure I am!—how could you make any doubts about it? [*Exit* WILLIAM.] Deny me to my old acquaintance, and favourite friend, Tom Contest!

Enter Mr CONTEST.

My dear Contest, I congratulate us both that your travels are completed, and that you are come to taste, for the remainder of your life, the joys of your own country.

Mr Con. Whether to taste joy or sorrow I am yet in doubt; for I am uncertain in what manner I shall be received by my father.

Lord Rake. Have not you seen him yet?

Mr Con. No: nor dare I, till I know in what humour he is.

Lord Rake. In a good one, you may depend upon it; for he is very lately married.

Mr Con. To my utter concern, I heard some time ago indeed, that it was his design to marry again; but as he has never condescended to make me acquainted with it himself, I know nothing further respecting the marriage than what public report has thrown in my way. Pray, can you tell me who my new mother is?

Lord Rake. I am told she is very young, extremely lively, and prodigiously beautiful. I am told too that she has been confined in the country, dressed, and treated like a child, till her present age of eighteen, in order to preserve the appearance of youth in her mother.

Mr Con. But who is her mother? Of what family is she?

Lord Rake. That I don't know—and I suppose your father did not consider of what family she was, but merely what family she was likely to bring him.

Mr Con. Yes, I have no doubt but he married on purpose to disinherit me, for having written to him, " that I had fixed my affections upon a widow of small fortune, but one who was so perfectly to my wishes, that even his commands could not force me to forsake her."

Lord Rake. And were you in earnest?

Mr Con. I thought I was then; but at present I am more humble. I have implored his pardon for those hasty expressions, and now only presume by supplication to obtain his approbation of my choice.

Lord Rake. Pray, who may your choice be? Is she a foreigner?

Mr Con. No ; an Englishwoman.   We met at Florence—parted at Venice—and she arrived in London just four days before me.

Lord Rake. And when will you introduce me to her?

Mr Con. Are you as much a man of gallantry as ever? If you are, you shall first promise me not to make love to her.

Lord Rake. As to that, my dear friend, you know I never make a promise, when I think there is the least probability of my breaking it.

Mr Con. Then positively you shall not see my choice till I am secure of her.   But I can tell you what I'll do—I'll introduce you to my young mother-in-law, if you like.

Lord Rake. My dear friend, that will do quite as well—nay, I don't know if it won't do better. Come, let us go directly.

Mr Con. Hold! not till I have obtained my father's leave: for, after offending him so highly as not to hear from him these six months, I thought it necessary to send a letter to him as soon as I arrived this morning, to beg his permission to wait upon him.

Enter WILLIAM, *and gives a Letter to* Mr CONTEST.

And here, I suppose, is his answer.

Wil. Your servant inquired for you, Sir, and left this.   [*Exit.*

[Mr CONTEST *breaks open the Letter hastily, and reads.*]

Mr Con. An invitation to go to his house immediately. *(He reads the remainder of the Letter, and then expressing surprise.)*—Why my father tells me he was only married this very morning! I heard he was married a week ago!

Lord Rake. And so did I—and so did half the

town. His marriage has even been in the newspapers these three days.

Mr Con. Ay, these things are always announced before they take place; and I most sincerely wish it had been delayed still longer.

Lord Rake. I do not—for I long to have a kiss of the bride.

Mr Con. Pshaw! my lord: as it is the wedding day, I cannot think of taking you now; it may be improper.

Lord Rake. Not at all, not at all. A wedding day is a public day; and Sir Adam knows upon what familiar terms you and I are. Indeed, my dear friend, my going will be considered but as neighbourly. I can take no denial—I must go.

Mr Con. Well, if it must be so, come then. [*Going, stops.*] Notwithstanding the cause I have for rejoicing at this kind invitation from my father, still I feel embarrassed at the thoughts of appearing before him, in the presence of his young wife; for I have no doubt but she'll take a dislike to me.

Lord Rake. And if she should, I have no doubt but she'll take a liking to *me*. So come away, and be in spirits.   [*Exeunt.*

SCENE II.—*An Apartment at Sir* ADAM CON-TEST'S.

Enter Sir ADAM, *drest in white clothes, like a Bridegroom.*

Sir Adam. Nothing is so provoking as to be in a situation where one is expected to be merry—it is like being asked in company " to tell a good story, and to be entertaining;" and then you are sure to be duller than ever you were in your life. Now, notwithstanding this is my wedding day, I am in such a blessed humour that I should like to make every person's life in this house a burthen to them. But I won't! [*Struggling with himself.*]—No, I won't!—Here comes my Lady Contest.

Enter Lady CONTEST *slowly and pensively, drest like a Bride.*

Sir Adam. [*Aside.*] Now I will be in a good humour, in spite of all my doubts and fears.

Lady Con. Did you send for me, Sir Adam?

Sir Adam. Yes, my dear; your guardian is just stept home, to bring his wife to dine with us; and I wished to have a few minutes conversation with you. Sit down. [*They sit.*] I observed, Lady Contest, (and it gave me uneasiness,) that at church this morning, while the ceremony was performing, you looked very pale. You have not yet wholly regained your colour; and instead of your usual cheerful countenance and air, I perceive a pensive, dejected—Come, look cheerful. [*Very sharply.*] Why don't you look cheerful? [*Checking himself, and softening his voice.*] Consider, every one should be happy upon their wedding day, for it is a day that seldom comes above once in a person's life.

Lady Con. But with *you*, Sir Adam, it has come twice.

Sir Adam. Very true—it has—and my *first* was a day indeed! I shall never forget it! My wife was as young as you are now—

Lady Con. And you were younger than you are now.

Sir Adam. [*Starts—then aside.*]—No, I won't be angry. [*To her.*] She was beautiful too—nay more, she was good; she possessed every quality. But this is not a proper topic on the present occasion; and so, my dear, let us change the subject.

Lady Con. Pray, Sir Adam, is it true that your son is come to town ?

Sir Adam. It is ; and I expect him here every moment.

Lady Con. And have you invited no other company all day ?

Sir Adam. Your guardian and his wife, Mr and Mrs Ploughman, you know, will be here ; and what other company would you wish for—besides me ?

Lady Con. In the country we had always fiddles and dancing at every wedding ; and I declare I have been merrier at other people's weddings, than I think I am likely to be at my own.

Sir Adam. If you loved me, Lady ˙ Contest, you would be merry in my company alone. *Do* you love me ? My first wife loved me dearly.

Lady Con. And so do I love you dearly—just the same as I would love my father, if he were alive.

Sir Adam. [*Aside.*] Now could I lay her at my feet for that sentence ! But I won't—I wont [*Struggling with himself.*] Answer me this—would you change husbands with any one of your acquaintance ?

Lady Con. What signifies now my answering such a question as that, when I am sure not one of my acquaintance would change with me ?

Sir Adam. What makes you think so ? [*Violently,*] [*Softening.*] Your equipage will be by far the most splendid of any lady's you will visit. I have made good my promise in respect to your jewels too ; and I hope you like them ?

Lady Con. Like them ! to be sure !—Oh my dear Sir Adam, *they* even make me like you.

Sir Adam. A very poor proof of your love, if you can give me no other.

Lady Con. But I'll give you fifty others.

Sir Adam. [*Anxiously.*] Name them.

Lady Con. First, I will always be obedient to you.

Sir Adam. That's well.

Lady Con. Second, I will never be angry with you if you should go out and stay for a month—nay, for a year—or for as long as ever you like.

Sir Adam. [*Aside, and struggling with his passion.*] Sure I was not born to commit murder? I had better go out of the room.

Lady Con. [*Humming a tune.*] " And old Robin Gray was kind to me."

Sir Adam. [*Rising in agitation.*] Oh my first wife, my first wife, what a treasure was she! But my treasure is gone. [*Sighing.*]

Lady Con. Not all your money, I hope, Sir Adam? for my guardian told me you had a great deal.

Sir Adam. And did you marry me for that? What makes you blush? Come, confess to me—for there was always a sincerity in your nature, which charmed me beyond your beauty. It was that sincerity, and that alone, which captivated me.

Lady Con. Then I am surprised you did not marry your chaplain's widow, good old Mrs Brown.

Sir Adam. Why so?

Lady Con. Because I have heard you say " there was not so *sincere* a woman on the face of the earth."

Sir Adam. [*Aside.*] And egad I almost wish I had married her.—By what I have now said, Lady Contest, I meant to let you know, that, in comparison with virtues, I have no esteem for a youthful or a beautiful face.

Lady Con. Oh dear! how you and I differ! for I here declare, I do love a beautiful youthful face, better than I love any thing in the whole world.

Sir Adam. [*In a half-smothered rage.*] Leave the room—leave the room instantly. [*After a violent struggle.*] No : Come back---come back, my dear--- [*Tenderly.*] [*Aside.*] I'll be in a good humour presently. I won't use her ill—I have sworn at the altar, not to use her ill, and I will keep my vow. [*He sits down affecting perfect composure, and after a pause.*] Pray, Lady Contest, pray, have not you heard from your mother yet?

Lady Con. Not a line, nor a word.

Sir Adam. It is wonderful that she should not send us a proper address! There is no doubt but that every letter we have sent to her since she has been abroad, has miscarried. However, it will be great joy and pride to her, when she hears of your marriage.

Lady Con. Yes—for she always said I was not born to make my fortune.

Sir Adam. Which prediction I have annulled.— And after all—Come hither—come hither—[*Takes her kindly by the hand.*] And after all, I do not repent that I have—for although I cannot say that you possess all those qualifications which my first wife did, yet you behave very well considering your age.

Lady Con. And I am sure so do you, considering yours.

Sir Adam. All my resolution is gone, and I can keep my temper no longer. [*Aside.*]—Go into your own chamber immediately. [*He takes her by the hand and puts her off.*] I'll—I'll—I'll—[*Threatening as if going to follow her—then stops short.*] No, I'll go another way. [*As he is going off at the opposite side, enter* JOHN.

John. My young master and another gentleman.
[*Exit.*

Enter Mr CONTEST *and Lord* RAKELAND.

Mr Con. [*To Sir* ADAM.] I kneel, Sir, for your pardon and your blessing.

Sir Adam. You have behaved very ill; but as you appear sensible of it, I forgive, and am glad to see

1

you. But I expect that your future conduct shall
give proof of your repentance.---My Lord Rakeland,
I beg pardon for introducing this subject before you;
but you are not wholly unacquainted with it, I suppose ?

Lord Rake. Mr Contest has partly informed me.
[*Aside to Mr* CONTEST.] Ask for your mother.

Mr Con. I sincerely congratulate you on your
nuptials, sir, and I hope Lady Contest is well.

Sir Adam. [*Going to the side of the Scene.*] Desire Lady Contest to walk this way.

Lord Rake. I sincerely congratulate you, too, Sir
Adam.

Sir Adam. Thank you, my lord, thank you.

Enter Lady CONTEST—*Sir* ADAM *takes her by the
hand, and presents Mr* CONTEST *to her.*

My dear, this is my son—and this, Tom, is your mother-in-law.

Lady Con. Dear Sir Adam, [*Half laughing.*] I
was never so surprised in my life ! Always when you
spoke of your son you called him Tom, and Tommy,
and I expected to see a little boy.

Sir Adam. And have you any objection to his being a man ?

Lady Con. Oh no, I think I like him the better.
[*To Mr* CONTEST.] Sir, I am very glad to see you.

Mr Con. I give your ladyship joy.
                          [*Salutes her hand.*

Lady Con. I shall be very fond of him, Sir Adam ;
I shall like him as well as if he were my own.

Sir Adam. [*Aside.*] Now am I in a rage, lest seeing my son a man, she should be more powerfully re-
minded that I am old.

Lord Rake. Sir Adam, you have not introduced
me to Lady Contest.

Lady Con. Is this another son ?

Sir Adam. What. could you be fond of him too?

Lady Con. Yes, I could.

Sir Adam. And like him as well as if he were your own?

Lady Con. Yes, I could.

Sir Adam. But he is not my son.

Lady Con. I can't help thinking he is.

[*Looking stedfastly at him.*

Sir Adam. I 'tell you he is not.

Lady Con. Nay, nay, you are joking—I am sure he is.

Sir Adam. [*Raising his voice.*] I tell you, no.

Lady Con. Why he is very like you. [*She goes up to Lord* RAKELAND, *and looks in his face.*] No, he is not so like when you are close.---I beg ten thousand pardons, sir; you are not at all like Sir Adam.

Sir Adam. [*Aside.*] Zounds, now I am jealous— and I am afraid my propensity will get the better of me. But no, it shan't—No, it *shall not.*---My lord, I beg your pardon, but I want half an hour's private conversation with my son; will you excuse us?

Lord Rake. Certainly, Sir Adam—I beg you will make no stranger of me.

Sir Adam. [*Taking Mr* CONTEST *by the hand.*] Come, Tom. [*Aside.*]---There, now, I have left them alone; and I think this is triumphing over my jealousy pretty well. Well done, Sir Adam, well done, well done. [*Exit with Mr* CONTEST, *Sir* ADAM *smiling with self-applause at the victory he has gain-ed.*]

Lord Rake. My dear Lady Contest, though I acknowledge I have not the happiness to be your son, yet, permit me to beg a blessing on my knees—'Tis this—Tell me when and where I shall have the happiness of seeing you again?

Lady Con. Dear Sir, without any compliment, the happiness will be done to me.

Lord Rake. Enchanting woman!—Appoint the time.

Lady Con. I'll ask Sir Adam.

Lord Rake. No; without his being present.

Lady Con. I don't know if I sha'n't like that full as well.

Lord Rake. Appoint a time, then; just to play a game at cribbage.

Lady Con. Or what do you think of " Beggar my Neighbour?"—would not that do as well?

Lord Rake. Perfectly as well.   The very thing.

Lady Con. But you must take care how you play; for it is a game you may lose a great deal of money by.

Lord Rake. But Sir Adam must not know of it.

Enter Sir ADAM, *and speaks aside.*

Sir Adam. Resolutions come and go—I wish I could have kept mine, and staid away a little longer. *(Affecting good humour.)* What, my lord, here still? holding conversation with this giddy woman?

Lord Rake. (Affecting coldness.) I assure you, Sir Adam, I am very well pleased with Lady Contest's conversation.

Lady Con. And I am sure, my lord, I am very much pleased with yours.

Lord Rake. We have been talking about a game at cards.

Lady Con. But you said Sir Adam was not to be of the party.

Lord Rake. Yes, Sir Adam—but not Mr Contest.

Lady Con. No, indeed you said Sir Adam.

Lord Rake. Oh no.

Lady Con. (Eagerly.) Yes—because, don't you remember I said—and you made answer—

Lord Rake. I don't remember any thing—

Lady Con. What! don't you remember kneeling for my blessing?

Sir Adam. How ? What!

Lord Rake. Sir Adam, it would be a breach of good manners were I to contradict Lady Contest a second time ; therefore I acknowledge that she is right —and that I have been in the wrong.

[*Exit, bowing with great respect.*

Lady Con. (*To Sir* ADAM *apart, and pulling his sleeve.*) Won't you ask him to dinner ?

Sir Adam. Ask him to dinner ! What a difference between you and my first wife!—Would *she* have wished me to ask him to dinner ? would *she* have suffered a man to kneel——

Lady Con. I did not suffer him to kneel a moment.

Sir Adam. But my first wife was a model of perfection, and it is unjust to reproach you with the comparison. Yet I cannot help saying—would she had lived !

Lady Con. And I am sure I wish so, with all my heart.

Sir Adam. (*Fetching a heavy sigh.*) But she was suddenly snatched from me.

Lady Con. How was it, Sir Adam ? Were you not at sea together ? And so a storm arose—and so you took to the long-boat—and she would stay in the ship—and so she called to you, and you would not go—and you called to her, and she would not come. And so your boat sailed, and her ship sunk.

Sir Adam. Don't, don't—I can't bear to hear it repeated. I loved her too sincerely. But the only proof I can now give of my affection, is to be kind to her son ; and as, by what he acknowledged to me, his heart I perceived was bent upon marriage, I have given him leave to introduce to me the lady on whom he has fixed his choice—and if I like her——

Lady Con. Has he fixed his choice ?—Who is the young lady ? What is her name ?

Sir Adam. I did not ask her name.

Lady Con. But I hope you will give your consent, whoever she is.

Sir Adam. And if I do, in a little time they may both wish I had not. Young people are so capricious they don't know their own minds half an hour. For instance, I dare say you think very highly of that young lord who was here just now ; but if you were to see him two or three times a-week, you would cease to admire him.

Lady Con. I should like to try. Do invite him here two or three times a week, on purpose to try.

Sir Adam. No, no ; it's an experiment I don't wish to try.

Enter JOHN.

John. Mr and Mrs Ploughman are come, sir, and dinner is almost ready.   [*Exit.*

Lady Con. (*Looking at her hand, gives a violent scream*) Oh ! Oh !—Oh dear ! Sir Adam—Oh dear ! Oh dear ! Oh dear !

Sir Adam. What's the matter ? What, in the name of heaven, is the matter?

Lady Con. I wish I may die if I have not lost my wedding ring—Oh ! 'tis a sure sign of some ill luck.

Sir Adam. Here, John !

Enter JOHN.

Go and look for your mistress's wedding ring : she has dropt it somewhere about the house.

Lady Con. I am afraid it was in the street, as I stepped out of my coach. Oh ! indeed, Sir Adam, it did not stick close. I remember I pulled my glove off just at that time :—Go and look there, John. [*Exit* JOHN.] Oh ! Sir Adam, some ill luck will certainly happen to one or both of us, you may depend upon it.

Sir Adam. Childish nonsense! What ill luck can happen to us while we are good?

Lady Con. But suppose we should not be good?

Sir Adam. We always may, if we please.

Lady Con. I know we may. But then sometimes 'tis a great deal of trouble.

Sir Adam. Come, don't frighten yourself about omens; you'll find your ring again.

Lady Con. Do you think that young lord mayn't have found it? Suppose we send to ask him?

Sir Adam. Did you miss it while he was here?

Lady Con. No, nor should not have missed any thing, if he had staid till midnight.

Sir Adam. (*Taking her by the hand.*) Come, come to dinner. (*Going, stops.*) But I must say this has been a very careless thing of you. My first wife would not have lost *her* wedding ring.

Lady Con. But indeed, Sir Adam, mine did not fit.   [*Exeunt.*

ACT II.

SCENE I.—*An Apartment at Mr* MILLDEN'S.

Enter Lady AUTUMN *and Mrs* HAMFORD.

Mrs Ham. My dear Lady Autumn, Mr Contest is not of a proper age for a lover, much less for a husband of yours.

Lady Aut. Mrs Hamford, I believe, old as you pretend to think me now, you thought me young but a few weeks ago at Venice; when, on your first landing there, you imposed upon me your romantic tale, and prevailed with me to bring you to England.

Mrs Ham. Hold, madam; do not conclude too hastily, that, because I have for a few days since my

arrival in my native country, deferred my promise of
revealing to you my real name and my connections
here, that I am for this reason an impostor.

Lady Aut. No; upon recollection, you certainly
have been living on a savage island for these ten or
twelve years, which gives you all these Hottentot
ideas in respect to the advanced age of women.

Enter *Mr* MILLDEN.

Mr Mil. Lady Autumn, I make no apology for
entering your apartment thus abruptly, because I
come with good news—Your daughter is married.

Lady Aut. Married! What! while I have been
abroad?

Mr Mil. No doubt—But I cannot give you any
particulars of the marriage, nor tell you even the
gentleman's name; for I only passed her guardian by
accident in his carriage, and I had not an opportunity to inquire, nor he to inform me further, than
" that it was a most advantageous union for your
daughter, for that her husband is a man of fortune
and title."

Mrs Ham. There, Lady Autumn! you find you
have a daughter old enough to be a wife.

Lady Aut. More shame for her.—Why was not
my consent asked?

Mr Mil. You were out of England, and no letters
reached you. However, your daughter's guardian
will call upon you in the evening, and explain to you
every particular.

Lady Aut. But now, my dear Mr Millden, and you,
my dear Mrs Hamford, don't let this marriage escape
your lips, if Mr Contest should call this evening; for
if my daughter's husband should not, after all, be a
man of some importance, I should wish to keep it a
secret from Mr Contest that I have a daughter married.   [*Exit.*

Mr Mil. Mrs Hamford, I observe a gloom upon your countenance; I hope no inquiries you have made concerning any part of your family since you have arrived in England—[*He takes her hand.*] You tremble! What's the matter?

Mrs Ham. I tremble till a visit which I am now going to make is over; and then, whatever is my destiny, I trust in that Power, which has supported me through numerous trials, to give me resignation.

[*Exeunt.*

SCENE II.—*An Apartment at Sir* ADAM CON-
TEST'S.

Enter Lady CONTEST, *followed by her Maid.*

Lady Con. [*Pulling off her cloak.*] Has any **body** called on me, Hannah, since I have been out?

Han. Yes, madam, an elderly gentlewoman; but she refused to leave her name. She begg'd very hard she might have the pleasure of seeing you the next time she came, as she said she had particular business, and wanted to speak to you in private.

Lady Con. Then pray let me see her when she comes again; for I am very fond of particular business.

Enter JOHN.

John. Lord Rakeland, if your ladyship is not engaged.

Lady Con. [*Drawing* HANNAH *on one side.*] Oh! Hannah, Hannah! is this the elderly gentlewoman? Oh! for shame, Hannah!—However, poor Hannah, don't be uneasy; I won't be very angry with you.—[*To* JOHN.] You may desire his lordship to walk up.

[*Exit* JOHN.

Enter Lord RAKELAND—*Exit* HANNAH.

Lord Rake. My adorable Lady Contest——

Lady Con. I hope you are very well; but I need not ask, for you look charmingly.

Lord Rake. And you look like a divinity! I met Sir Adam this moment in his carriage going out, and that emboldened me——

Lady Con. Yes, sir, he is gone out for a little while with my guardian; but he'll soon be back. I suppose, sir, you called to play an hand of cards.

Lord Rake. No; my errand was to tell you—I love you; I adore you; and to plead for your love in return.

Lady Con. But that is not in my power to give.

Lord Rake. You cannot possibly have given it to Sir Adam!

Lady Con. I sha'n't tell you what I have done with it.

Lord Rake. You could love me; I know you could.

Lady Con. If you were my husband, I would try: and then, perhaps, take all the pains I would, I could not.

Lord Rake. Oh! that I *were* your husband.
                                    [*Kneeling.*

Lady Con. You would not kneel so if you were—not even on the wedding day.

Lord Rake. No, but I would clasp you thus.
                        [*Throwing his arms about her.*

Lady Con. Oh dear! Oh dear! I am afraid Sir Adam's first wife would not have suffered this!

Lord Rake. Why talk of Sir Adam? Oh! that you were mine, instead of his!

Lady Con. And would you really marry me if I were single?

Lord Rake. Would I?—yes—this instant, were

you unmarried—this instant, with rapture, I would become your happy bridegroom.

Lady Con. I wonder what Sir Adam would say were he to hear you talk thus! He suspected you were in love with me at the very first—I can't say I did—I suspected nothing—but I have found a great deal.

Lord Rake. Nothing to my disadvantage, I hope?

Lady Con. No—nor any thing that shall be of disadvantage to Sir Adam.

Lord Rake. Why are you perpetually talking of your husband?

Lady Con. Because, when I am in your company, I am always thinking of him.

Lord Rake. Do I make you think of your husband?

Lady Con. Yes—and you make me tremble for him.

Lord Rake. Never be unhappy about Sir Adam.

Lady Con. I won't—and he shall never have cause to be unhappy about me—for I'll go lock myself up till he comes home. Never—no, never will I see you again, unless Sir Adam makes one of the company.

[*Going.*

Lord Rake. [*Holding her.*] What are you alarmed at? Is there any thing to terrify you either in my countenance or address?—In your presence, I feel myself an object of pity, not of terror.

Lady Con. Ay, but this may be all make-believe, like the poor little boy in the song.

SONG—*Lady* CONTEST.

I.

In the dead of the night, when with labour opprest,
All mortals enjoy the calm blessing of ease,
Cupid knock'd at my window, disturbing my rest,
Who's there? I demanded—begone, if you please.

II.

He answered so meekly, so modest, and mild,
Dear ma'am, it is I, an unfortunate child;
'Tis a Cold rainy night, I am wet to the skin;
I have lost my way, ma'am, so pray let me in.

III.

No sooner from wet and from cold he got ease,
When, taking his bow, he said, ma'am, if you please—
If you please, ma'am, I would by experiment know,
If the rain has not damaged the string of my bow.

IV.

Then away skipped the urchin, as brisk as a bee,
And, laughing, I wish you much joy, ma'am, said he;
My bow is undamaged, for true went the dart,
But you will have trouble enough with your heart.
                                        [*Going.*

Enter JOHN.

John. A lady, a stranger, who Mrs Hannah says
your ladyship gave orders should be admitted—

Lady Con. Very true—Desire her to walk in—
show her up.   [*Exit* JOHN.

Lord Rake. Who is it?

Lady Con. I don't know—I can't tell—I thought
you had been her; but I was mistaken.

Lord Rake. Will she stay long?

Lady Con. I don't know any thing about her.

Lord Rake. Dear Lady Contest, do not let me
meet her on the stairs; conceal me somewhere till
she is gone. Here, I'll go into this dressing-room.

[*He goes to a door which leads to the next chamber.*

Lady Con. Then you will hear our discourse.

Lord Rake. No matter; I will keep it a secret.

Lady Con. No, no; you must go away—out of the
house.

Lord Rake. I can't—I wo'nt—don't expose yourself before the lady.

Enter Mrs HAMFORD.

[*Lord* RAKELAND *goes into the next room ; but stands at the door, and listens to the conversation of the ensuing scene.*

Mrs Ham. [*Courtseying to Lady* CONTEST.] I beg pardon, madam.

Lady Con. [*Curtseying.*] No apologies, madam.

Mrs Ham. I am afraid I am not right.
[*Looking round.*

Lady Con. Yes, madam—Pray, are not you the lady who called this afternoon, and said you had particular business ?

Mrs Ham. I am. [*Looking earnestly at her.*] And are you Lady Contest ?

Lady Contest. Yes, ma'am.

Mrs Ham. Sir Adam's wife ? [*In surprise.*

Lady Con. Yes, ma'am, Sir Adam's wife—Won't you please to sit down ? [*They sit.*

Mrs Ham. There is then, Lady Contest, a very material circumstance in my life, that I wish to reveal to you ; and to receive from *you* advice how to act. I am an elderly woman, and unfit for the enjoyment of many delights, which this world bestows ; yet would I soften, with the utmost tenderness and caution, every sorrow likely to fall upon the young. Such is the nature of my present errand to you : but to my great surprise, I find you so very, very young—

Lady Con. Yes, ma'am, thank heaven.

Mrs Ham. And you are very happy, I presume ?

Lady Con. [*Hesitating.*] Y-e-s, ma'am—yes, very happy, all things considered.

Mrs Ham. I am sorry then to be the messenger of news that will, most probably, destroy that happiness for ever.

Lady Con. Dear me! what news? You frighten me out of my wits!   [*Rising.*

Mrs Ham. You are now, Lady Contest, newly married; in the height of youth, health, prosperity; and I am the fatal object who, in one moment, may crush all those joys!

Lady Con. Oh! then pray don't—you'll break my heart if you do. What have I done? or what has happened to take away from me all my joys?— Where's my pocket handkerchief?
    [*Feeling in her pocket.*

Mrs Ham. Here, take mine, and compose yourself.

Lady Con. [*Taking it.*] Thank you, ma'am.

Mrs Ham. And now, my dear, I will inform you— and at the same time flatter myself that you will deal frankly with me, and not restrain any of those sensations which my tale may cause.

Lady. Con. Dear madam, I never conceal any of my sensations—I can't if I would.

Mrs. Ham. Then what will they be when I tell you—I am Sir Adam Contest's wife—his wife whom he thinks drowned; but who was preserved and restored to life, though not till now restored to my own country.

Lady Con. Dear madam, I don't know any body on earth I should be happier to see!
    [*Runs to her, embraces, and hugs her repeatedly.*

Mrs Ham. But consider, my dear, *you* are no longer wife to Sir Adam!

Lady Con. And is that all?—here, take your handkerchief again. [*Returns it her.*]—And come you out of your hiding place. [*She goes to the chamber where Lord* RAKELAND *is—He enters confused, and bowing to Mrs* HAMFORD.]—Come, come, for you need no longer conceal yourself now, or be miserable; for I have no longer a husband to prevent my being your wife, or to prevent me from loving you ;—for oh! oh! I do—[*Checks herself.*] though I durst not say so before.

Mrs Ham. May I enquire who this gentleman is ?

Lady Con. A poor man that has been dying for love of me, even though he thought it a sin.

Lord Rake. I wish you a good evening. I beg pardon, and promise never to be guilty for the future.

Lady Con. You are not going away ?

Lord Rake. I have an engagement it is impossible to postpone.—Good evening.

Lady Con. But you will soon come back, I hope ? for I suppose you hold your mind to be my husband?

Lord Rake. Alas! that is a happiness above my hopes.

Lady Con. Above your hopes !

Lord Rake. It is.

Lady Con. Then it shall be *beneath* mine.

Lord Rake. I wish you a good evening.

[*He bows, and exit.*

Mrs Ham. And is it possible that you can think of parting with Sir Adam without the least reluctance.

Lady Con. Pray, madam, when did you see Sir Adam last ?

Mrs. Ham. Above fifteen years ago.

Lady Con. He is greatly altered since that time.

Mrs Ham. Still will my affection be the same.

Lady Con. And so it ought; for he loves you still; he is for ever talking of you ; and declares he never knew what happiness was since he lost you.—Oh! he will be so pleased to change *me* for *you!* I wish he was at home. Oh, how I long to see him !

Mrs Ham. I hope you do not flatter me !

Lady Con. I am sure I don't;—I expect him at home every minute, and then you'll see !

Mrs Ham. Excuse me; at present I could not

support an interview. I will take my leave till I
hear from you; and will confide in your artless and
ingenuous friendship to inform Sir Adam of my escape.

Lady Con. You may depend upon me, Lady Contest.

Mrs Ham. Adieu!   [*Going.*

Lady Con. Dear madam, I would insist on waiting
upon you down stairs; but I won't stand upon any
ceremony with you in your own house.

                      [*Exit Mrs* HAMFORD.

> [*As Lady* CONTEST *is going off at the opposite
> side, she stops on hearing Sir* ADAM's *voice
> without.*

Sir Adam. Nobody so plagued as I am with servants!

Enter Sir ADAM.

Lady Con. Bless me, Sir Adam, I did not know
you were come home!

Sir Adam. I have been at home this quarter of an
hour. The coachman has made himself tipsy on the
joyful occasion of our marriage, and was very near
dashing out my brains in turning a corner.

Lady Con. And is that worth being in such an ill
temper about?—Ah! you would not be so cross, if
you knew something.

Sir Adam. Knew what? I have a piece of news to
tell you.

Lady Con. And I have a piece of news to tell *you.*

Sir Adam. Your mother is arrived in town: your
guardian heard so this morning, but he did not mention it to you nor to me till this moment, because he
thinks it is proper for him to wait upon, and acquaint
her with our marriage in form, before I throw myself
at her feet, to ask her blessing.

Lady Con. Very well—with all my heart. And now, Sir Adam—what do you think ?

Sir Adam. What do I think !

Lady Con. What will you give me to tell you something, that will make you go almost out of your wits with joy ?

Sir Adam. What do you mean ?—Have I got another estate left me ?

Lady Con. No : something better.

Sir Adam. Better than that !

Lady Con. A great deal better—*you* will think.

Sir Adam. [*Eagerly.*] Has the county meeting agreed to elect me their representative ?

Lady Con. No.

Sir Adam. What, any thing better than that ?

Lady Con. A great deal better than that—and something the most surprising !—Guess again.

Sir Adam. Pshaw ! I'll guess no more—I hate such teasing—it is unmannerly :—Would my first wife have served me so ?

Lady Con. Now you have hit upon it.

Sir Adam. Upon what ?

Lady Con. Your first wife.

Sir Adam. Ay, I shall never see her like again !

Lady Con. No, but you may see her——

Sir Adam. Eh ! What ! what ! what !

Lady Con. She is alive, and you may have her home as soon as you please.

Sir Adam. What the deuce does the woman mean ?
                              [*Trembling.*

Lady Con. Your first wife—escaped in the long boat—as surprising a story as Robinson Crusoe !—I have seen her, and she longs to see you.

Sir Adam. Why, what do you mean ? [*Still trembling.*] Alive ?

Lady Con. As much alive as I am.

Sir Adam. And what does she intend to do? [*Trembling.*] Poor woman! poor creature! where does she intend to go?

Lady Con. Go! come home, to be sure.

Sir Adam. Home!—What does she call her home?

Lady Con. You are her home.

Sir Adam. I her home!—Come to me!—What can I do with her?—and what is to become of you?

Lady Con. Oh! never mind me.

Sir Adam. Yes, but I can't think to part with you. [*Ready to cry.*] I can't think to turn a poor young creature like you upon the wide world.—Her age will secure her: *she* won't be in half the danger.

Lady Con. Poor soul! if you knew what she has suffered——

Sir Adam. And have not I suffered too?—I am sure I have lamented her loss every hour of my life; —you have heard me.

Lady Con. And yet you don't seem half so much pleased at her return as I am.

Sir Adam. I cannot help being concerned to think, what a melancholy twelve or fourteen years the poor woman has experienced! most likely upon some desert island, instead of being in heaven!

Lady Con. But if you are concerned upon her account, you ought to be pleased upon your own, my dear—[*Checks herself.*] I beg pardon; I mean Sir Adam.

Sir Adam. No, no, call me " my dear,"—do not show reserve to me already; for if you do, you will break my heart.—Can you resolve to part from me?

Lady Con. Yes; because I know you will be so much happier with your first wife.

Sir Adam. But if our parting should give you any uneasiness——

Lady Con. It won't a bit.

Sir Adam. No!

Lady Con. No ; [*Soothing.*] not when I know you are with that good, prudent woman, your first wife.—Will you give me leave to write to her, a kind letter for you, and invite her to come hither directly ?

Sir Adam. [*After a struggle.*] You may do as you like.

Lady Con. Ay, I shan't be with you long, and so you may as well let me have my own way while I stay.—[*She writes—he walks about, starts, and shows various signs of uneasiness during the time.*]—Here they are ; only a few words, but very kind ; telling her to " fly to your impatient wishes."—Here, John—[*Enter* JOHN.] Take this letter to Mr Millden's immediately. [*Exit* JOHN—*She goes to Sir* ADAM.]—Come, look pleased ; consider how charming it is for old friends to meet.

Sir Adam. Yes, if they are not too old.

Enter JOHN.

John. Lady Autumn and Mr Contest.

Enter Mr CONTEST and Lady AUTUMN.

Mr Con. Sir Adam, according to your permission, I have brought the lady on whom I have placed my affections, to receive from——

Lady Con. Oh, my dear mother, how do you do ?
                              [*Running to Lady* AUTUMN.

Mr Con. Mother !—Your mother !

Lady Con. Yes—though she looks very well, does not she ?

Mr Con. This is the lady on whom I have fixed my choice.

Lady Con. What, on my mother !

Sir Adam. And my mother ! your father's mother !—Why you are as bad as the man in the farce—fall in love with your grandmother.

Lady Con. Dear mamma, don't make yourself uneasy, if you have a mind to marry my son; for there is a lady now at Mr Millden's, and who is coming here, that will claim him for *her* son, and make me no longer wife to Sir Adam.

Enter Mr MILLDEN.

Mr Mil. Mr Contest, will you step for' a moment to the person in the next room.

                [*Exit Mr* CONTEST.

Sir Adam Contest, I come to inform you, that there is a lady in the next room who has been near fainting at the sound of your voice.

Sir Adam. And I believe I *shall* faint at the sound of her's.

Mr Mil. Her son is supporting her to you.

Enter Mrs HAMFORD *leaning on Mr* CONTEST.

Lady Con. Dear Sir Adam, fly and embrace your first wife.—[*She goes to her.*] Dear Lady Contest, notwithstanding his seeming insensibility, he loves you to distraction: a thousand times has he declared to me, he did not think there was such a woman in the world.

Sir Adam. And I did flatter myself there was not.

Mrs Ham. [*Seeing Sir* ADAM *advance towards her.*] Oh! Sir Adam!

Sir Adam. Oh, my dear! If you knew what I have suffered, and what I still suffer on your account, you would pity me.

Lady Aut. Sir Adam, I give you joy of a wife that suits your own age.

Sir Adam. And such a one shall my son marry, when he has my consent.

Lady Con. [*Crying till she sobs.*] Good b'ye, Sir Adam—good b'ye—I did love you a little, upon my word; and if I was not sure you were going to be so much happier with your first wife, I should never know a moment's peace.

Sir Adam. I thank you. And at parting, all I have to request of you is—that you will not marry again till I die.

Lady Con. Indeed Sir Adam, I will not—but then you won't make it long?—And my next husband, whoever he is, shall be of my own age ; but he shall resemble you, Sir Adam, in your principles of honour. And then, if my wedding ring should unhappily sit loose, I will guard it with unwearied discretion ; and I will hold it *sacred*—even though it should *pinch* my finger.

[*Exeunt.*

Wives as They Were and Maids as They Are
Act IV, Scene III. Sir William: There is
your prisoner

WIVES AS THEY WERE,

AND

MAIDS AS THEY ARE.

A COMEDY,

IN FIVE ACTS;

By Mrs INCHBALD.

AS PERFORMED AT THE

THEATRE ROYAL, COVENT GARDEN.

PRINTED UNDER THE AUTHORITY OF THE MANAGERS

FROM THE PROMPT BOOK.

WITH REMARKS

BY THE AUTHOR.

———

LONDON:

PRINTED FOR LONGMAN, HURST, REES, ORME, AND
BROWN, PATERNOSTER-ROW.

EDINBURGH :
Printed by James Ballantyne and Co.

REMARKS.

THE writer of this drama seems to have had a tolerable good notion of that which a play ought to be; but has here failed in the execution of a proper design.

Here are both fable and characters to constitute a good comedy; but incidents, the very essence of a dramatic work, are at times wanting, at other times ineffectual.

The first act promises a genuine comedy; and the authoress appears to have yielded up her own hopes with reluctance. In the dearth of true comic invention, she has had recourse, at the end of her second act, to farce; though she certainly knew, that the natural and the extravagant always unite so ill, that in the combination, the one is sure to become insipid, or the other revolting.

Aware of this consequence, and wanting humour to proceed in the beaten track of burlesque, she then essays successively, the serious, the pathetic, and the refined comic; failing by turns in them all, though by turns producing chance effect; but without accomplishing evident intentions, or gratifying certain expectations indiscreetly raised.

The outline of a good play is a dangerous drawing to give to the public,—a feeble plan is the surest safe-guard for an indifferent work: want of talent is never so forcibly perceived as when certain parts are im-perfect, whilst the rest demand eulogium. Critics are nice, and sometimes enraged where they find at once, ability, and imbecile attempt to explain vigor-ous conceptions.

Happy the author whose imagination extends no farther than the produce of his own anxious efforts! Such an one knows not his danger—his incapacity; and escaping censure, enjoys with triumph implied success, or receives animadversion with a sense of injury: whilst the more judicious, though more hum-ble writer, often shrinks from praise as unmerited, yet bears with still heavier heart the critic's reproach as his due.

There are some just sentiments, some repartees, a little pathos, and an excellent moral in this produc-tion;—but there are also vapid scenes, and impro-bable events, which, perhaps, more than counterba-lance those which are lively and natural

Had the punishment of the two fashionable women been inflicted by a less disgraceful means than a prison for debt, and had the singular conduct of Lord and Lady Priory been supported by occurrences as plea-santly singular, this might have ranked among some very deserving comedies: Yet even in its present imperfect state, assisted by the art of excellent act-ing, it was most favourably received on the stage; and may now, without the charm of scenic aid, af-ford an hour's amusement to the reader.

The character of Miss Dorillon is by far the most prominent and interesting one in the piece; and appears to have been formed of the same matter and spirit as compose the body and mind of the heroine of the " Simple Story,"—a woman of fashion with a heart—a lively comprehens on, and no reflection:—an understanding, but no thought.— Virtues abounding from disposition, education, feeling :—Vices obtruding from habit and example.

This part was written purposely for Miss Farren; but the very season she should have performed it, she quitted the stage, to appear in a more elevated character.

DRAMATIS PERSONÆ.

LORD PRIORY	Mr Quick.
SIR WILLIAM DORRILLON	Mr Munden.
SIR GEORGE EVELYN	Mr Pope.
MR BRONZELY	Mr Lewis.
MR NORBERRY	Mr Waddy.
OLIVER	Mr Fawcett.
NABSON	Mr Thompson.
LADY PRIORY	Miss Chapman.
LADY MARY RAFFLE	Mrs Mattocks.
MISS DORRILLON	Miss Wallis.

Several SERVANTS, *&c.*

Scene—London.

WIVES AS THEY WERE,

AND

MAIDS AS THEY ARE.

ACT THE FIRST.

SCENE I.

An Apartment at Mr Norberry's.

Enter Sir William Dorrillon, *followed by* Mr
Norberry.

Mr Nor. Why blame me?—Why blame me?—
My sister had the sole management of your daughter
by your own authority, from the age of six years,
till within eight months of the present time, when,
in consequence of my sister's death, she was trans-
ferred to my protection.

Sir W. Your sister, Mr Norberry, was a prudent
good woman—she never could instruct her in all this
vice.

Mr Nor. Depend upon it, my dear friend, that
Miss Dorrillon, your daughter, came to my house
just the same heedless woman of fashion you now see
her.

Sir W. [*Impatiently.*] Very well—'Tis very well.
—But, when I think on my disappointment——

Mr Nor. There is nothing which may not be re-
paired. Maria, with you for a guide——

Sir W. Me! She turns me into ridicule—laughs at me: This morning, as she was enumerating some of her frivolous expenses, she observed me lift up my hands and sigh; on which she named fifty other extravagances she had no occasion to mention, merely to enjoy the pang, which every folly of her's sends to my heart.

Mr Nor. But do not charge this conduct of your daughter to the want of filial love :—did she know you were Sir William Dorrillon, did she know you were her father, every word you uttered, every look you glanced, would be received with gentleness and submission :—but your present rebukes from Mr Mandred (as you are called,) from a perfect stranger, as she supposes, she considers as an impertinence, which she has a right to resent.

Sir W. I wish I had continued abroad. And yet, the hope of beholding her, and of bestowing upon her the riches I had acquired, was my sole support through all the toils by which I gained them.

Mr Nor. And, considering her present course of life, your riches could not come more opportunely.

Sir W. She shall never have a farthing of them. Do you think I have encountered the perils of almost every climate, to squander my hard-earned fortune upon the paltry vicious pleasures in which she delights? No; I have been now in your house exactly a month—I will stay but one day longer—and then, without telling her who I am, I will leave the kingdom and her for ever——Nor shall she know that this insignificant merchant, whom she despises, was her father, till he is gone, never to be recalled.

Mr Nor. You are offended with some justice; but, as I have often told you, your excessive delicacy, respecting the conduct of the other sex, degenerates into rigour.

Sir W. True; for what I see so near perfection as woman, I want to see perfect. We, Mr Norberry, can never be perfect : but surely women, women, might easily be made angels !

Mr Nor. And if they were, we should soon be glad to make them into women again.

Sir W. [*Inattentive to* MR NORBERRY]—She sets the example. She gives the fashion !—and now your whole house, and all your visitors, in imitation of her, treat me with levity, or with contempt.—But I'll go away to-morrow.

Mr Nor. Can you desert your child in the moment she most wants your protection ? That exquisite beauty just now mature——

Sir W. There's my difficulty '—There's my struggle !—If she were not so like her mother, I could leave her without a pang—cast her off, and think no more of her.—But that shape ! that face ! those speaking looks ' Yet, how reversed !—Where is the diffidence, the humility—where is the simplicity of my beloved wife ? Buried in her grave.

Mr Nor. And, in all this great town, you may never see even its apparition

Sir W. I rejoice, however, at the stratagem by which I have gained a knowledge of her heart ; deprived of the means of searching it in her early years, had I come at present as her father, she might have deceived me with counterfeit manners, till time disclosed the imposition.——Now, at least, I am not imposed upon.

Enter SERVANT.

Serv. Lord Priory.   [*Exit.*
Sir W. Lord Priory !

Mr Nor. An old acquaintance of mine, though we seldom meet. He has some singularities ; and yet, perhaps——

Enter LORD PRIORY.

Mr Nor. My dear lord, I am glad to see you.
Mr Mandred. [*Introducing* SIR WILLIAM.] My lord,
I hope I see you in perfect health ?

Lord P. Yes; but in very ill humour. I came to
London early this morning with my family for the
winter, and found my house, after going through only
a slight repair, so damp, that I dare not sleep in it :
and so I am now sending and going all over the town
to seek for lodgings.

Mr Nor. Then seek no further, but take up your
lodgings here.

Lord P. To be plain with you, I called in hopes
you would ask me ; for I am so delicately scrupulous
in respect to Lady Priory, that I could not bear the
thought of taking her to an hotel.

Mr Nor. Then pray return home, and bring her
hither immediately, with all your luggage.

Lord P. I am most extremely obliged to you ;
[*Very fervently.*] for into no one house belonging to
any of my acquaintance would I take my wife so
soon as into yours. I have now been married eleven
years, and during all that time I have made it a rule
never to go on a visit, so as to domesticate, in the
house of a married man.

Sir W. May I inquire the reason of that ?

Lord P. It is because I am married myself; and
having always treated my wife according to the ancient mode of treating wives, I would rather she
should never be an eye-witness to modern household
management.

Sir W. The ancients, I believe, were very affectionate to their wives.

Lord P. And they had reason to be so ; for their
wives obeyed them. The ancients seldom gave them
the liberty to do wrong : but modern wives do as they
like.

Mr Nor. And don't you suffer Lady Priory to do as she likes?

Lord P. Yes, when it is what I like too. But never, never else.

Sir W. Does not this draw upon you the character of an unkind husband?

Lord P. That I am proud of. Did you never observe, that seldom a breach of fidelity in a wife is exposed, where the unfortunate husband is not said to be "the best creature in the world! Poor man, so good-natured!—Dotingly fond of his wife!—Indulged her in every thing!—How cruel in her to serve him so!" Now, if I am served so, it shall not be for my good-nature.

Mr Nor. But I hope you equally disapprove of every severity.

Lord P. [*Rapidly.*] What do you mean by severity?

Mr Nor. You know you used to be rather violent in your temper.

Lord P. So I am still—apt to be hasty and passionate; but that is rather of advantage to me as a husband—it causes me to be obeyed without hesitation—no liberty for contention, tears, or repining. I insure conjugal sunshine, by now and then introducing a storm; while some husbands never see any thing but a cloudy sky, and all for the want of a little domestic thunder to clear away the vapours.

Sir W. I have long conceived indulgence to be the bane of female happiness.

Lord P. And so it is.—I know several women of fashion, who will visit six places of different amusement on the same night, have company at home besides, and yet, for want of something more, they'll be out of spirits: my wife never goes to a public place, has scarce ever company at home, and yet is always in spirits.

Sir W. Never visits operas, or balls, or routs?

Lord P. How should she? She goes to bed every night exactly at ten.

Mr Nor. In the name of wonder, how have you been able to bring her to that?

Lord P. By making her rise every morning at five.

Mr Nor. And so she becomes tired before night?

Lord P. Tired to death. Or, if I see her eyes completely open at bed time, and she asks me to play one game more at piquet, the next morning I jog her elbow at half after four.

Mr Nor. But suppose she does not reply to the signal?

Lord P. Then I turn the key of the door when I leave the chamber; and there I find her when I come home in the evening.

Sir W. And without her having seen a creature all day?

Lord P. That is in my favour: for not having seen a single soul, she is rejoiced even to see me.

Mr Nor. And will she speak to you after such usage?

Lord P. If you only considered how much a woman longs to speak after being kept a whole day silent, you would not ask that question.

Mr Nor. Well! this is the most surprising method!

Lord P. Not at all. In ancient days, when manners were simple and pure, did not wives wait at the table of their husbands? and did not angels witness the subordination? I have taught Lady Priory to practise the same humble docile obedience—to pay respect to her husband in every shape and every form—no careless inattention to me—no smiling politeness to others in preference to me—no putting me up in a corner—in all assemblies, she considers her husband as the first person.

Sir W. I am impatient to see her.

Lord P. But don't expect a fine lady with high

SCENE I.]   AND MAIDS AS THEY ARE.   13

feathers, and the et cætera of an eastern concubine; you will see a modest plain Englishwoman, with a cap on her head, a handkerchief on her neck, and a gown of our own manufacture.

Sir W. My friend Norberry, what a contrast must there be between Lady Priory and the ladies in this house!

Lord P. [*Starting*] Have you ladies in this house?

Mr Nor. Don't be alarmed; they are both single, and can give Lady Priory no ideas concerning the marriage state.

Lord P. Are you sure of that? Some single women are more informed than their friends believe.

Mr Nor. For these ladies, notwithstanding a few, what you would call, excesses, I will answer.

Lord P. Well, then, I and my wife will be with you about nine in the evening; you know we go to bed at ten.

Mr Nor. But remember you bring your own servants to wait on you at five in the morning.

Lord P. I shall bring but one—my old servant, Oliver, who knows all my customs so well, that I never go any where without him.

Mr Nor. And is that old servant your valet still?

Lord P. No, he is now a kind of gentleman in waiting. I have had no employment for a valet since I married:—my wife, for want of dissipation, has not only time to attend upon herself, but upon me Do you think I could suffer a clumsy man to tie on my neckcloth, or comb out my hair, when the soft, delicate, and tender hands of my wife are at my command?   [*Exit.*

Sir W. After this amiable description of a woman, how can I endure to see her, whom reason bids me detest, but whom nature still——

Mr Nor. Here she comes; and her companion in folly along with her.

Sir W. There's another woman! that Lady Mary

B

Raffle! How can you suffer such people in your house?

Mr Nor. She is only on a visit for a few months—she comes every winter, as her family and mine have long been intimately connected.

Sir W. Let us go—let us go. I cannot bear the sight of them.   [*Going.*

Mr Nor. Stay, and for once behave with politeness and good humour to your daughter—do—and I dare venture my life she will neither insult nor treat you with disrespect. You know you always begin first.

Sir W. Have not I a right to begin first?

Mr Nor. But that is a right of which she is ignorant.

Sir W. And deserves to be so, and ever shall be so. I stay and treat her with politeness and good humour! No—rather let her kneel and implore my pardon.

Mr Nor. Suffer me to reveal who you are, and so she will.

Sir W. If you expose me only by one insinuation to her knowledge, our friendship is at that moment at an end.

Mr Nor. [*Firmly.*] I have already given you my promise on that subject, and you may rely upon it.

Sir W. I thank you—I believe you—and I thank you.   [*Exeunt* SIR WILLIAM *and* MR NORBERRY.

Enter LADY MARY RAFFLE *and* MISS DORRILLON.

Miss Dor. [*Stealing on as* MR NORBERRY *and* SIR WILLIAM *leave the stage.*] They are gone. Thank Heaven they are gone out of this room, for I expect a dozen visitors! and Mr Norberry looks so gloomy upon me, he puts me out of spirits: while that Mr Mandred's peevishness is not to be borne.

Lady R. Be satisfied; for you were tolerably severe upon him this morning in your turn.

Miss Dor. Why, I am vexed; and I don't like to be found fault with in my best humour, much less when I have so many things to tease me.

Lady R. What are they?

Miss Dor. I have now lost all my money, and all my jewels at play; it is almost two years since I have received a single remittance from my father; and Mr Norberry refuses to advance me a shilling more. —What I shall do to discharge a debt, which must be paid either to-day or to-morrow, Heaven only knows!—Dear Lady Mary, you could not lend me a small sum, could you?

Lady R. Who, I! [*With surprise.*]—My dear creature, it was the very thing I was going to ask of you: for when you have money, I know no one so willing to disperse it among her friends.

Miss Dor. Am not I?—I protest I love to part with my money; for I know with what pleasure I receive it myself; and I like to see that joy sparkle in another's eye, which has so often brightened my own. But last night ruined me—I must have money somewhere.——As you cannot assist me, I must ask Mr Norberry for his carriage, and immediately go in search of some friend that can lend me four, or five, or six, or seven hundred pounds. But the worst is, I have lost my credit—Is not that dreadful?

Lady R. Yes, yes; I know what it is.

[*Shaking her Head.*

Miss Dor. What will become of me?

Lady R. Why don't you marry, and throw all your misfortunes upon your husband?

Miss Dor. Why don't you marry? for you have as many to throw.

Lady R. But not so many lovers who would be willing to receive the load. I have no Sir George Evelyn with ten thousand pounds a year—no Mr Bronzely.

Miss Dor. If you have not now, you once had:

for I am sure Bronzely once paid his addresses to
you

Lady R. And you have the vanity to suppose you
took him from me ?

Miss Dor. Silence.—Reserve your anger to defend
and not to attack me.   We should be allies by the
common ties of poverty: and 'tis time to arm, for
here's the enemy.

Enter Sir William, *with* Mr Norberry.

Sir W. They are here still.
        [*Aside to* Mr Norberry, *and offering to go
        back.*
Mr Nor. [*Preventing him.*] No, no.
Miss Dor. I have been waiting here, Mr Nor-
berry, to ask a favour of you. [*He and* Sir William
come forward.] Will you be so kind as to lend me your
carriage for a couple of hours ?
Mr Nor. Mr Mandred [*Pointing to* Sir William] has just asked me for it to take him into the
city.
Lady R. Oh, Mr Mandred will give it up to Miss
Dorrillon, I am sure : he can defer his business till
to-morrow.
Sir W. No, madam, she may as well put off her's.
I have money to receive, and I can't do it.
Miss Dor. I have money to pay, and I can't do it.
Lady R If one is going to receive, and the other
to pay money, I think the best way is for you to go
together; and then, what deficiency there is on one
side, the other may supply.
Miss Dor. Will you consent, Mr Mandred ?—
Come, do, and I'll be friends with you.
Sir W. [*Aside.*] " She'll be friends with me!"
Miss Dor. Will you ?
Sir W. No.
Miss Dor. Well, I certainly can ask a favour of

Mr Mandred better than I can of any person in the world.

Mr Nor. Why so, Maria?

Miss Dor. Because, instead of pain, I can see it gives him pleasure to refuse me.

Sir W. I never confer a favour, of the most trivial kind, where I have no esteem.

Miss Dor. [*Proudly.*] Nor would I receive a favour, of the most trivial kind, from one who has not liberality to esteem me.

Mr Nor. Come, Miss Dorrillon, do not grow serious : laugh as much as you please, but say nothing that——

Sir W. [*To her, impatiently.*] From whom, then, can you ever receive favours, except from the vain, the idle, and the depraved?—from those whose lives are passed in begging them of others?

Miss Dor. They are the persons who know best how to bestow them: for my part, had I not sometimes felt what it was to want a friend, I might never have had humanity to be the friend of another.

Enter SERVANT.

Serv. Sir George Evelyn.

Mr Nor. And pray, my dear, whose friend have you ever been?

Enter SIR GEORGE EVELYN.

Not Sir George Evelyn's, I am sure ; and yet he, of all others, deserves your friendship most.

Miss Dor. But friendship will not content him : as soon as he thought he had gained that——

Sir G. He aspired to the supreme happiness of your love.

Miss Dor. Now you talk of " supreme happiness," have you procured tickets for the fête on Thursday?

Sir G. I have; provided you have obtained Mr Norberry's leave to go.

Mr Nor. That I cannot grant.

Miss Dor. Nay, my dear sir, do not force me to go without it.

Sir W. [*With Violence.*] Would you dare?

Miss Dor. [*Looking with Surprise.*] " Would I dare," Mr Mandred!—and what have *you* to say if I do?

Sir W. [*Recollecting himself.*] I was only going to say, that if you did, and I were Mr Norberry——

Miss Dor. And if you *were* Mr Norberry, and treated me in the manner you now do, depend upon it, I should not think your approbation or disapprobation, your pleasure or displeasure, of the slightest consequence.

Sir W. [*Greatly agitated.*] I dare say not—I dare say not. Good morning, Sir George—I dare say not.—Good morning, Mr Norberry.   [*Going.*

Mr Nor. Stop a moment.—Maria, you have offended Mr Mandred.

Miss Dor. He has offended me.

Sir W. [*At the Door, going off.*] I sha'n't offend you long.

Mr Nor. [*Going to him, and taking him by the Arm.*] Stay, Mr Mandred: Miss Dorrillon, make an apology: Mr Mandred is my friend, and you must not treat him with this levity.

Lady R. No, no apology.

Miss Dor. No, no apology. But I'll tell you what I'll do. [*Goes up to* SIR WILLIAM.] If Mr Mandred likes, I'll shake hands with him—and we'll be good friends for the future. But then, don't find fault with me—I can't bear it. *You* don't like to be found fault with yourself—You look as cross as any thing every time I say the least word against you. Come, shake hands, and don't let us see one another's failings for the future.

Sir W. There is no future for the trial.

Miss Dor. How do you mean?

Mr Nor. Mr Mandred sets off again for India to-morrow.

Miss Dor. Indeed! I thought he was come to live in England. I am sorry you are going.

Sir W. [*With earnestness.*] Why sorry?

Miss Dor. Because we have so frequently quarrelled. I am always unhappy when I am going to be separated from a person with whom I have disagreed; I often think I could part with less regret from a friend.

Sir G. Not, I suppose, if the quarrel is forgiven?

Miss Dor. Ah! but Mr Mandred does not forgive! no! in his looks I can always see resentment. —Sometimes, indeed, I have traced a spark of kindness, and have gently tried to blow it to a little flame of friendship; when, with one hasty puff, I have put it out.

Sir W. You are right. It is—I believe—extinguished.

[*Exit* SIR WILLIAM—MR NORBERRY *following.*

Sir G. A very singular man.

Lady R. Oh! if he was not rich, there would be no bearing him—Indeed, he seems to have lost all his friends; for, during the month he has been here, I never found he had any one acquaintance out of this house.

Miss Dor. And, what is very strange, he has taken an aversion to me.—But it is still more strange, that, although I know he has, yet in my heart I like *him.* He is morose to an insufferable degree: but then, when by chance he speaks kind, you cannot imagine how it sooths me.—He wants compassion and all the tender virtues; and yet, I frequently think, that if any serious misfortune were to befall me, he would be the first person to whom I should fly to complain.

Lady R. Then why don't you fly, and tell him of your misfortune last night?

Sir G. [*Starting.*] What misfortune?

Miss Dor. [*To* LADY RAFFLE] Hush!

Lady R. A loss at play.—[*To* Miss DORRILLON.]
—I beg your pardon, but it was out before you said
hush!

Sir G. Ah, Maria! will you still risk your own
and my happiness? For mine is so firmly fixed on
you, it can only exist in yours.

Lady R. Then, when she is married to Mr Bronzely, you will be happy, because she will be so?

Sir G. Bronzely! has he dared?

Miss Dor. Have not *you* dared, sir?

Lady R. But I believe Mr Bronzely is the most
daring of the two.—[*Aside to* Sir GEORGE.] Take
care of him.   [*Exit.*

Sir G. Miss Dorrillon, I will not affront you by
supposing that you mean seriously to receive the addresses of Mr Bronzely; but I warn you against giving others, who know you less than I do, occasion
to think so.

Miss Dor. I never wish to deceive any one—I do
admit of Mr Bronzely's addresses.

Sir G. Why, he is the professed lover of your
friend Lady Mary; or, granting he denies it, and that
I even pass over the frivolity of the coxcomb, still he
is unworthy of you.

Miss Dor. He says the same of you; and half a
dozen more say exactly the same of each other. If
you like, I'll discard every one of you as unworthy;
but, if I retain you, I will retain the rest. Which do
you chuse?

Sir G. I submit to any thing, rather than the total
loss of you—But remember, that your felicity—

Miss Dor. " Felicity! felicity!"—ah! that is a
word not to be found in the vocabulary of my sensations!—   [*Sighing.*

Sir G. I believe you, and have always regarded
you with a compassion that has augmented my love.
In your infancy, deprived of the watchful eye and
anxious tenderness of a mother; the manly caution

and authority of a father; misled by the brilliant vapour of fashion; surrounded by enemies in the garb
of friends——Ah! do you weep? blessed, blessed be
the sign!—Suffer me to dry those tears I have caused, and to give you a knowledge of true felicity.

Miss Dor. [*Recovering*] I am very angry with myself.—Don't, I beg, tell Mr Norberry or Mr Mandred you saw me cry—they'll suppose I have been
more indiscreet [*Stifling her Tears.*] than I really
have. For in reality I have nothing——

Sir G. Do not endeavour to conceal from me, what
my tender concern for you has given me the means to
become acquainted with. I know you are plunged in
difficulties by your father neither sending nor coming,
as you once expected : I know you are still deeper
plunged by your fondness for play.

Miss Dor. Very well, sir! proceed.

Sir G. Thus then—Suffer me to send my steward
to you this morning; he shall regulate your accounts,
and place them in a state that shall protect you
from further embarrassment till your father sends to
you; or shall protect you from his reproaches, should
he arrive.

Miss Dor. Sir George, I have listened to your de-
tail of the vices, which I acknowledge, with patience,
with humility—but your suspicion of those which I
have *not*, I treat with pride, with indignation.

Sir G. How! suspicion!

Miss Dor. What part of my conduct, sir, has made
you dare to suppose I would extricate myself from
the difficulties that surround me, by the influence I
hold over the weakness of a lover?

[*Exeunt, separately.*

ACT THE SECOND.

SCENE I.

Another Apartment at MR NORBERRY'S.

Enter Two PORTERS *from an upper Entrance, bring-ing in Trunks;* LORD PRIORY *and* MR NORBERRY *following.*

Mr Nor. Here, Stephens, why are you out of the way? Show the men with these boxes into the dress-ing-room appointed for my Lord Priory.

    [*A* SERVANT *enters on the opposite Side, and the* PORTERS *follow him off at a lower En-trance on that Side.*

Enter SIR WILLIAM DORRILLON.

Sir W. My lord, I hope I see you well this even-ing.

Lord P. Yes, sir—and you find I have literally accepted Mr Norberry's invitation, and am come to him with all my luggage.

Enter OLIVER, *with a small Box in each Hand.*

Lord P. Follow those men with the trunks, Oliver.
Mr Nor. Ah, Mr Oliver, how do you do?
Oliver. Pretty well—tolerably well—I thank you, sir.   [*Exit.*

Enter SERVANT.

Serv. Lady Priory.

Enter LADY PRIORY.

Lord P. [*To her.*] Mr Norberry, our worthy host ; and Mr Mandred.   [*She courtesies.*

Mr Nor. I hope your ladyship will find my house so little inconvenient to you, as to induce you to make no very short visit.

Lady P. I have no doubt, sir, but I shall find, from your friendship, every comfort in this house which it is possible for me to enjoy out of my own.

Enter LADY MARY RAFFLE *and* MISS DORRILLON.

Mr Nor. [*Introducing them.*] Lady Priory—Lady Mary Raffle—Miss Dorrillon—Lord Priory.

Lady R. Permit me, Lady Priory, to take you to the next room ; we are going to have tea immediately.

Lady P. I have drank tea, madam.

Miss Dor. Already ! it is only nine o'clock.

Lady P. Then it is near my hour of going to bed.
          [LORD PRIORY, SIR WILLIAM, *and* MR
             NORBERRY, *retire to the Back of the Stage,
             and talk apart.*

Lady R. Go to bed already ! in the name of wonder, what time did you rise this morning ?

Lady P. Why, I do think it was almost six o'clock.

Lady R. [*In amaze.*] And were you up at six this morning ?

Lady P. Yes.

Miss Dor. At six in the month of January !

Lady R. It is not light till eight : and what good, now, could you possibly be doing for two hours by candle-light ?

Lady P. Pray, Lady Mary, at what time did you go to bed ?

Lady R. About three this morning.

Lady P. And what good could you possibly be doing for eleven hours by candle-light ?

Lady R. Good! it's as much as can be expected from a woman of fashion, that she does no harm.

Lady P. But I should fear you would do a great deal of harm to your health, your spirits, and the tranquillity of your mind.

[MR NORBERRY *goes off*—LORD PRIORY and SIR WILLIAM *come forward.*

Lady R. Oh, my Lord Priory, I really find all the accounts I have heard of your education for a wife to be actually true!—and I can't help laughing to think, if you and I had chanced to have married together, what a different creature you most likely would have made of me to what I am at present!

Lord P. Yes; and what a different creature you most likely would have made of *me*, to what I am at present.

Sir W. Lady Priory, I am not accustomed to pay compliments, or to speak my approbation, even when praise is a just tribute; but your virtues compel me to an eulogium.—That wise submission to a husband that loves you, that cheerful smile so expressive of content, and that plain dress, which indicates the elegance, as well as the simplicity, of your mind, are all symbols of a heart so unlike to those which the present fashion of the day misleads——

Miss Dor. Why look so stedfastly on me, Mr Mandred? Do you pretend to see my heart?

Sir W. Have you any?

Miss Dor. Yes; and one large enough to hold— even my enemy.

Enter SERVANT.

Serv. Mr Bronzely.

Miss Dor. Show him into the other room. [*Exit* SERVANT.] Come, Lady Priory, we must introduce you to Mr Bronzely: he is one of the most fashionable, agreeable, pleasant, whimsical, unthinking, and spirited creatures in all the world : you'll be charmed——

Lady P. I dare say it's near ten o'clock. I am afraid I sha'n't be able to keep awake.

Miss Dor. You must—We are going to have a little concert—'Twill be impossible to sleep.

[*Exit* MISS DORRILLON, *leading off* LADY PRIORY.

Lady R. Upon my word, my lord, your plan of management has made your wife unfit for company.

Lord P. So much more fit to be a wife.

Lady R. She is absolutely fatigued with hard labour—for shame!—How does household drudgery become her hand?

Lord P. Much better than cards and dice do yours.

[*Exit* LADY MARY, *followed by* LORD PRIORY —SIR WILLIAM *is left on the Stage alone.*

Sir W. She " has a heart large enough to receive her enemy."—And by that enemy she means her father. [*He sits down, and shows Marks of Inquietude.*

Enter SIR GEORGE EVELYN.

Sir G. I beg your pardon, Mr Mandred—I hope I don't interrupt you—I only wished to speak to Miss Dorrillon.

Sir W. She is just gone into the next room.

Sir G. To the concert?

Sir W. Are not you invited?

Sir G. Yes ; but before I go in, I wish to know who are the company.——Can you tell whether—a Mr Bronzely is there?

Sir W. I know he is.

Sir G. Are you acquainted with him?

Sir W. I have met him here frequently .

Sir G. And are you *certain* he is here at present?

Sir W. I have reason to be certain.

Sir G. Any particular reason?

c

Sir W. Your mistress, when his name was announced, went out, exclaiming, " he was the most charming and accomplished man in the world."

Sir G. [*Greatly agitated.*] She loves him, sir—I have reason to believe—to know she loves him. Thus she gives up my happiness and her own, to gratify the vanity of a man, who has no real regard for her ; but whose predominant passion is to enjoy the villainous name of a general seducer.

Sir W. [*Rising.*] Why do you suffer it ?

Sir G. Hush ! Don't repeat what I have said, or I lose her for ever. I am at present suffering under her resentment ; and have just sent into the next room, to ask, if she were there, to speak with her.

Enter MISS DORRILLON.

Miss Dor. And is it possible I was sent for by you ?

Sir G. Don't be offended, that I should be uneasy, and come to atone——

Miss Dor. I can't forgive you, sir ; 'tis impossible.
[*Going.*

Sir G. You pardon those, Maria, who offend you more.

Sir W. But an ungrateful mind always prefers the unworthy.

Miss Dor. Ah ! Mr Mandred, are you there ? [*Playfully.*] And have you undertaken to be Sir George's counsel ? If you have, I believe he must lose his cause.—To fit you for the tender task of advocate in the suit of love, have you ever been admitted an honourable member of that court ? Have you, with all that solemn wisdom of which you are master, studied Ovid, as our great lawyers study Blackstone ? If you have—show cause—why plaintiff has a right to defendant's heart.

Sir W. A man of fortune, of family, and of character, ought at least to be treated with respect and with honour.

Miss Dor. You mean to say, " That if A is beloved by B, why should not A be constrained to return B's love?" Counsellor for defendant—"Because, moreover, and besides B, who has a claim on defendant's heart, there are also C, D, E, F, and G; all of whom put in their separate claims—and what, in this case, can poor A do? She is willing to part and divide her love, share and share alike; but B will have all, or none: so poor A must remain A, by herself, A."

Sir G. Do you think I would accept a share of your heart?

Miss Dor. Do you think I could afford to give it you all? " Besides," says defendant's counsellor, " I will prove that plaintiff B has no heart to give defendant in return—he has, indeed, a pulsation on the left side; but as it never beat with any thing but suspicion and jealousy; in the laws of love, it is not termed, admitted, or considered—a heart." [*Going.*

Sir G. Where are you going?

Miss Dor. To the music-room, to be sure: and if you follow me, it shall be to see me treat every person there better than yourself—and Mr Bronzely, whom you hate, to see me treat him best of all.

[*Exit.*

Sir G. I must follow you, though to death. [*Exit.*

Sir W. Fool! And yet am not I nearly as weak as he is, else why do I linger in this house? Why feed my hopes with some propitious moment to waken her to repentance? Why still anxiously wish to ward off some dreaded fate?—If she would marry Sir George, now—if she would give me only *one* proof of discretion, I think I would endeavour to own her for my child.

Enter MR BRONZELY, *in haste.*

Mr Bron. My dear sir, will you do me the greatest favour in the world?—you must do it in an instant too. Do, my dear sir, ask no questions; but lend me your coat for a single moment, and take mine—only for a moment—I cannot explain my reasons now, my impatience is so great ;—but, the instant you have complied, I will inform you of the whole secret ; and you will for ever rejoice that you granted my request.   [*Pulling off his Coat.*

Sir W. [*Aside, with great Scorn.*] And this very contemptible fellow is the favoured lover of my daughter?—I'll—[*After a Struggle.*]—yes—I'll make myself master of his secret—it may possibly concern her—my child—my child's safety may depend upon it.

Mr Bron. Dear Mr Mandred, no time is to be lost !

Sir W. This is rather a strange request, Mr Bronzely. However, your fervency convinces me you must have some very forcible reason.—There's my coat, sir.   [*Gives it him.*

Mr Bron. Thank you, dear sir, a thousand times. —This goodness I shall for ever remember—this binds me to you for ever! [*Putting it on.*] Thank you, sir, a thousand times ! [*Bowing, dressed, and composed.*

Sir W. [*After putting on the other Coat.*] And now, sir, explain the cause of this metamorphosis ?—let me have the satisfaction to know what advantage will accrue from it, and in what I have to rejoice?

Mr Bron. Will you promise me not to reveal the secret, if I trust you with it?

Sir W. Would you add conditions after the bargain is made ? I must know your secret instantly.
                [*Threatening.*

Mr Bron. Then I will disclose it to you voluntarily ; and rely on your honour to keep it.

Sir W. [*Attentively.*] Well, sir.

Mr Bron. Hark ! I thought I heard somebody coming !   [*Offers to go.*

Sir W. I insist upon the information.

                 [*Laying hold of him.*

Mr Bron. Well, then, sir—well—you shall—you shall.—Then, sir——in the small gallery, which separates the music-room from the rest of these apartments—in that little gallery, the lamp is just, unfortunately, gone out.—I was (as unfortunately) coming along, when the whisking of a woman's gown made me give a sudden start!—I found a person was in the gallery with me, and in the dark.

Sir W. Well, sir!

Mr Bron. And so, confidently assuring myself that it was Miss Dorrillon's waiting-maid, or Lady Mary's waiting-maid, I most unluckily clasped my arms around her, and took one kiss.

Sir W. Only one?

Mr Bron. There might be half a dozen! I won't pretend to swear to one. We'll say half a dozen, before I knew who she was. My rapidity would not let her breathe at first, and she was fairly speechless.— But the moment she recovered her breath, she cried, "Villain, whoever you are, you shall repent this :"— and I found it was the voice of a lady to whom I had just been introduced in the concert-room, one Lady Priory! It seems, she was stealing to bed at the time we unhappily met.

Sir W. But what has this to do with your coat?

Mr Bron. A great deal, sir—you will find, a great deal.—As I perceived she did not know me, I carefully held my tongue—but she, with her prudish notions, called "Help !" and "Murder !" On which, I flew to the door, to get away before the lights could be brought—she flew after me ; and, as I went out, exclaimed—"Don't hope to conceal yourself; I shall know you among the whole concert room ; for I carry scissars hanging at my side, and I have cut a piece off your coat."—[SIR WILLIAM *looks hastily at his Coat.*

                 c 2

—*on which* BRONZELY *holds up the Part cut.*]—And, sure enough, so she had !

Sir W. [*In Anger.*] And what, sir, am I to have the shame——

Mr Bron. Either you or I must.

Sir W. And do you dare——

Mr Bron. Consider, my dear sir, how much less the fault is, if perpetrated by you than by me! This is the first offence of the kind which, I dare say, you have committed this many a year; and it will be overlooked in *you.* But I have been suspected of two or three things of the same sort within a very short time ; and I should never be forgiven.

Sir W. Nor ought you to be forgiven—it would be scandalous in me to connive——

Mr Bron. But would it not be more scandalous to reveal the secret of a person who confided in you ? —who flew to you in distress, as his friend, the partner of his cares ?

Sir W. Your impertinence to me, but more your offence to a woman of virtue, deserves punishment. Yet I think the punishment of death, in the way that a man of my Lord Priory's temper might inflict it, much too honourable for your deserts ; so I save your life for some less creditable end. I lend you my coat, to disgrace you by existence : and will go to my chamber, and put on another myself.

[*Passes* BRONZELY, *in order to retire to his Chamber.*

Enter LORD PRIORY, *who meets him.* SIR WILLIAM *starts.*

Mr Bron. [*Going up to* LORD PRIORY.] Ah, my lord ! is the concert over ? charming music ! that *solo* was divine.

[SIR WILLIAM *steals to a Chair, and sits down to hide his Coat.*

Lord P. [*After looking inquisitively at* BRONZE-
LY's *Dress.*] It is time the concert should be over—
it had been better had it never begun ; for there have
been some very improper persons admitted.

[*In great Anger.*

Mr Bron. [*Affecting surprise.*] Indeed!

Lord P. [*Trembling with Rage.*] I am at a loss how
to act. [*Draws a Chair with violence, and places himself down by* SIR WILLIAM—SIR WILLIAM *appears
disconcerted and uneasy.*] But if I could find the man
to whom this piece of cloth belongs——

Mr Bron. What ! that small piece of woollen
cloth ?

Lord P. Yes ; then I should know how to act· In
the mean time, Mr Mandred, as I know you are a
great admirer of my wife, [SIR WILLIAM *starts.*] and
a grave prudent man of honour, I come to ask your
advice, how I am the most likely to find out the villain who has dared to insult her: for a gross insult
she has received from one of Mr Norberry's visitors,
wearing a coat of which this is a part.

Mr Bron. The villain, no doubt, stole out of the
house immediately.

Lord P. I ordered the street-door to be guarded
that instant—and you, Mr Bronzely, are now the
last man whose habit I have examined.

Mr Bron. And you see I am perfectly whole.

[*Turning round.*

Lord P. I do see——I do see.

[SIR WILLIAM *moves about on his Chair, and appears greatly embarrassed.* LORD PRIORY
starts up in a violent Passion—SIR WILLIAM
starts up with him.

Lord P. I'll find him out if he be on earth—I'll find
him out if——My passion carries me away—I
have not coolness to detect him myself—I'll employ
another—I'll send Oliver in search. Oliver ! [*Cal.*

ing.] Oliver ! here, Oliver ! Why don't you answer when you are called, you stupid, dull, idle, forgetful, blundering, obstinate, careless, self-sufficient——

[*Exit in a Fury.*

Sir W. [*Rising with great Dignity*] And now, Mr Bronzely, how do you think you are to repay me, for having felt one transitory moment of shame ? Understand, sir, that shame is one of the misfortunes to which I have never——

Enter LADY MARY RAFFLE.

Mr Bron. [*Aside to* SIR WILLIAM.] Sit down, sit down, sit down—hold your tongue, and sit down.

[SIR WILLIAM *reluctantly retires to a Chair.*

Lady R. Well, I do most cordially rejoice, when peevish, suspicious, and censorious people meet with humiliation ! I could die with laughing at the incident, which has put both my Lord and my Lady Priory into the greatest terror, grief, and rage.

Sir W. [*Rising.*] I am out of all patience ! The malicious depravity of persons in a certain sphere of life is not to be borne. [*With firmness and Solemnity.*] Lady Mary—Mr Bronzely——

Mr Bron. [*In a half Whisper to him.*] Go away—don't expose yourself—steal out of the room—take my advice, and go to bed—hide yourself. So great is my respect for you, I would not have you detected for the world.

Sir W. I am going to retire, sir. I would not throw my friend's house into confusion and broils; therefore I am as well pleased not to be detected as you can be. [*Goes to the Door, then turns.*] But before I quit the room, I am irresistibly impelled to say—Mr Bronzely ! Lady Mary ! while you continue to ridicule all that is virtuous, estimable, dignified, your vices most assuredly will plunge you into that very disgrace.——

Enter OLIVER, *and places the Piece of Cloth against* SIR WILLIAM's *Coat.*

Oliver. 'Tis as exact a match as ever was—it fits to a thread. Ha! ha! ha!—Ha! ha! ha!

Sir W. Rascal!

Mr Bron. Did not I entreat you to go to bed?

Lady R. Oh, this is the highest gratification I ever knew! My lord! my lord!   [*Calling.*

Mr Bron. Hush, hush!—hold, for Heaven's sake.

Oliver. But, mercy and goodness defend us! who would have thought of this grave gentleman? Ha! ha! ha!—I can tell you what, sir; my lord will be in a terrible passion with you. This house won't hold you both; and I am sure I hate to make mischief.— Mum—I'll say nothing about it. [*Clapping* SIR WILLIAM *on the Shoulder.*] And so make yourself easy.

Mr Bron. [*On the other side of* SIR WILLIAM.] Yes, make yourself easy.

Oliver. A good servant should sometimes be a peacemaker—for my part, I have faults of my own, and so, I dare say, has that gentleman—and so, I dare say, has that gentlewoman. But of all the birds in the wood, how came you to make up to my lady? ha! ha! ha! ha! ha!

Mr Bron. No jests—no jests. Mr Mandred is my friend—my very good friend—and he is not so much to blame as you think for.—Good night, my dear sir.—Heaven bless you.—I thank you a thousand times.—Good night.

[*Shaking Hands with* SIR WILLIAM, *and leading him towards the Door.*

Sir W. [*With steady Composure.*] Good night.— Good night, Lady Mary.   [*Exit.*

Oliver. Why, he never so much as once said he was obliged to me.

5

Lady R. I am sure, if you do not discover this to your master, I will.

Oliver. Oh! as that old gentleman had not manners to say, "Thank you for your kindness," I'll go tell my lord directly.   [*Exit.*

Mr Bron. [*Running after him.*] No, no, no—stop, Oliver. He is gone.

Lady R. What makes you thus anxious and concerned, Bronzely? Now, may I suffer death, if, till I came into this room, I did not think you were the offender.

Mr Bron. I! I indeed!—No, if I could have been tempted to offend any woman in this house in a similar manner, it could have been none but you.

                     [*Bowing.*

Lady R. No, Bronzely, no; I have been too partial to you, to have any remaining claims——Hark! don't I hear Lord Priory's voice in a dreadful rage?

Mr Bron. Then Oliver has informed him. What shall I do to prevent mischief? Dear Lady Mary, as it is not proper for me to stay here any longer uninvited, do you run and try to pacify my Lord Priory. Tell him Mandred does not sleep here to-night; and in the morning you are sure he will make an apology.

Lady R. I will do as you desire—but I know Mr Mandred so well, that I am sure he will not apologise.   [*Exit.*

Mr Bron. Then I will for him. Early in the morning, I'll wait on Lady Priory, and beg pardon in his name, without his knowing it. Yes, I have got poor Mandred into a difficulty, and it is my duty to get him out of it. And then, I shall not only serve him, but have one more interview with that heavenly woman.   [*Exit.*

ACT THE THIRD.

SCENE I.

An Apartment at Mr Norberry's.

Enter Mr Bronzely, *followed by a* Servant.

Mr Bron. [*Looking at his Watch.*] I am early, I know; but Lady Priory is the only person I wish to see. Is my lord with her?

Serv. No, sir, Lord Priory sat up very late, and is yet in bed.

Mr Bron. Acquaint Lady Priory, a person who comes on urgent business, begs to speak with her. If she asks my name, you know it. [*Exit* Servant.] Pray Heaven she may bless me with her sight! Never was so enchanted by a woman in my life!—and never played such a trick in my life. I am half inflamed by love, and half by spite, once more to attempt her.

Enter Lady Priory—*he bows most respectfully—she courtesies.*

Mr Bron. Lady Priory, I come—I come upon rather an awkward, yet a very serious business; it was my misfortune to be among that company yesterday evening, where an unworthy member of it had the insolence to offer an affront to your resplendent virtue.

Lady P. I have some household accounts to ar-

range, and breakfast to make for my lord as soon as
he leaves his chamber : therefore, if you please, sir,
proceed to the business on which you came, without
thinking it necessary to interrupt it by any compliment to me

Mr Bron. I will be concise, madam.—In a word,
I wait upon you from Mr Mandred, with the most
humble apology for his late conduct, which he ac-
knowledges to have been indecorous and unwarrantable : but he trusts, that, in consequence of the con-
cession which I now make for him, the whole matter
will, from this hour, be buried in oblivion.

Lady P. [*Going to the side of the Scene, and speaking.*] If my lord be at leisure, tell him here is a gentleman would be glad to speak with him——[*To*
BRONZELY.] I am sorry, sir, you should know so
little of the rules of our family, as to suppose, that I
could give an answer upon any subject in which my
husband condescends to be engaged.   [*Going.*

Mr Bron. Lady Priory, stop   You can at least
use your power to soften Lord Priory's resentment ;
and unless this apology is accepted, a challenge must
follow, and possibly he may fall.

Lady P. Possibly !   [*Sighing.*

Mr Bron. You are interested for your husband's
life ?

Lady P. Certainly. But I set equal value on his
reputation.   [*Going.*

Mr Bron. Hear me one sentence more.—I cannot part from her. [*Aside.*] Oh, I have something of
such importance to communicate to you—and yet—
I know not how !

Lady P. Then tell it to my husband.

Mr Bron. Hem—hem. [*Aside.*] Oh, Lady Priory,
if the insult of last night has given you offence, should
you not wish to be informed of a plan laid for yet
greater violence ?   [*She starts.*

Lady P. Good Heaven !

Mr Bron. This is neither time nor place to disclose what I wish to say ; nor do I know how to find an opportunity to speak with you alone, free from the possibility of intrusion ; where I could reveal a secret to you, which is connected with your happiness —with your future peace.

Lady P. You alarm me beyond expression! I am going to my own house about twelve o'clock, for a couple of hours—follow me there.

Mr Bron. And I shall be admitted ?

Lady P. Certainly—for you have excited my curiosity, and I am all impatience to hear what you have to communicate that so much concerns me!

Mr Bron. Promise, then, no person but yourself shall ever know of it. [*She hesitates.*] Unless you promise this, I dare not trust you.

Lady P. [*After a second Hesitation.*] I do promise —I promise faithfully.

Mr Bron. Your word is sacred, I rely ?

Lady P. Most sacred.

Mr Bron. And you promise that no one but yourself shall know of the appointment we have now made at your house, nor of the secret which I will then disclose to you ?

Lady P. I promise faithfully, that no one but myself shall ever know of either.

Mr Bron. Remember then to be there alone, precisely at—

Lady P. At one o'clock.

Mr Bron. And that your servants have orders to show me to you.

Lady P. I am too much interested to forget a single circumstance.

Mr Bron. Go now, then, to Lord Priory with Mandred's apology—and urge his acceptance of it with all that persuasion by which you are formed to govern, while you appear to obey.

Lady P. I will present the apology as I received

it from you ; but do not imagine I dare give my opinion upon it, unless I am desired.

Mr Bron. But if you are desired, you will then say——

Lady P. Exactly what I think.   [*Exit.*

Mr Bron. I'll do a meritorious act this very day. This poor woman lives in slavery with her husband. I'll give her an opportunity to run away from him. When we meet, I'll have a post-chaise waiting a few doors from her house ; boldly tell her that I love her ; and——

Enter Miss Dorrillon.

My dear Miss Dorrillon, I could not sleep all night, and am come thus early on purpose to complain of your treatment of me during the whole of yesterday evening. Not one look did you glance towards me— and there I sat in miserable solitude up in one corner the whole time of the concert.

Miss Dor. I protest I did not see you!—and stranger still !—never thought of you.

· *Mr Bron.* You then like another better than you like me ?

Miss Dor. I do.

Mr Bron. Do you tell him so ?

Miss Dor. No.

Mr Bron. You tell him you like me the best ?

Miss Dor. Yes.

Mr Bron. Then I will believe what you say to him, and not what you say to me.—And though you charge me with inconstancy, yet I swear to you, my beloved Maria, [*Taking her Hand.*] that no woman, no woman but yourself———

Enter Sir William, *and starts at seeing his Daughter in such close conversation with* Bronzely.

Sir W. Aside.] How familiar !—my eyes could not be shocked with a sight half so wounding to my heart as this!

Mr Bron. [*Apart to* Miss DORRILLON.] Hush! you have heard the story; but don't laugh at him now. He is in a devilish ill humour, and it will all fall on me. Go away.—It's a very good story, but laugh at him another him.

Miss Dor. I don't believe a word of the story; yet, as a received opinion, it is an excellent weapon for an enemy, and I long to use it.

Mr Bron. Not now, not now—because I have some business with him, and 'twill put him out of temper.

[*He hands her to the Door.*—*Exit* Miss DORRILLON.

Sir W. [*Looking steadfastly after her.* Poor girl! poor girl! I am not yet so enraged against her, but that I compassionate her for her choice —Is this the man who is to be, for life, her companion, her protector?

Mr Bron. Well, Mr Mandred, I believe I have settled it.

Sir W. Settled what?   [*Anxiously.*

Mr Bron. At least I have done all in my power to serve you: perhaps you don't know that Mr Oliver divulged the whole affair. But I have waited on my Lady Priory, and I do believe I have settled it with her, to manage it so with my lord, that every thing shall be hushed up. You may expect a few jests among your female acquaintance, and a few epigrams in the newspapers : but I verily believe every thing material is safe.—Is there any further satisfaction which you demand from me?

Sir W Not at present—a man is easily satisfied who possesses both courage and strength to do himself right, whenever he feels his wrongs oppressive. I have as yet found but little inconvenience from the liberties you have taken with me; and what, just at this time, far more engages my attention than revenge, is an application to you for intelligence. Without further preface, do you pay your addresses to the young lady who lives in this house?

Mr Bron. Yes I do, sir—I do.

Sir W. You know, I suppose, which of the two ladies I mean?

Mr Bron. Which ever you mean, sir, 'tis all the same; for I pay my addresses to them both.

Sir W. [*Starting.*] To them both!

Mr Bron. I always do.

Sir W. And pray, which of them do you love?

Mr Bron. Both, sir—upon my word, both—I assure you, both.

Sir W. But you don't intend to marry both?

Mr Bron. I don't intend to marry either: and, indeed, the woman whom I love best in the world has a husband already. Do you suppose I could confine my affections to Lady Mary, or Miss Dorrillon, after Lady Priory appeared? do you suppose I did not know who it was I met last night in the dark? wherever I visit, Mr Mandred, I always make love to every woman in the house: and I assure you, they expect it—I assure you, sir, they all expect it.

[Sir WILLIAM *walks about in Anger.*
Have you any further commands for me?

Sir W. Yes, one word more.——And you really have no regard for this girl who parted from you as I came in?

Mr Bron. Oh yes, pardon me—I admire, I adore, I love her to distraction; and if I had not been so long acquainted with Lady Mary, nor had seen my Lady Priory last night, I should certainly call Sir George Evelyn to an account for being so perpetually with her.

Sir W. [*Anxiously.*] Do you think he loves her?

Mr Bron. Yes, I dare say as well as I do.

Sir W. Do you think she likes him?

Mr Bron. I think she likes me.

Sir W. But, according to your method of affection, she may like him too.

Mr Bron. She may, she may.—In short, there is

no answering for what she likes—all whim and flight-
iness—acquainted with every body—coquetting with
every body—and in debt with every body. Her mind
distracted between the claims of lovers, and the claims
of creditors,—the anger of Mr Norberry, and the
want of intelligence from her father.

Sir W. She is in a hopeful way!

Mr Bron. Oh, it would be impossible to think of
marrying her in her present state—for my part, I
can't—and I question whether Sir George would.—
But if her father come home, and give her the fortune
that was once expected, why, then I may possibly
marry her myself.

Sir W [*Firmly.*] She will never have any fortune.
—I came from India lately, you know; and you may
take my word, her father is not coming over, nor will
he ever come.

Mr Bron. Are you sure of that?

Sir W. Very sure.

Mr Bron. Then keep it a secret—don't tell her so
—poor thing! it would break her heart. She is dotingly fond of her father.

Sir W. Hah! how!—oh no, she can have no remembrance of him.

Mr Bron. Not of his person, perhaps; but he has
constantly corresponded with her—sent her presents
and affectionate letters—and you know a woman's
heart is easily impressed.

Sir W. I never heard her mention her father.

Mr Bron. Not to you; but to us who are kind to
her she talks of him continually. She cried bitterly
the other day when the last ship came home, and
there was no account of him.

Sir W. Did she? did she? [*Eagerly.*] Ay, I suppose she is alarmed lest he should be dead, and all
his riches lost.

Mr Bron. No, I believe her affection for him is

totally unconnected with any interested views. I have
watched her upon that head, and I believe she loves
her father sincerely.

Sir W. [*Wiping a Tear from his Eye.*] I believe
it does not matter whom she loves.

Mr Bron. By the bye, she hates you.

Sir W. I thought so.

Mr Bron. Yes, you may be satisfied of that. Yes,
she even quarrelled with me the other day for speaking in your favour: you had put her in a passion,
and she said, no one that loved *her*, ought to have
any respect for you.

Sir W. I am much obliged to her—very much
obliged to her. Did she say nothing more?

Mr Bron. Only, that you were ill-natured, dog-
matic, cruel, and insolent. Nothing more.——And
say what she will against you, you know you can be
even with her.

Sir W. Yes, I can be even with her, and I will be
even with her.

Enter LORD PRIORY, *and takes* BRONZELY *on one
Side.*

Lord P. I have accepted this man's apology :—I
will not call him to a serious account ; but he shall
not escape every kind of resentment.—I am resolved
to laugh at him; to turn the whole affair into mirth
and good humour ; at the same time to gall him to
the heart. Good morning, Mr Mandred : how do
you do this morning, Mr Mandred?—Let me go,
[*Violently to* BRONZELY.] I must joke with him.

Mr Bron. But neither your voice nor your looks
agree with your words.

Lord P. Mr Mandred, I did intend to be angry,
but it would give too respectable an air to a base action, and so I am come to laugh at you.

Enter LADY RAFFLE.

And I am sure you, Lady Mary, will join even me,
in laughing at this man of gallantry.

Lady R. Oh, I am absolutely afraid to come near
the Tarquin.

Sir W. You need not, Lady Mary; for there can
be no Tarquin without a Lucretia.

Lord P. However, Mr Mandred, it is proper I
should tell you, I accept the apology you have made :
but at the same time——

Sir W. [*Hastily.*] What do you mean, my lord? I
have made no apology.

Mr Bron. Yes, yes, you have—I called and made
one for you.

Sir W. Made an apology for me! You have just
gone one step too far then; and I insist——

Mr Bron [*Drawing* SIR WILLIAM *on one Side.*]
I will—I will—I will set every thing to rights. It
would be base in me if I did not; and I will. [*Turns
to* LORD PRIORY *and* LADY MARY.] Yes, Mr Mandred, I will retrieve your character at the expence
of my own. I am more able to contend with the
phrenzy of a jealous husband than you are.

Enter MISS DORRILLON *and* SIR GEORGE EVELYN.

I am happy to see you—you are just come in time to
hear me clear the grave, the respectable character of
my friend, Mr Mandred, and to stigmatise my own.——
My lord, vent all your anger and your satire upon
me. It was I (pray believe me, I beg you will; don't
doubt my word,) it was I who committed the offence,
of which my friend, the man I respect and reverence,
stands accused—It was I who offended my Lady
Priory, and then——

Lord P. It cannot be—I won't be imposed upon.

Lady R. But how generous and noble in him to
take it upon himself!

Mr Bron. [*To* SIR WILLIAM.] There! what can
I do more? You see they won't believe me!—Tell
me what I can do more? Can I do any thing more?
—My feelings are wounded on your account, more
than on my own, and compel me, though reluctantly, to quit the room.   [*Exit.*

Sir G. I am at a loss which to admire most, the
warmth of Mr Bronzely's friendship, or the coldness
of Mr Mandred's gratitude.

Lady R. Oh! if it were not for that happy steadi-
ness of feature he could not preach rectitude of conduct as he does.

Lord P. [*Going up to* SIR WILLIAM.] Eloquent
admonisher of youth!

Miss Dor [*Going to him.*] Indeed, my rigid monitor, I cannot but express admiration, that under
those austere looks, and that sullen brow, there still
should lurk——

Sir W. Have a care—don't proceed—stop where
you are—dare not you complete a sentence that is
meant to mock me.——I have borne the impertinence
of this whole company with patience—with contempt;
but dare you to breathe an accent suspicious of my
conduct, and I will instantly teach you how to respect me, and to shrink with horror from yourself.
                    [*She stands motionless in Surprise.*

Lord P. What a passion he is in! Compose yourself, Mr Mandred.

Miss Dor. I protest, Mr Mandred——

Sir W. Silence! [*Raising his Voice.*] Dare not to
address yourself to me.

Lady R. Did you ever hear the like?—And I vow
she looks awed by him!

Lord P How strange, that a man cannot command
his temper!

Sir G. Mr Mandred, permit me to say, I have
ever wished to treat you with respect—nor would I
be rash in laying that wish aside; yet I must now

take upon me to assure you, that if you think to offend every lady in this house with impunity, you are
mistaken.

Sir W. Sir George, if you mean to frighten me by
your threats, I laugh at you—but if your warmth is
really kindled, and by an attachment to that unworthy object, [*Pointing to* Miss Dorrillon.] I only
pity you.

Sir G. Insufferable !—[*Going up to him.*]—Instantly make an atonement for what you have said, or expect the consequence!

Sir W. And pray, Sir George, what atonement
does your justice demand ?

Sir G. Retract your words—Acknowledge you
were grossly deceived when you said Miss Dorrillon
was unworthy.

Sir W. Retract my words !

Sir G. Were they not unjust ?—Is it a reproach,
that, enveloped in the maze of fashionable life, she
has yet preserved her virtue unsuspected ? That, en-
cumbered with the expenses consequent to her situation, she has proudly disdained, even from me, the
honourable offer of pecuniary aid ? That her fond
hope still fixes on the return of an absent parent,
whose blessing she impatiently expects ? and that I,
who have watched her whole conduct with an eye
of scrutinizing jealousy, have yet only beheld that
which makes me aspire, as the summit of earthly
happiness, to become her husband ?

Sir W. Young man, I admire your warmth. [*With
great Fervour and Affection.*] There is much compassion and benevolence, and charity, in sometimes
mistaking the vicious for the virtuous ;—and if in the
heat of contention I have said a word reflecting on
your character, I am ready to avow my error ; and,
before this company, to beg your pardon.

Sir G. That is not enough, sir,—[*Taking* Miss

DORRILLON *by the Hand, and leading her forward.*]—
you must ask this lady's pardon.

      [SIR WILLIAM *starts, and turns his Face away,*
        strongly impressed.

Sir W. Ask her pardon ! Though I forgive some
insults, I will not this.—Ask her pardon !—

Miss Dor. Nay, nay, Sir George, you have no business with Mr Mandred's quarrels and mine.—Reserve your heroic courage for some nobler purpose
than a poor woman's reputation.

Sir G. Point out a nobler, and I'll give up this.

Lady R. There is none so noble! And I wish, Sir
George, you would undertake to vindicate mine

Lord P. Come, Lady Mary, let us retire, and leave
these two irritable men to themselves.

Lady R. Come, Maria, let us leave them alone.
He'll teach Mr Mandred to be civil for the future.

Miss Dor. [*In great Agitation.*] Dear madam, I
would not leave them alone for the world !

Lady R. Then, my lord, you and I will; they
have no offensive weapons, so we may venture to
leave them.

Lord P. This comes of being too warm in conversation ! This comes of being in a passion !

      [*Exeunt* LORD PRIORY *and* LADY MARY.

Sir G. While there is a female present, I have only
to say——good morning, Mr Mandred.   [*Going*

Miss Dor. [*Catching hold of him*] For once I give
up my pride to soften yours Come, do not look
thus determined !—I am sure Mr Mandred did not
mean to offend me ; the words he made use of fell
from his lips by accident.

Sir W. They did not—I meant them—I mean
them still—and I repeat them.

Miss Dor. [*To* SIR WILLIAM.] Now, how can you
be so provoking ?—Nay, hold, Sir George, [*He offers
to go.*] you shall not go away with that frowning

brow. [*She draws him gently towards* Sir William; *then takes* Sir William's *Hand.*] Nor you, with that sullen aspect.—Come, shake hands, for my sake. —— Now, as I live, Sir George, Mr Mandred's hand feels warmer and kinder than yours—he tries to draw it back, but he has not the heart. [Sir William *snatches it away, as by compulsion.*] Thou art a strange personage!—thou wilt not suffer me either to praise or to dispraise thee.——Come, Sir George, make up this difference—for if you were to fight, and Mr Mandred was to fall——

Sir W. What then?

Miss Dor. Why, " I could better spare a better man."

Sir W. How!

Miss Dor. I see you are both gloomy, both obstinate, and I have but one resource.—Sir George, if you aspire to my hand, dare not to lift yours against Mr Mandred. He and I profess to be enemies: but if I may judge of his feelings by my own, we have but passing enmities.—I bear him no malice, nor he me, I dare be sworn. Therefore, sir, lift but your arm against him, or insult him with another word, and our intercourse is for ever at an end.   [*Exit.*

[Sir George *and* Sir William *stand for some time silent.*

Sir G. Why is it in the power of one woman to make two men look ridiculously?

Sir W. I am at a loss to know, sir, whether you and I part friends or enemies.—However, call on me in the way you best like, and you will find me ready to meet you, either as an enemy, or as a friend.

[*Exeunt separately.*

ACT THE FOURTH.

SCENE I.

A Hall at LORD PRIORY'S.

Two SERVANTS *discovered sitting.—Another enters.*

1 *Serv.* Do you hear, Mr Porter? you are to admit
no person but Mr Bronzely.

2 *Serv.* Mr Bronzely—very well—[*A loud rapping.*]
—and there I suppose he is.

1 *Serv.* [*Looking through the Window.*] Yes; that,
I believe, is his carriage.—[*To third* SERVANT.]—
Let my lady know.   [*Exit third* SERVANT.

Enter MR BRONZELY.

Mr Bron. You are sure Lady Priory is at home?

1 *Serv.* Yes, sir, and gave orders to admit nobody
but you.

Mr Bron. Has she been some time at home?

1 *Serv.* Yes, sir; I dare say my lady came from
Mr Norberry's half an hour ago.

Mr Bron. Waiting for me half an hour—[*Aside.*]
—Show me to her instantly.

[*Exit, following the* SERVANT *hastily.*

SCENE II.

An Apartment at LORD PRIORY'S.

Enter BRONZELY *and* LADY PRIORY, *on opposite
Sides.*

Mr Bron. My dear Lady Priory, how kind you are,
not to have forgotten your promise.

Lady P. How was it possible I should? I have
been so anxious for the intelligence you have to
communicate, that it was pain to wait till the time
arrived.

Mr Bron. Thus invited, encouraged to speak, I
will speak boldly—and I call Heaven to witness, that
what I am going to say——

Lady P. No, stay a moment longer—don't tell me
just yet—[*Listening towards the Side of the Scenes.*]
—for I wish him to hear the very beginning.

Mr Bron. Who hear the very beginning?

Enter LORD PRIORY.—BRONZELY *starts.*

Lord P. I have not kept you waiting, I hope. My
lawyer stopped me on business, or I should have been
here sooner.—My dear Mr Bronzely, [*Going up to
him.*] I thank you a thousand times for the interest
you take in my concerns; and I come prepared with
proper coolness and composure, to hear the secret
with which you are going to entrust us.

Mr Bron. The secret!—yes, sir—the secret which
I was going to disclose to my Lady Priory—Ha! ha!
ha!—But, my lord, I am afraid it is of too frivolous
a nature for your attention.

Lord P. I account nothing frivolous which concerns my wife.

E

Mr Bron. Certainly, my lord, certainly not.

Lora P. Besides, she told me it was of the utmost importance. Did not you?   [*Angrily.*

Lady P. He said so.

Mr Bron. And so it was—it was of importance then—just at the very time I was speaking to Lady Priory on the subject.

Lady P. You said so but this very moment.

Lord P. Come, come, tell it immediately, whatever it is. Come, let us hear it.—[*After waiting some time.*] Why, sir, you look as if you were ashamed of what you are going to say! What can be the meaning of this?

Mr Bron. To be plain, my lord, my secret will disclose the folly of a person for whom I have a sincere regard.

Lord P. No matter—let every fool look like a fool, and every villain be known for what he is—Tell your story.

Lady P. How can you deprive me of the pleasure you promised? You said it would prevent every future care.

Lord P. Explain, sir.—I begin to feel myself not quite so composed as I expected. You never, perhaps, saw me in a passion—she has—and if you were once to see me really angry——

Mr Bron. Then, my lord, I am apt to be passionate too—and I boldly tell you, that what I had to reveal, though perfectly proper, was meant for Lady Priory alone to hear. I entreated your ladyship not to mention to my lord that I had any thing to communicate, and you gave me a solemn promise you would not.

Lady P. Upon my honour, during our whole conversation upon that subject, you never named my Lord Priory's name.

Mr Bron. I charged you to keep what I had to tell you a profound secret.

Lady P. Yes; but I thought you understood I could have no secrets from my husband.

SCENE II.] AND MAIDS AS THEY ARE.

Mr Bron. You promised no one should know it but yourself.

Lady P. He is myself.

Lord P. How, Mr Bronzely, did you suppose she and I were two? Perhaps you did, and that we wanted a third Well, I quite forgive you for your silly mistake, and laugh at you, ha! ha! ha! as I did at Mr Mandred —[*Seriously.*]—Did you suppose, sir, we lived like people of fashion of the modern time? Did you imagine that a woman of her character could have a wish, a desire, even a thought, that was a secret from her husband?

Mr Bron It is amazing to find so much fidelity the reward of tyranny!

Lady P. Sir—I speak with humility—I would not wish to give offence.—[*Timidly.*]—But, to the best of my observation and unders anding, your sex, in respect to us, are all tyrants. I was born to be the slave of some of you—I make the choice to obey my husband.

Lord P. Yes, Mr Bronzely; and I believe it is more for her happiness to be my slave, than your friend—to live in fear of me, than in love with you. Lady Priory, leave the room. [*Exit* LADY PRIORY.] Do you see—did you observe the glow of truth and candour which testifies that woman's faith? and do you not blush at having attempted it?—Call me a tyrant! Where are the signs? Oh, if every married man would follow my system in the management of his wife, every impertinent lover would look just as foolish as you!

Mr Brn. This is all boasting, my lord—you live in continual fear—for (without meaning any offence to LadyPriory's honour) you know you dare not trust her for one hour alone with any man under sixty.

Lord P. I dare trust her at any time with a coxcomb.

Mr Bron. That is declaring I am not one—for I am certain you dare not leave her alone with me.

Lord P. [*In a Passion.*] Yes, with fifty such.

Mr Bron. But not with one—and you are right —it might be dangerous.

Lord P. [*Angrily.*] No, it would not.

Mr Bron. [*Significantly.*] Yes, it would.

Lord P. Have not you had a trial?

Mr Bron. But you were present. You constantly follow all her steps, watch all she says and does. But I believe you are right—wives are not to be trusted.

Lord P. Mine is.

Mr Bron. No, my dear Lord Priory, you must first become gentle, before you can positively confide in her affection—before you can trust her in a house, or in any place, alone.

Lord P. [*Hastily.*] To prove you are mistaken, I'll instantly go back to my friend Norberry's, and leave you here to tell her the secret you boasted. Pay your addresses to her, if that be the secret; you have my free consent.

Mr Bron. My dear friend, I'll accept it.

Lord P. Ay, I see you have hopes of supplanting me, by calling me your friend.—But can you conceive now that she'll listen to you?

Mr Bron. You have given me leave to try, and can't recall it.

Lord P. But depend upon it, you will meet with some terrible humiliation.

Mr Bron. Either you or I shall.

Lord P. I shall laugh to hear you tumbled down stairs.

Mr Bron. You are not to remain on the watch here: you are to return to Mr Norberry's.

Lord P. Was that the bargain?

Mr Bron. Don't you remember? You said so.

Lord P. Well, if that will give you any satisfaction——

Mr Bron. It will give me great satisfaction.

Lord P. Heaven forgive me, but your confidence makes me laugh. Ha! ha! ha!

Mr Bron. And yours makes me laugh. Ha! ha! ha!

Enter OLIVER.

Lord P. Hah! What brings you here, Oliver? Lady Priory and I are only come home for a few hours.

Oliver. I know it, my lord. I thought, nevertheless, I might be wanted.

Mr Bron. And so you are, good Mr Oliver. Your lord desires you to conduct me to your lady in the next room, and acquaint her it is with his permission I am come to conclude the conversation which was just now interrupted —Is not that right, my lord? Are not those words exactly corresponding with your kind promise?

Lord P. I believe they are.

Oliver. —I am " to take Mr Bronzely to my lady, and tell her you sent him." [*Exit* OLIVER.

Mr Bron. Now this is perfect fashion: and while I step to Lady Priory, do you go and comfort my intended wife Lady Mary.

Lord P. I hate the fashion—and were I not sure you would now be received in a very unfashionable manner——

Mr Bron. No rough dealings, I hope?

Lord P. Oh, you begin to be afraid, do you?

Mr Bron No—but I have met with an accident or two lately—and I am not so well acquainted with ancient usages as to know in what manner a man of my pursuits would have been treated in former times.

Lord P. A man of your pursuits, Mr Bronzely, is

E 2

of a very late date ; and to be shamed out of them by
a wife like mine.

Mr Bron. Then we shall all three be old-fashioned.
[*Exit, following* OLIVER.

Lord P. [*Returning, and looking anxiously after*
BRONZELY.] I am passionate—I am precipitate—I
have no command over my temper.—However, if a
man cannot govern himself, yet he will never make
any very despicable figure as long as he knows how
to govern his wife.   [*Exit, on the opposite Side.*

SCENE III.

SIR WILLIAM'S *Apartment at* MR NORBERRY'S.

Several Trunks and travelling Boxes.—SIR WILLIAM
discovered, packing Writings into a Portfolio.

Sir W. And here is the end of my voyage to England !—a voyage, which, for years, my mind had
dwelt on with delight !—I pictured to myself a daughter grown to womanhood, beautiful ! and so she is.—
Accomplished ! and so she is.—Virtuous ! and so she
is.—Am I of a discontented nature, then, that I am
not satisfied ?—Am I too nice ?—Perhaps I am.—
Soothing thought !—I will for a moment cherish it,
and dwell with some little gratitude upon her late
anxiety for my safety.
[*He walks about in a thoughtful musing manner.—A loud thrusting and rapping is heard
at his Chamber Door.*

Enter MISS DORRILLON *hastily, and in affright.*

Miss Dor. Oh, Mr Mandred, I beg your pardon

—I did not know this was your apartment. But suffer me to lock the door; [*She locks it.*] and conceal
me for a moment, for Heaven's sake.

Sir W. What's the matter? Why have you locked
my door?

Miss Dor. [*Trembling.*] I dare not tell you.

Sir W. I insist upon knowing.

Miss Dor. Why then—I am pursued by a——I
cannot name the horrid name——

Nabson. [*Without.*] She went into this room.

Miss Dor. [*To* SIR WILLIAM.] Go to the door,
and say I did not.

Sir W. How!

Nabson. [*Without.*] Please to open the door.

Miss Dor. Threaten to beat him if he won't go
away.

Sir W. Give me the key, and let me see from whom
you want to fly.—[*Commanding.*]—Give me the key.

Miss Dor. [*Collecting firmness.*] I will not.

Sir W. [*Starting.*] "Will not"——Will not, when
I desire you?

Miss Dor. No—since you refuse me protection,
I'll protect myself.

Sir W. But you had better not have made use of
that expression to me—you had better not.   Recall
it by giving me the key.

Miss Dor. If I do, will you let me conceal myself
behind that bookcase, and say I am not here?

Sir W. Utter a falsehood!

Miss Dor. I would for you.

[*A hammering at the Door.*

Sir W. They are breaking open the door.—Give
me the key, I command you.

Miss Dor. "Command me!" "command me!"
However, there it is. [*Gives it him.*] And now, if you
are a gentleman, give me up if you dare!

Sir W. " If I am a gentleman !" Hem, hem—" If I am a gentleman !" Dares me too !

[*Going slowly towards the Door.*

Miss Dor. Yes. I have now thrown myself upon your protection ; and if you deliver me to my enemies——

Sir W. What enemies ? What business have you with enemies ?

Miss Dor. 'Tis they have business with me.

Sir W. [*To them without.*] I am coming. The door shall be opened.

Miss Dor [*Follows and lays hold of him.*] Oh, for Heaven's sake, have pity on me—they are merciless creditors—I shall be dragged to a prison. Do not deliver me up—I am unfortunate—I am overwhelmed with misfortunes—have compassion on me !

[*She falls on her Knees.*

Sir W. [*In great agitation.*] Don't *kneel* to me !—I don't mean you to kneel to me !—What makes you think of kneeling to *me ?*—I must do my duty.

[*He unlocks the Door.*

Enter NABSON—MISS DORRILLON *steals behind a Bookcase.*

Sir W. What did you want, sir ?

Nabson. A lady that I have just this minute made my prisoner ; but she ran from me, and locked herself in here.

Sir W. [*With surprise*] Arrested a lady !

Nabson. Yes, sir ; and if you mean to deny her being here, I must make bold to search the room.

Sir W. Let me look at your credentials.—[*Takes the Writ.*]—" Elizabeth Dorrillon for six hundred pounds." Pray, sir, is it customary to have female names on pieces of paper of this denomination ?

Nabson. Oh yes, sir, very customary. There are as many ladies who will run into tradesmen's books as there are gentlemen ; and when one goes to take

the ladies, they are a thousand times more slippery
to catch than the men.

Sir W. Abominable !—Well, sir, your present prisoner shall not slip through your hands, if I can prevent it. I scorn to defend a worthless woman as much
as I should glory in preserving a good one ; and I give
myself joy in being the instrument of your executing
justice.—*He goes and leads* MISS DORRILLON *from
the place where she was concealed—she casts down her
Head.*]—What ! do you droop ? Do you tremble ?
You, who at the ball to-night would have danced
lightly, though your poor creditor had been perishing
with want ! You, who never asked yourself if your
extravagance might not send an industrious father of
a family to prison, can you feel on the prospect of
going thither yourself ?

Miss Dor. For what cause am I the object of your
perpetual persecution ?

Nabson. Lord ! Madam, the gentleman means to
bail you after all : I can see it by his looks.

Sir W. How, rascal, dare you suppose, or imagine,
or hint, such a thing ?   [*Going up to him in Anger.*

Miss Dor. That's right, beat him out of the house.

Sir W. No, madam, he shall not go out of the house
without taking you along with him. . Punishment
may effect in your disposition what indulgence has
no hope of producing.——There is your prisoner,
[*Handing her over to him.*] and you may take my
word, that she will not be released by me, or by any
one : and it will be only adding to a debt she can
never pay, to take her to any house previous to a prison. [*With the Emotion of Resentment, yet deep Sorrow.*

Nabson. Is that true, my lady ?

Miss Dor. [*After a Pause.*] Very true. I have but
one friend—but one relation in the world—and he is
far away.   [*Weeps.*—SIR WILLIAM *wipes his Eyes.*

Nabson. More's the pity.

Sir W. No, sir, no—no pity at all—for if fewer

fine ladies had friends, we should have fewer exam-
ples of profligacy.

[*She walks to the Door, then turns to* SIR WILLIAM.

Miss Dor. I forgive you.

[*Exit, followed by* NABSON.

Sir W. [*Looking after her.*] And perhaps I *could*
forgive you. But I must not. No, this is justice—
this is doing my duty—this is strength of mind—this
is fortitude—fortitude—fortitude.

[*He walks proudly across the Room, then stops,
takes out his Handkerchief, throws his Head
into it, and is going off.*

Enter LADY RAFFLE—*a Man following at a distance.*

Lady R. Mr Mandred, Mr Mandred ! [*He turns.*]
Sir—Mr Mandred—Sir—[*In a supplicating Tone.*] I
presume—I presume, sir——

Sir W. What, madam ? what ?

Lady R. I came, sir, to request a favour of you.

Sir W. So it should seem, by that novel deportment.

Lady R. If you would for once consider with lenity, the frailty incidental to a woman who lives in
the gay world——

Sir W. Well, madam !

Lady R. How much she is led away by the temptation of fine clothes, fine coaches, and fine things.

Sir W. Come, to the business.

Lady R. You are rich, we all know, though you
endeavour to disguise the truth.

Sir W. I can't stay to hear you, if you don't proceed.

Lady R. My request is—save from the dreadful
horrors of a gaol, a woman who has no friend near
her—a woman who may have inadvertently offended
you, but who never——

Sir W 'Tis in vain for you to plead on her account—she knows my sentiments upon her conduct

—she knows the opinion I have formed of her; and you cannot prevail on me to change it.

Lady R. Do you suppose I come to plead for Miss Dorrillon?

Sir W. Certainly.

Lady R. No, I am pleading for myself. I am unfortunately involved in similar circumstances—I have a similar debt to the self-same tradesman, and we are both at present in the self-same predicament.

Sir W. And upon what pretence did you suppose I would be indulgent to you more than to her?

Lady R. Because you have always treated me with less severity; and because I overheard you just now say, you "should glory in delivering from difficulty a good woman."

Sir W And so I should.

Lady R. How unlike the world!

Sir W. No—whatever the discontented may please to say, the world is affectionate, is generous, to the good: more especially to the good of the female sex; for it is only an exception to a general rule, when a good woman is in pecuniary distress.

[*Exit* Sir William.

Enter Lord Priory, *humming a tune, but with a very serious face: he pulls out his Watch, with evident marks of anxiety—coughs—rubs his forehead—and gives various other marks of discontent and agitation.—*Lady Raffle *observes him with attention, then sidles up to him.*

Lady R. By the good humour you appear in, my lord, I venture to mention to you my distresses. I know the virtues of Lady Priory make my failings conspicuous; but then consider the different modes to which we have been habituated—she excluded from temptation——

Lord P. No—she shuns temptation. Has she not in this very house been compelled to make exertions?

Has she not detected and exposed both Mr Mandred and Mr Bronzely?

Lady R. Bronzely! Bronzely! How! [*Aside.*] Another rival?

Lord P. She has not done with *him* yet, I believe; for, to tell the truth, he is now with her at my house in Park Street. He taxed me with being jealous of my wife—to prove in what contempt I held the accusation, I left them together, and bid him make love to her.

Lady R. Is that possible?

Lord P. I can't say I would have done so rash an action, had I been married to some women—to you, for instance——but I have not a doubt of Lady Priory's safety: her mind, I know, is secure, and I have servants in the house to protect her from personal outrage. The only fear is, lest he should have received one; for 'tis now near two hours [*Looking at his Watch.*] since I came away, and I have neither seen nor heard any thing of either of them!—But to your ladyship's concerns.

Lady R. I am at this instant, my lord, in the power of an implacable creditor; and unless some friend will give bond for a certain sum, I must—I blush to name it—be taken to a prison.

Lord P. I am not at all surprised at the circumstance, madam; but it amazes me that you should apply to me for deliverance. You have a brother in town; why not send to him?

Lady R. He was my friend the very last time a distress of this kind befell me.   [*Weeps.*

Lord P. Ask Mr Norberry.

Lady R. He was my friend the time before.

Lord P. Mr Bronzely, then.

Lady R. And Bronzely the time before that.

Enter OLIVER.

Lord P. Ah, Oliver! I am glad to see you, my

good fellow. Ah! what have you done with Mr Bronzely?

Oliver. Nay, my lord, that I can't tell. I can't tell what he has done with himself.

Lord P. How long has he been gone from my house?

Oliver. He is not gone yet, as I know of; for none of the servants let him out.

Lord P. Not gone! and you can't tell where he is!

Oliver. No, that we can't: we have looked in every room for him, and can't find him any where.

Lord P. Not find him! [*Recollecting himself.*] Ho! ho! I thought how it would be—I thought he'd have some trick played him. Where's your lady?

Oliver. That I can't tell neither. We have looked in every room, and can't find *her*.

Lord P. How!

Oliver. 'Tis as sure as I am alive. I and the butler, two footmen, and all the maids have been looking in parlours, chambers, and garrets, every crick and corner, and no where can we find either Mr Bronzely or my lady: but, wherever they are, there's no doubt but they are together. Ha! ha!

Lady R. No doubt at all, Mr Oliver.

Lord P. Together! together! and not in my house! You tell a falsehood. I'll go myself and find them.

Oliver. You must look sharp, then.

Lord P. How came you to miss them?

Oliver. I chanced to go into the next room, to see if there was a proper fire to get it well aired; I knew I had taken Mr Bronzely to my lady in the inner room, and I had heard them both laughing not a quarter of an hour before; but now, all on a sudden, there was neither laughing nor talking, nor any noise at all—every thing was quiet.

Lord P. [*Anxiously*] Well!

Oliver. And so I thought to myself, thought I, I'll sit down here, for my lady will be ringing soon; however, there was no ringing for a whole half hour; and so then I thought I would e'en rap at the door; but nobody called " Come in." So then I went in of my own accord, and there I found——

Lord P. What?

Oliver. Nobody! not a soul to be seen!

Lord P. [*Affecting indifference.*] Oh! she has been playing Bronzely some trick! She has been hiding him; and in some miserable place!

Oliver. But why need she hide herself along with him?

Enter Mr Norberry.

Mr Nor. My dear friend, my dear Lord Priory, let me speak with you alone.—I come upon business that——

Lord P. You look pale! What is your business? Tell it me at once.

Mr Nor. It is of so delicate a nature——

Lord P. I know my wife is with Mr Bronzely— I left them together. I know he is a depraved man; but I know she is an innocent woman.—Now, what have you to tell me?

Mr Nor. What I have just learnt from one of your servants. About a quarter of an hour after you left them, they stole softly out at the back of your house, ran to a post-chaise and four that was in waiting, and drove off together full speed.

Lord P. Gone! eloped! run away from me! left me! left the tenderest, kindest, most indulgent husband, that ever woman had!

Lady R. That we can all witness.

Lord P. I was too fond of her—my affection ruined her—women are ungrateful—I did not exert a husband's authority—I was not strict enough—I hu-

12

moured and spoiled her!—Bless me! what a thick
mist is come over my eyes!

Lady R. No, my lord, it is clearing away.

Lord P Lead me to my room.

[*He is led off by* MR NORBERRY, *exhausted
with grief and anger.*—OLIVER *looks after*
LORD PRIORY, *then takes out his Handkerchief, and follows him off, crying.*

Lady R. Ha! ha! ha! Oh, how I enjoy this distress! Ha! ha! ha!

[*The* OFFICER *who has attended her during
the Scene, and kept at the further part of
the Stage, now comes forward, and bows to
her. She starts on seeing him—takes out
her Handkerchief, and goes crying off at the
opposite side, he following.*

ACT THE FIFTH.

SCENE I.

An Apartment at MR BRONZELY'S.

Enter HOUSEKEEPER *and* FOOTMAN.

House. Dinner enough for twelve, and only two to
sit down to it! Come home without one preparation
—not a bed aired, or the furniture uncovered!

Foot. This is not the first time he has done so.

House. No: for 'tis always thus when a woman's
in the case. Well, I do say that my own sex are—

Foot. Hush! here they are. Run away. [*Exeunt.*

Enter LADY PRIORY *and* MR BRONZELY.

Lady P. Only twelve miles from London?

Mr Bron. No more, be assured.

Lady P. And you avow that I did not come hither by the commands of my husband, but was deceived into that belief by you.

Mr Bron. Still it was by his commands your servant introduced me to you; and, upon an errand, which I feared to deliver till I arrived at a house of my own.

Lady P. What is the errand?

Mr Bron. To tell you that——I love you.

Lady P. Do you assert, Lord Priory sent you to me for this?

Mr Bron. I assert, that, in triumph at your betraying to him our private appointment, he gave me leave to have a second trial. If, then, you have ever harboured one wish to revenge and forsake a churlish ungrateful partner, never return to him more—but remain with me.

Lady P. And what shall I have gained by the exchange, when you become churlish, when you become ungrateful? My children's shame! the world's contempt! and yours! [*Smiling.*] Come, come; you are but jesting, Mr Bronzely! You would not affront my little share of common sense, by making the serious offer of so bad a bargain. Come, own the jest, and take me home immediately.

Mr Bron. Is it impossible for me to excite your tenderness?

Lady P. Utterly impossible.

Mr Bron. I will then rouse your terror.

Lady P. Even that I defy.

Mr Bron. Lady Priory, you are in a lonely house of mine, where I am sole master, and all the servants slaves to my will.

[LADY PRIORY *calmly takes out her Knitting, draws a Chair, and sits down to knit.*

Mr Bron. [*Aside.*] This composure is worse than reproach—a woman who meant to yield would be outrageous.—[*Goes to speak to her, then turns away.*] By Heaven she looks so respectable in that employment, I am afraid to insult her. [*After a struggle with himself.*] Ah! do not you fear me?

Lady P. No—for *your* fears will protect me—I have no occasion for mine.

Mr Bron. What have I to fear?

Lady P. You fear to lounge no more at routs, at balls, at operas, and in Bond Street; no more to dance in circles, chat in side-boxes, or roar at taverns : for you have observed enough upon the events of life to know—that an atrocious offence, like violence to a woman, never escapes condign punishment.

Mr Bron. Oh! for once let your mind be feminine as your person—hear the vows—

[*He seizes her Hand—she rises—he starts back.*

Lady P. Ah! did not I tell you, you were afraid? 'Tis you who are afraid of me. [*He looks abashed.*] Come, you are ashamed, too—I see you are, and I pardon you.—In requital, suffer me to return home immediately. [*He shakes his Head.*]——How! are not you ashamed to detain me here?

Mr Bron. I was not this moment—But now you urge the subject, I think I am.

Lady P. Repent your folly, then, and take me home.   [*Hastily.*

Mr Bron. Can you wish to go back to the man who has made this trial of your fidelity, and not resent his conduct?

Lady P. Most assuredly I wish to return. But if you deliver me safe, perfectly safe, from further insult, it will be impossible for me not to show resentment to Lord Priory.

Mr Bron. Why only in that case?

Lady P. Because, only in that case, you will make

F 2

an impression on my heart—and I will resent his having exposed me to such a temptation.

Mr Bron. Oh ! I'll take you home directly—this moment—Any thing, any sacrifice to make an impression on your heart. William !—[*Calling.*]—I'll take you home directly. Here, John, Thomas, William—[*Calling.*] But, upon my life, it will be a hard task—I cannot do it—I am afraid—I am afraid I cannot.—Besides, what are we to say when we go back?—No matter what, so you will but think kindly of me.

Enter SERVANT.

Order the horses to be put to the chaise; I am going back to London immediately. Quick! quick! Bid the man not be a moment, for fear I should change my mind.

Serv. The chaise is ready now, sir; for the post-boy was going back without unharnessing his horses.

Mr Bron. Then tell him he must perform his journey in half an hour—If he is a moment longer, my resolution will stop on the road [*Exit* SERVANT.] I feel my good designs stealing away already—now they are flying rapidly. [*Taking* LADY PRIORY'S *Hand.*] —Please to look another way—I shall certainly recant if I see you. [*Going.*]—And now, should I have the resolution to take you straight to your husband, you will have made a more contemptible figure of me by this last act, than by any one you have led me to.

[*Exit, leading her off.*

Mr Bron. [*Without.*] Tell the post-boy he need not wait—I have changed my mind—I shall not go to London to-night.

A Room in a Prison.

Enter MISS DORRILLON *and* MR NORBERRY.

Mr Nor. You ought to have known it was vain to send for me. Have not I repeatedly declared that, till I heard from your father, you should receive nothing more from me than a bare subsistence ?—I promise to allow you thus much, even in this miserable place : but do not indulge a hope that I can release you from it. *She weeps—he goes to the Door—then returns.*] I forgot to mention, that Mr Mandred goes on board to-morrow, for India ; and, little as you may think of his sensibility, he seems concerned at the thought of quitting England in resentment, without just bidding you a parting farewell. He came with me hither— shall I send him up ?

Miss Dor. Oh, no ! for Heaven's sake ! Deliver me from his asperity, as you would save me from distraction.

Mr Nor. Nay, 'tis for the last time—you had better see him. You may be sorry, perhaps, you did not, when he is gone.

Miss Dor. No, no : I sha'n't be sorry.—Go, and excuse me—Go, and prevent his coming. I cannot see him.—[*Exit* MR NORBERRY.]—This would be aggravation of punishment, to shut me in a prison, and yet not shelter me from the insults of the world !

Enter SIR WILLIAM.—*She starts.*

Sir W. I know you have desired not to be troubled with my visit ; and I come with all humility——I do not come, be assured, to reproach you.

2

Miss Dor. Unexpected mercy!

Sir W No; though I have watched your course with anger, yet I do not behold its end with triumph.

Miss Dor. It is not to your honour, that you think necessary to give this statement of your mind.

Sir W. May be——but I never boasted of perfection, though I can boast of grief that I am so far beneath it. I can boast too, that, though I frequently give offence to others, I could never part with any one for ever (as I now shall with you,) without endeavouring to make some atonement.

Miss Dor. You acknowledge then your cruelty to me?

Sir W. I acknowledge I have taken upon me to advise, beyond the liberty allowed, by custom, to one who has no apparent interest or authority.——But, not to repeat what is passed, I come with the approbation of your friend Mr Norberry, to make a proposal to you for the future.

　　　　　　　　[He draws Chairs, and they sit.

Miss Dor. What proposal?—What is it?

　　　　　　　　　　　　　　[Eagerly.

Sir W. Mr Norberry will not give either his money or his word to release you.—But as I am rich—have lost my only child—and wish to do some good with my fortune, I will instantly lay down the money of which you are in want, upon certain conditions.

Miss Dor. Do I hear right! Is it possible I can find a friend in you!—a friend to relieve me from the depth of misery! Oh, Mr Mandred!

Sir W. Before you return thanks, hear the conditions on which I make my offer.

Miss Dor. Any conditions—What you please!

Sir W. You must promise, solemnly promise, never to return to your former follies and extravagancies. *[She looks down.]* Do you hesitate? Do you refuse?—Won't you promise?

Miss Dor. I would, willingly—but for one reason.

Sir W. And what is that?

Miss Dor. The fear I should not keep my word.

Sir W. You will, if your fear be real.

Miss Dor. It is real—it is even so great, that I have no hope.

Sir W. You refuse my offer, then, and dismiss me?
[*Rises.*

Miss Dor. [*Rising also.*] With much reluctance. —But I cannot,—indeed I cannot make a promise, unless I were to feel my heart wholly subdued, and my mind entirely convinced that I should never break it.—Sir, I am most sincerely obliged to you for the good which I am sure you designed me; but do not tempt me with the proposal again—do not place me in a situation that might add to all my other afflictions, the remorse of having deceived you.

Sir W. [*After a Pause.*] Well, I will dispense with this condition—but there is another I must substitute in its stead.—Resolve to pass the remainder of your life, some few ensuing years at least, in the country. [*She starts.*] Do you start at that?

Miss Dor. I do not love the country. I am always miserable while I am from London. Besides, there are no follies or extravagancies in the country.—Dear sir, this is giving me up the first condition, and then forcing me to keep it by the second.

Sir W. There, madam, [*Taking out his Pocket-book.*] I scorn to hold out hopes, and then destroy them. There is a thousand pounds free of all constraint— [*She takes it.*]—extricate yourself from this situation, and be your own mistress to return to it when you please.   [*Going.*

Miss Dor. Oh, my benefactor! bid me farewell at parting—do not leave me in anger.

Sir W. How! will you dictate terms to me, while you reject all mine?

Miss Dor. Then only suffer me to express my gratitude—

Sir W. I will not hear you.   [*Going.*

Miss Dor. Hear me then on another subject : a subject of much importance—indeed it is.

Sir W. Well !

Miss Dor. You are going to India immediately— it is possible that there, or at some place where you will land on your way, you may meet with my father.

Sir. W. Well !

Miss Dor. You have heard that I have expected him home for some time past, and that I still live in hopes——

Sir W. Well !   [*Anxiously.*

Miss Dor. If you should see him, and should be in his company—don't mention me.

Sir W. Not mention you !

Miss Dor. At least, not my indiscretions——Oh ! I should die, if I thought he would ever know of them.

Sir W. Do you think he would not discover them himself, should he ever see you ?

Miss Dor. But he would not discover them all at once—I should be on my guard when he first came —My ill habits would steal on him progressively, and not be half so shocking, as if you were to vociferate them all in a breath.

Sir W. To put you out of apprehension at once— your father is not coming home—nor will he ever return to his own country.

Miss Dor. [*Starting.*] You seem to speak from certain knowledge—Oh, Heavens ! is he not living ?

Sir W. Yes, living—but under severe affliction— fortune has changed, and all his hopes are blasted.

Miss Dor. Fortune changed !—in poverty !—my father in poverty !—[*Weeping.*]—Oh, sir ! excuse what may, perhaps, appear an ill compliment to your bounty ; but to me, the greatest reverence I can pay to it.—You are going to that part of the world where he is ; take this precious gift back, search out my fa-

ther, and let him be the object of your beneficence.
—[*Forces the Bank Note into his Hand.*]—I shall be
happy in this prison, indeed I shall, so I can but give
a momentary relief to my dear, dear father.—[SIR
WILLIAM *takes out his Handkerchief*]—You weep!—
This present possibly may be but poor alleviation of
his sufferings—perhaps he is in sickness; or perhaps a
prisoner! Oh! if he is, release me instantly, and take
me with you to the place of his confinement.

Sir W. What! quit the joys of London?

Miss Dor. On such an errand I would quit them
all without a sigh—and here I make a solemn promise to you—— [*Kneeling.*]

Sir W. Hold, you may wish to break it.

Miss Dor. Never—exact what vow you will on
this occasion, I will make and keep it.

Enter MR NORBERRY.—*She rises.*

——Oh, Mr Norberry! he has been telling me such
things of my father——

Mr Nor. Has he? Then kneel again—call *him* by
that name—and implore him not to disown you for
his child.

Miss Dor. Good Heaven!—I dare not—I dare not
do as you require. [*She faints on* NORBERRY.]

Sir W. [*Going to her.*] My daughter!—my child!

Mr Nor. At those names she revives.—[*She raises
her Head, but expresses great Agitation.*]—Come, let
us quit this wretched place—she will be better then.
My carriage is at the door. You will follow us?
[*Exit, leading off* MISS DORRILLON.]

Sir W. Follow you!—Yes—and I perceive that, in
spite of philosophy, justice, or resolution, I would follow you all the world over. [*Exit.*]

SCENE II.

Another Room in the Prison.

LADY RAFFLE *discovered sitting in a dejected Posture.*

Lady R. Provoking! not an answer to one of my pathetic letters!—not a creature to come and condole with me!—Oh that I could but regain my liberty before my disgrace is announced in the public prints! —I could then boldly contradict every paragraph that asserted it—by—*We have authority to say, no such event ever took place.*

Enter a MAN *belonging to the Prison.*

Man. One Sir George Evelyn is here, madam; he will not name your name, because it sha'n't be made public; but he desires you will permit him to come and speak a few words to you, provided you are the young lady from Grosvenor Street, with whom he has the pleasure of being acquainted.

Lady R. Yes, yes, I am the young lady from Grosvenor Street—my compliments to Sir George, I am that lady—intimately acquainted with him; and entreat he will walk up. [*Exit the* MAN] This is a most fortunate incident in my tragedy! Sir George no doubt takes me for Miss Dorrillon; yet I am sure he is too much the man of gallantry and good breeding to leave me in this place, although he visits me by mistake.

Enter SIR GEORGE EVELYN, *speaking as he enters.*

Sir G. Madam, you are free—the doors of the prison are open—my word is passed for the——
        [*He stops—looks around—expresses Surprise and Confusion.*

Lady R. [*Courtesying very low.*] Sir George, I am under the most infinite obligation!—Words are too poor to convey the sense I have of this act of friendship—but I trust my gratitude will for ever——

Sir G. [*Confused.*] Madam—really—I ought to apologize for the liberty I have taken.

Lady R. No liberty at all, Sir George—at least no apology is necessary—I insist on hearing no excuses. A virtuous action requires no preface, no prologue, no ceremony—and surely, if one action be more noble and generous than another, it must be that one, where an act of benevolence is conferred, and the object, an object of total indifference to the liberal benefactor.—Generous man, good evening.—Call me a coach. [*Going.*

Sir G. Stay, madam—I beg leave to say——

Lady R. Not a word—I won't hear a word—my thanks shall drown whatever you have to say.

Enter the former MAN.

Sir G. Pray, sir, did not you tell me, you had a very young lady under your care?

Man. Yes, sir, so I had—but she, it seems, has just been released, and is gone away with the gentleman who paid the debt.

Lady R. Do you mean Miss Dorrillon?

Man. I mean the other lady from Grosvenor Street.

Sir G. Who can have released her?

Lady R. Some friend of mine, I dare say, by mistake.—Well, if it be so, she is extremely welcome to the good fortune which was designed for me. For my part, I could not submit to an obligation from every one—scarcely from any one—and from no one with so little regret as I submit to it from Sir George Evelyn. [*Exit, courtesying to* SIR GEORGE.

Sir G. Distraction! the first disappointment is nothing to this last! to the reflection, that Miss Dorrillon has been set at liberty by any man on earth except myself. [*Exit.*

SCENE IV.

An Apartment at MR NORBERRY'*s.*

Enter LORD PRIORY.

Lord P. What a situation is mine! I cannot bear solitude, and am ashamed to see company! I cannot bear to think on the ungrateful woman, and yet I can think on nothing else! It was her conduct which I imagined had alone charmed me; but I perceive her power over my heart, though that conduct be changed!

Enter MR NORBERRY, SIR WILLIAM *and* MISS DORRILLON.

Mr Nor. My dear Lord Priory, exert your spirits to receive and congratulate a friend of mine. Sir William Dorrillon, [*Presenting him.*] father to this young woman, whose failings he has endeavoured to correct under the borrowed name of Mandred.

Sir W. And with that fictitious name, I hope to disburden myself of the imputation of having ever offered an affront to my Lord Priory.

[*He takes* LORD PRIORY *aside, and they talk together.*

Enter SIR GEORGE EVELYN.

Sir G. Is it possible what I have heard can be true? Is it Mr Mandred who has restored Miss Dorrillon to the protection of Mr Norberry?

Sir W. [*Coming forward.*] No, Sir George; I have now taken her under my own protection.

Sir G. By what title, sir?

Sir W. A very tender one—don't be alarmed—I am her father.

Sir G. Sir William Dorrillon? [*They talk apart.*

Enter LADY RAFFLE.

Lady R. Has there been any intelligence of my
Lady Priory yet? [*Sees* MISS DORRILLON.] My dear
Dorrillon, a lover of yours has done the civilest thing
by me!—As I live, here he is. How do you do, Sir
George? I suppose you have all heard the news of
Bronzely running away with——
Miss Dor. Hush!—Lord Priory is here.
Lady R. Oh, he knows it—and it is not improper
to remind him of it—it will teach him humility.
Lord P. I *am* humble, Lady Mary; and own I
have had a better opinion of your sex than I ought
to have had.
Lady R. You mean, of your management of us; of
your instructions, restrictions, and corrections.

Enter SERVANT.

Serv. Lady Priory and Mr Bronzely.
Lady R. What of them?
Serv. They are here.
Lord P. I said she'd preserve her fidelity! Did not
I always say so? Have I wavered once? Did I not
always tell you, that she was only making scoff of
Bronzely? Did I not tell you all so?

Enter BRONZELY *and* LADY PRIORY.

Mr Bron. Then, indeed, my lord, you said truly;
for I return the arrantest blockhead——
Lord P. I always said you would: But how is it?
Where have you been? What occasion for a post-
chaise? Instantly explain, or I shall forfeit that dignity of a husband, to which, in these degenerate
times, I have almost an exclusive right.
Mr Bron. To reinstate you. my lord, in those honours, I accompany Lady Priory; and beg public

pardon for the opinion I once publicly professed of
your want of influence over her affections.

Lord P. Do you hear? Do you hear? Lady Mary,
do you hear?

Mr Bron. Taking advantage of your permission to
call on her, by stratagem I induced her to quit your
house, lest restraint might there act as my enemy.
But your authority, your prerogative, your honour
attached to her under my roof. She has held those
rights sacred, and compelled even me to revere them.

Lord P. Do you all hear? I was sure it would turn
out so!

Lady R. This is the first time I ever knew a woman's honour vindicated by the good word of her
gallant.

Lord P. I will take her own word—the tongue
which, for eleven years, has never in the slightest instance deceived me, I will believe upon all occasions.
My dear wife, boldly pronounce, before this company, that you return to me with the same affection
and respect, and the self-same contempt for this man
—[*To* BRONZELY]—you ever had.

[*A short Pause.*]

Lady R. She makes no answer.

Lord P. Hush! hush? She is going to speak.—
[*Another Pause.*]—Why, why don't you speak?

Lady P. Because I am at a loss what to say.

Lady R. Hear, hear, hear—do you all hear?

Lord P. Can you be at a loss to declare you hate
Mr Bronzely?

Lady P. I do *not* hate him.

Lady R. I was sure it would turn out so.

Lord P. Can you be at a loss to say you love me?

[*She appears embarrassed.*]

Lady R. She *is* at a loss.

Lord P. How? don't you fear me?

Lady P. Yes.

Lady R. She speaks plainly to that question.

Lord P. You know I love truth—speak plainly to all their curiosity requires.

Lady P. Since you command it then, my lord— I confess that Mr Bronzely's conduct towards me has caused a sentiment in my heart——

Lord P. How? What?

Lady R. You must believe her—" she has told you truth for eleven years."

Lady P. A sensation which——

Lord P. Stop—any truth but this I could have borne.—Reflect on what you are saying—Consider what you are doing—Are these your primitive manners?

Lady P. I should have continued those manners, had I known none but primitive men. But to preserve ancient austerity, while, by my husband's consent, I am assailed by modern gallantry, would be the task of a stoic, and not of his female slave.

Lady R. Do you hear? do you all hear? My lord, do *you* hear?

Lord P. I do—I do—and though the sound distracts me, I cannot doubt her word.

Lady P. It gives me excessive joy to hear you say so: because you will not then doubt me when I add —that gratitude, for his restoring me so soon to you, is the only sentiment he has inspired.

Lord P. Then my management of a wife is right after all!

Mr Nor. Mr Bronzely, as your present behaviour has in great measure atoned for your former actions, I will introduce to your acquaintance, my friend Sir William Dorrillon.

Mr Bron. Mandred, Sir William Dorrillon!

Sir W. And considering, sir, that, upon one or two occasions, I have been honoured with your confidence, you will not be surprised, if the first command I lay upon my daughter is—to take refuge from your pursuits, in the protection of Sir George Evelyn.

Sir G. And may I hope, Maria——

Miss Dor. No—I will instantly put an end to all your hopes.

Sir G How?

Sir W. By raising you to the summit of your wishes. Alarmed at my severity, she has owned her readiness to become the subject of a milder government.

Sir G. She shall never repine at the election she has made.

Lord P. But, Sir George, if you are a prudent man, you will fix your eyes on my little domestic state, and guard against a rebellion.

Lady P. Not all the rigour of its laws has ever induced me to wish them abolished.

Mr Bron. [*To* LADY PRIORY.] Dear lady, you have made me think with reverence on the matrimonial compact : and I demand of you, Lady Mary—if, in consequence of former overtures, I should establish a legal authority over you, and become your chief magistrate—would you submit to the same control to which Lady Priory submits ?

Lady R. Any control, rather than have no chief magistrate at all.

Sir G. [*To* MISS DORRILLON.] And what do you say to this?

Miss Dor. Simply one sentence—A maid of the present day, shall become a wife like those—of former times.   [*Exeunt.*

THE END.